"Directors have needed a book like this since D.W. Griffith invented the close-up. We directors have to pass along to other directors our hard-learned lessons about actors. Maybe then they won't have to start from total ignorance like I did, like you did, like we all did."
— John Frankenheimer, Director (*The Manchurian Candidate, Grand Prix, Seconds*)

"With humor and humility, director John Badham takes you inside the most intimate of filmmaking relationships — the endless joust between director and actor for control, recognition, and respect. His candor is like a rifle shot straight to the heart — it pierces pretension and strikes at what matters, with the kind of honesty that is often lacking in Hollywood. *I'll Be in My Trailer* understands what it takes to build trust and avoid the game-playing rituals of stars, studios, and casting the producer's girlfriend."
— Robert Bassett, Dean, Dodge School of Film & Media Arts, Chapman University

"'Blow smoke and you'll get busted,' advises John Badham in this hilarious and outstanding guide that heeds its own advice. Having picked the brains of some of the finest directors and actors working today, Badham's book offers directors the chance to cut through the agony and aggravation of dealing with actors and get to work."
— Gilbert Cates, former President, Directors Guild of America; former Dean of the Film School at UCLA; Artistic Director, The Geffen Theatre

"Most young directors are afraid of actors. They come from film school with a heavy technical background, but they don't know how to deal with an actor. Even many experienced directors barely talk to their actors."
— Oliver Stone, Director (*JFK, Platoon, Wall Street, Born on the Fourth of July*)

"In this outstanding book, John Badham proves not only superbly authoritative but wonderfully wise: deft in conveying the conflicted negotiations that characterize the actor-director relationship, and enchanting in his appreciation of the artistic spirit that he has nurtured and shaped throughout his remarkable directing career. His profound love of actors — and working with them — radiates through the book on every page. *I'll Be in My Trailer* will prove an invaluable text for filmmaking students, scholars and professionals alike."
— Dr. Robert Cohen, Trevor Professor of Drama, University of California, Irvine

"Here is a book by a master director that strips away the layers of confusion about how to make a movie and how to deal with the people and the problems. With wit and wisdom and practical examples taken from the experience of a variety of filmmakers (that include me!), John and his co-writ
the novice and the established."
— Jeremy Kagan, Director, Professor of Cinem

"I'll Be in My Trailer is an entertaining primer on what and what not to say to actors, replete with horror stories from many well-known actors and directors. John Badham has great war stories from the movie set and the scars to prove it! A highly entertaining book and should be mandatory reading for anyone who's considering a career as a director. Highly recommended!"
— Wayne Crawford, Producer/Writer/Director (*Valley Girl, Night of the Comet, Jake Speed*)

"This is a unique and practical resource for directors — as well as actors, producers, and anyone else interested in how good dramatic storytelling is done. An enormously talented and humane director has assembled a cogent approach to acting and directing, highlighted by insights from leading professional artists who are unrivalled in their frankness and diversity of views. Actors, directors, and producers seeking to deepen their own craft, and to better understand the craft of their collaborators, will do well to read this book now — and return to it regularly for future reference."
— James Bundy, Dean, Yale School of Drama/Artist Director, Yale Repertory Theater

"This book is a terrific read for both the beginner and the seasoned professional."
— Peter Hunt, Tony Award winner for Best Director, *1776*

"Where was this book forty years ago when I started directing?"
— Arthur Hiller, former President, Academy of Motion Pictures & Directors Guild of America

"GREAT opening and lead chapter. One of the many things John Badham does right is grab so many other voices and viewpoints of talented pros. The 'historical worth' of this read is enough to make me happy in and of itself."
— James Grady, Novelist (*Six Days of the Condor, White Flame, River of Darkness*)

"I'll Be in My Trailer conveys the inspiration and heartache of being a career director, with Mr. Badham accomplishing one of the most difficult things in writing: to actually make the reader feel as though they have absorbed his hard-earned experience. Reading this book is the next best thing to having a microchip with John Badham's memories installed in your brain. A must read for any director at any stage of their career."
— Jeremy Hanke, Editor, *Microfilmmaker* Magazine

"An excellent book about the sometimes dysfunctional relationships between actors and directors. It's about time someone wrote this book. Badham proves himself as good a writer as he is a director."
— Matthew Terry, Screenwriter/Teacher/Columnist for *www.hollywoodlitsales.com*

"John Badham and Craig Modderno have crafted an insider's guide to the care and feeding of actors. It's a fascinating page-turner that draws the fine line between art and therapy. It's sure to become a classic and should be required reading for anyone who even thinks about stepping foot on a movie set."
— Catherine Clinch, Associate Publisher, *Creative Screenwriting* Magazine

I'll Be in My Trailer

THE CREATIVE WARS
between Directors and Actors

JOHN BADHAM
AND CRAIG MODDERNO

MICHAEL WIESE PRODUCTIONS

Published by Michael Wiese Productions
11288 Ventura Boulevard
Suite #621
Studio City, CA 91604
(818) 379-8799, (818) 986-3408 (FAX).
mw@mwp.com
www.mwp.com

Cover design by MWP
Interior design by William Morosi
Copyedited by Paul Norlen
Printed by McNaughton & Gunn

Library of Congress Cataloging-in-Publication Data

Badham, John, 1939-
I'll be in my trailer : the creative wars between directors & actors / John Badham and Craig Modderno.
     p. cm.
Includes index.
ISBN 1-932907-14-9
1. Motion pictures--Production and direction. 2. Motion picture acting. I. Modderno, Craig, 1950- II. Title.
PN1993.9.P7B273 2006
791.4302'33--dc22
                                2006013455

*In memory of John Frankenheimer (1930-2002)
and Michael Ritchie (1938-2001), directors whose talent,
intelligence, creativity, and toughness of spirit will always be
an inspiration to directors everywhere*

Dedication

This book is lovingly dedicated to my mother,
Mary I. Badham (1916-1972),
an actress of great talent and soul whose inspirations and vitality
continue to inspire both my sister, Mary Badham, and me.

Dedication

To my parents, who encouraged my love of movies, and to
the many, many film artists who continue to make my life
more enjoyable with their on-screen creations.

Craig Modderno

Table of Contents

How to Hide
The Moral of This Tale Is?
Novice Director Meets Richard Pryor
Career in the Dumper
Summary

Universal Peeves
Summary

The Magic, Please
Summary

If It Looks So Easy, You Try It
Craziness Clarified
Just a Bunch of Children?
"Never Act with Dogs or Kids"
Crybabies Too?

Actors Are Different Than You and Me
Summary

Active Action Verbs
Rehearsing Emotional Scenes
This'll Shut 'em Up
Napoleon's One-Minute Manager
Phantom Kibitzers
Summary

What's the First Shot?
Six-Hundred-Pound Gorillas
Forget Them, What About Me?
It's About Respect
Summary

Get a Stuntman
Who Made You God of Ideas?
Summary

Result Directing
Tricky, Tricky
Skip the Bullshit, What Do You Want?
Off the Wall
Rx for Stage Actors
Film Actors Can't Throw Stones
Summary

Obvious Possibilities
The Dog Ate My Dialogue
This Scene Is Stupid
Can't Play It Truthfully
What Is the Real Emotion?
Fear of Failure
They Are Not There
I'm Not Saying This
I'm Not Doing This

Acknowledgments

Until writing this book I never appreciated how much support and help a writer needs.

My dear wife, Julia Badham, who not only read and gave tough feedback on draft after draft but understandingly did without my company on many evenings and weekends, though my G4 laptop was often the object of many curses. My daughter, Kelley Badham, who used her skills as a photographer, museum curator, and publicist to organize and restore the piles of photographs in the book into some sense of order. Director Vanessa Ruane, who tirelessly chased after many elusive directors, actors, and studios to get their signatures and permissions. My manager, Todd Harris, and agent, Jill Gillett, who encouraged me to complete the book even though it meant having to turn down some more lucrative assignments. My students and teaching assistants Stacey Kattman and Marissa Mueller at the Dodge School of Film and Media at Chapman University, who read every chapter and gave me intelligent and constructive feedback. "Colonel" Lee Rosenberg, my agent for 25 years, whose fountain of wisdom continues to guide my life.

I am very grateful to the many photographers who gave us permission to use their photographs and especially to Paramount Pictures senior advisor Robert Friedman, who generously donated permission to use all the photos from *Saturday Night Fever*, *Drop Zone*, and *Nick of Time*.

And finally, love and thanks to our two Westies, Barkely and Fanny, who stayed by my PowerBook for years and refused to let me feel like a "lonely writer."

John Badham

I'd like to acknowledge the support and friendship of Frances Doel, Carl Gottlieb, Paul Shefrin, Michael Cipely, Paul Ventura, Dr. Jerry Buss, Ed Asner, Kurtwood Smith, Evan Fong, Bob Strauss, Alan and Laura Davy, Buck Henry, Marvin Levy and my parents in encouraging me to be the best person I could be... at least creatively!

Craig Modderno

Preface

I was teaching a directing class at the American Film Institute in 1997 where we were discussing different techniques of staging film scenes between actors. The subject was whether it was better for the director to tell actors where to stand and move or to allow them to discover it for themselves. Suddenly a hand went up in the back of the class. A very serious and beautiful young woman queried, "Yes, but what do you do when actors won't do what you tell them to do?"

I've been asked tougher questions before. But asking why actors sometimes won't listen could take a reealllly long time to answer. While I fumbled for a concise reply, an amazing thing happened: The entire class came to attention. Their ears seemed to extend towards me like trumpets while they waited. It was as though I was going to tell them surefire ways to win at blackjack in Las Vegas. This was a *big* topic for them. They understood everything about cameras, lights and sound equipment. CGI-Special Effects is child's play. But ACTORS??!! Remembering my own awkwardness and terror as a beginning director working with actors who always had their own ideas about what to do, I couldn't blame any tyro director for feeling the same way. I could, however, pass on a lot of practical knowledge.

The next day I called my longtime friend, journalist Craig Modderno, who has been doing interviews for many years with both film and sports celebrities for the *Los Angeles Times*, the *New York Times*, entertainment magazines and even *Penthouse*. Though he was not about to introduce me to any cool girls from *Penthouse*, his skill at interviewing would be invaluable for finding out as much about working with actors as we could.

We did not want to write a dry textbook but something that anyone who loves movies could read and appreciate. Between me and the many directors and actors we interviewed, we heard lots of funny and not-funny-at-all war stories of disasters and catastrophes, as well as success stories. These anecdotes are entertaining for anyone who loves movies and has a taste for gossip gussied up as educational.

We interviewed as many of the talented and skilled directors as we could corner like Oliver Stone, Michael Mann, Sydney Pollack, and Steven Soderbergh to get their perspectives on this elusive art: working with actors. We were fortunate to talk to the late John Frankenheimer shortly before his untimely passing. It seemed to us at the time that he was determined to pass along as much of his vast knowledge as he could while he still had time.

We also talked to actor/directors like Jack Nicholson, Richard Dreyfuss, Anne Bancroft, James Woods, Mel Gibson and Mark Rydell so we could present a fully rounded picture, combining their knowledge with my thirty-plus years of directing experience. They willingly shared their hard-earned knowledge, spending hours articulating the kinds of things that go wrong and right in that often acrimonious marriage between an actor and a director.

We looked for answers to questions like: What does an actor want to hear from a director as he is rehearsing or performing his role? What do directors do that alienates actors? What does the actor never want to hear from a director?

In this book we'll talk about the ten worst and the ten best things you can say to an actor. We will explore the nature of an actor's temperament and the true nature of his contributions. We want to understand the nature of creativity and its many pitfalls. We will go through the processes of casting and rehearsal. We will watch what happens in an actor's mind during a performance, whether it is on a proscenium stage on Broadway or the 007 Stage at Pinewood.

Who knew all this would take five years to accomplish? Getting time with these very busy people was always difficult. Just as we would get on a roll with interviews, either Craig or I would get another day job that would have to take precedence. Craig wrote hundreds of articles for different media and I directed five movies and several TV episodes in this time. The good part was that I could both interview the actors I was working with — like Candice Bergen, Michael Chiklis, Don Johnson, James Garner, Jeanne Tripplehorn, Jenna Elfman, Sam Robards, Bryan Brown, George Eads and Jamie Pressly — and also put into practice many of the things I was learning from them.

Finally, lest anyone take offense at the tone of the book, much of it is written with tongue firmly implanted in cheek. My love for actors is deep and sincere. Though I may write about them as though I were one of those cynics who mistrust and mock the acting profession, it does not reflect my personal admiration for what actors are capable of and their dedication to a difficult craft. Regarding any actor with less than honest respect would be a serious flaw for any director.

Author's note: In this age of gender neutrality, I have alternated references between masculine and feminine when referring to directors and actors.

Introduction

by Craig Modderno

Like most love affairs, mine with movies didn't start very well. My father took me to see *Dr. Jekyll and Mr. Hyde* at the local cinema in Mount Holly, North Carolina. The story of a crazed genius with two conflicting personalities, *Dr. Jekyll and Mr. Hyde* was an omen of seemingly every third person I've ever encountered in Hollywood. But to a preteen who at the time had never even watched television, the terrifying sight of Spencer Tracy basically transforming himself from man to monster elicited screams and tears from your frightened author. The next time my parents took me to the movies Ma and Pa Kettle were on the screen showcasing animals on a farm. The experience was almost like having sex for the second time; one knew it couldn't be as scary as the first encounter, so you let what you were facing work its magic.

(When I did the first major interview in print with Steven Spielberg for *Penthouse* magazine in 1977 he told me that when he watched his first adult movie for the next five minutes the legendary director wanted to have sex with anything and then he watched five more minutes and was convinced that he never wanted to have sex again! To quote Chief Dan George in the movie *Little Big Man*: "Sometimes the magic works and sometimes it doesn't.")

Later my father moved us to Italy. (My father worked for the military or the Mafia, but I was never sure which. All I know is when we moved it would always be late at night and halfway around the world.) A classmate told me to come to his house after school to see a movie being shot down the street. Sex and cinema were then bonded forever in my slowly expanding teenage brain as I watched Sophia Loren acting in *Yesterday, Today and Tomorrow*. She was then, now, and always will be one of the most beautiful women in the world. Ms. Loren, who grew up in the slums of a nearby Italian city, joked and played with the local kids during breaks in filming. Unfortunately I was mute and unable to move, which Burt Reynolds years later told me was his response as an adult upon meeting the magnetic Ms. Loren. (When I came to Hollywood in 1975 I was told there are only two people in show business who will have sex appeal until they die: Sophia Loren and Paul Newman! Nobody has ever refuted that statement to me almost thirty years later.)

After we moved to the San Francisco Bay Area in 1965 I took several jobs while in high school to support our family once my father died two years later. My love of movies only increased as I worked at one of the first domed theatres in California (Century 21 in Pleasant Hill) and the Concord Drive-In, which has long since been destroyed but remains visible forever in the scene where the airplane carrying Richard Dreyfuss to college departs at the end of *American Graffiti*.

At the drive-in we changed programs once a week. I worked at the Dome almost eight months and we played only three pictures: *The Graduate*, *Camelot*, and *Grand Prix*. When we opened *Candy* on Christmas I quit that evening rather than face four months of viewing this horrible film every day. Working as a doorman and assistant manager at the Dome, particularly during the summer of 1968 when *The Graduate* played there exclusively, taught me so much about why people go to the movies and what they look for in their entertainment pursuits.

The thought of Anne Bancroft seducing me into an affair with an older woman was far more appealing to this newly turned high school graduate than President Lyndon Johnson getting me to play the draft lottery as the conflict in Vietnam escalated into a debilitating war. A happy-to-be child of the sixties, I, like other people of my generation, looked to movies to help explain the military madness engulfing our rapidly changing times.

Films like *Cool Hand Luke*, *M.A.S.H.*, *Bullitt*, *Z*, *The Graduate*, *Woodstock*, *Midnight Cowboy*, *In the Heat of the Night*, *Goodbye Columbus*, *Easy Rider*, *The Wild Bunch*, *Petulia*, *Joe*, *Summer of '42*, *Patton*, *Faces*, *Bonnie and Clyde*, and *2001: A Space Odyssey* were excellent entertainments which managed to speak directly to the public in a way few politicians (who hadn't been murdered) were able to do at the time or since.

In today's Hollywood, movies are often made as merchandising-driven vehicles bolstered by multimillion-dollar media-manipulated hype. If you want to compare the difference in a Hollywood that encouraged risk-taking creativity and the current one aimed at fulfilling fifteen-year-old boys' fantasies, then ask yourself two questions: "When was the last time you saw a movie whose ending you couldn't predict within ten minutes?" and "What was the last new film that you saw which had an impact on your life?"

Don Farrar, a longtime friend and a film buyer for almost forty years, always reminded me never to underestimate the intelligence of a movie audience... something today's Hollywood hierarchy often does as they pander their youthful trendy topics to an extremely fickle public.

Explains Farrar: "The best hype in the world can never compete with good or bad word-of-mouth. At times it's almost as if somebody called someone that they didn't even know and said: 'You don't know me and I live many miles away from you, but there's a movie coming out Friday (think *The Cat in the Hat* for example) that you shouldn't bother seeing!'"

Woody Allen, who was my first professional interview, later gave me a job working for him as he directed his first film *Take the Money and Run* in San Francisco in 1968. Whenever I got away from school in the final days of my senior year and the first months of summer I would call the production office to find out where the company was shooting. Woody paid me out of his own pocket for gas and bridge tolls for having me assist him when needed. Since I was an only child whose father had died two weeks prior to the start of my senior year and a prime lottery candidate for a winning ticket to the front lines of Vietnam, Woody's extreme kindness and patience while explaining his filmmaking process was a noble gesture towards a confused young man seeking his way in life.

Stars in the sixties were generally much nicer to ordinary people attempting to break into the business, earn a living, or merely seeking a kind word. Paul Newman gave me an interview for my high school newspaper in the lobby of the famed Fairmont Hotel. Director Richard Lester, who directed the classic Beatles films *A Hard Day's Night* and *Help!*, stopped a security guard from kicking me out of an underground garage in San Francisco where he was directing George C. Scott and a drop-dead gorgeous Julie Christie in his emotionally powerful picture *Petulia*. When Robert Redford was starring in Michael Ritchie's *The Candidate* in the Bay Area, he let me follow him around for a few days for a story in my college newspaper, and, like Woody Allen, offered detailed encouragement and advice on pursuing an artistic career.

One should not leave with the mistaken impression that all celebrities have the class and courtesy exhibited early in my career by Mr. Allen, Mr. Lester, and Mr. Newman. Conversely, I am not someone who will defend the media carte blanche from celebrity complaints, especially so-called celebrity journalists when faced with a complaint by a celebrity. Still, people should know the damage a rude, egotistical, or dishonest celebrity can do to a writer's career and relationships. Two examples are thus offered.

When I was a freelancer working for *TV Guide* over a decade ago, I got an assignment to do a cover story with Paul Reiser, who was hosting the Grammy Awards. Reiser agreed to do the interview, then kept putting it off for no apparent reason and making me wait three days at home for his phone call, which never came. When Reiser was asked by a mutual friend of ours why he treated me so unprofessionally, Reiser angrily replied: "I don't give a... about what I did. The story wasn't going to put another dollar in my pocket!"

Another insensitive actor I spent a day interviewing was Matthew Perry, whom I experienced first hand enjoying making enemies rather than friends during his initial celebrity exposure. I took Perry to a Los Angeles Kings game, which he suggested we do, to talk to him about hockey during the contest for a story in the team's magazine. Young fans sent over food and sodas to Perry, seeking only a smile or a wave in return. "You eat this stuff. Why do these people keep bothering me when I'm only here to watch the game?" Perry angrily asked me.

Why is personality and image so important to an actor or a politician in dealing with the public? Because that's generally what they're selling. Humphrey Bogart, James Cagney, and Steve McQueen were just a few legendary actors who didn't make hit movies all the time, but did, nonetheless, attract a loyal audience even to their lesser efforts because these true superstars had an on and off-screen persona which the public admired.

"What are they really like?" is the question I'm most asked of the celebrities I've spoken with. Today's celebrity is given superstar status too quickly by a starving, insatiable internet-led media needing to be fed 24-7 around the world. Thus many people knew the reason Britney Spears got divorced even before they realized she had been married.

We may all lead a simple life, but Hollywood does its best to shed some perspective on the glamorous life that we're missing. So when John Badham, a nice and bright man who has directed several films that I like, asked me to co-write this book with him I was instantly interested. We took the actors and directors to the restaurant of their choice or brought food to them.

Since today's filmmakers rarely discuss their craft unless they're addressing a class, several of our actors and directors kept asking if we were getting what we needed.

The annual tribute at the Academy Awards to the people in show business who have died since the previous Oscars is extremely emotional. Like any movie fan, I often find myself asking questions about certain actors and directors, long since departed, who worked with my interview subject. I never get tired of actor/author/director/screenwriter Carl Gottlieb, who co-wrote *Jaws* and *The Jerk* amongst a long list of impressive credits, telling me about a scene John Huston directed with him and Jack Nicholson, which didn't make the final cut of *Prizzi's Honor*. Or asking Carl about how larger-than-life actor Robert Shaw endured the daily problems the mechanical, malfunctioning shark caused the cast, crew and director Steven Spielberg on the set of *Jaws*, all of which Gottlieb detailed in his must-read book *The Jaws Log*. Looking at the memorial tribute at the Academy Awards through the years I recalled personal and pleasant memories dealing with the dearly departed John Alonzo, George Burns, Frank Capra, Richard Crenna, Richard Harris, Jack Lemmon, Frank Sinatra, Bette Davis, Robert Stack, Richard Sylbert, John Wayne, and Natalie Wood, just to name a few filmmakers who were kind to me beyond the need to conduct the business we were doing.

And then there were the legends who, much like the artists interviewed in this book, taught me about their craft during an interview with special stories that I'd like to pass on. Burt Lancaster said Montgomery Clift was the only actor he ever feared because his *From Here to Eternity* co-star didn't know how good he was; citing an example to me of the scene in the World War II drama where Clift merely had to listen to his military superior's personal problems. Recalled Lancaster: "Clift listened so intensely and compassionately to me that when I saw the movie even I was drawn to watching him on screen and it was my big scene!"

Bette Davis, who had a respect for and love of her craft even long after she was offered the quality roles in which to prove it, told me: "If you can't be emotionally and physically naked in front of strangers then don't act. Actors generally express the emotions publicly which most people can't even deal with privately."

Hopefully this book will give some fresh insights to the often-creative war between actors and directors, the games if you will that artists often play in order to get the results they seek. There's a memorable still photo from *North by Northwest* where Cary Grant is being attacked by a crop duster plane. The body language Grant exhibits in the shot is amazing and quite athletic. Grant's looking over his shoulder and yet half his body is frozen, ready to run at a moment's notice. Grant told me he was a close friend of Hitchcock, but like most directors the master of suspense would do whatever necessary to get the results on film that he wanted. For that particular scene Hitchcock had told the pilot to fly lower than Grant was expecting. The terror on the actor's face is real and the physical conflict genuine because Grant is looking for the assistant director to give him the off-camera cue to start running. But as the plane flies closer and lower than Grant was told, the frightened actor — ever the professional — wouldn't move until given the pre-arranged, off-camera signal to do so.

When he was just starting acting in films, Robert Mitchum told me his agents advised him not to play villains because he might get typecast. Mitchum's approach to this important aspect of his business and craft was to balk at any suggestion of image management.

Mitchum recalled years later with a sardonic grin: "I loved playing villains, especially as a young actor. A villain doesn't get cut out of the picture and he generally has a contract that runs through the course of the movie. If the hero and the screenwriter and the director do any kind of half-ass job, your work as a villain is almost done with just a little effort on your part. Plus, more women are attracted to bad guys than they'll admit. It's good pay for basically showing up and acting like you would if someone threw a bucket of water on you while you're sleeping."

Mitchum's laid-back acting style and I-don't-give-a-damn attitude suckered many a filmmaker into underestimating him until they saw his performance on screen. Gregory Peck, Mitchum's co-star in and the unofficial producer of the original *Cape Fear*, didn't make that mistake. Peck candidly told me of his admiration for Mitchum's acting ability. "I usually eat a meal each shooting day with my co-star or director just to get to know them better and discuss any problems they might have with the picture. But I didn't do that with Bob on *Cape Fear*. I knew when I bought the book that the villain was the best part. Even though I portray the hero, I'm not on equal footing with Bob's character until the finale of the film when we're fighting. So if I were to have breakfast with Bob and he were to ask me how I was feeling and I'd tell him I had a fight with the wife last night he would put his arm around me and say 'Tell me all about it Greg. I'm in the doghouse with my wife every night!' Bob would be nice, helpful, and then whatever I told him he'd somehow use in his character against me in our next scenes together. Bob is an extremely underrated actor because his technique is not obvious or visibly apparent. As a result of that Bob forces you to be at your best in every scene you're in with him or you'll come out second best while he'll come off as natural as someone could be."

While not inclined to get into a philosophical discussion of acting, Mitchum later responded to what Peck told me. "Greg knows there's a little evil in every hero, which is why he's always believable playing both. He understands on a basic level what good and evil is all about. Greg's also a very nice man, which makes the audience like him instantly and the villain's job harder in trying to find his character's weakness."

Having acted in one film, the boxing comedy *The Great White Hype*, my respect for actors and directors only increased. I was witness to the creative preparations of and acted with Samuel L. Jackson, Jeff Goldblum, Damon Wayans, Jon Lovitz, Cheech Marin, Pete Berg, Jamie Foxx, Rocky Carroll, Albert Hall, Salli Richardson, Corbin Bernsen, and John Rhys-Davies. The actors and director Reggie Hudlin may not remember me and my impressive on camera ad-lib, but the filmmaking lessons I got from talking to and observing them at work made me more understanding of what the artists in this book passionately articulated. Still, acting isn't brain surgery unless you're playing a brain surgeon, and directing can't be that difficult since each porn film has at least one credited director!

But as Woody Allen once said, "Sex between two people is a meaningless experience, but as meaningless experiences go it's one of the best." With all proper respect, I think actors and directors echo Woody's observation in regards to their craft at some point in their career. Thus my sincere thanks to the filmmakers in this book for letting us share their personal experiences and thoughts on creative differences.

Contributors

Without the generous help of all the following people, this book would not have the wisdom they shared. We cannot thank them enough.

Ed Asner is the only actor to win Emmys for playing the same character (Lou Grant) in both a comedy (*The Mary Tyler Moore Show*, 1970) and a drama (*Lou Grant*, 1977).

Anne Bancroft won an Academy Award for her performance in *The Miracle Worker* and stunned audiences with her mature sexuality as Mrs. Robinson in *The Graduate*. She directed the movie *Fatso*.

Candice Bergen has won five Emmy Awards for her work in the eponymous *Murphy Brown*. She is renowned for her exquisite photographs of Africa.

Scott Brazil is an executive producer and director of multiple episodes of *The Shield*.

Gary Busey was nominated for an Oscar for his portrayal of Buddy Holly in *The Buddy Holly Story*. He creates astounding and unusual characters in his many films such as *Lethal Weapon*, *The Bear*, *Point Break*, *Under Siege*, *Big Wednesday*, as well as John Badham's *Drop Zone* and *The Law*.

Robert Butler, Emmy and DGA-winning director of *Hill Street Blues* and *The Waltons*, is one of the most sought-after directors in series television. Whether it is the pilot of *Moonlighting*, *Sisters*, or *The New Adventures of Superman* that he is directing, he always brings a solid and talented sensibility to whatever he does.

Michael Chiklis, the Emmy-winning star and director of *The Shield*, came to prominence in 1989 playing John Belushi in *Wired*. He starred in *The Commish* and *Daddio*.

Rob Cohen became head of Motown Films at the young age of twenty-five. After an impressive start producing *Lady Sings the Blues*, *The Bingo Long Traveling All-Stars and Motor Kings*, *The Witches of Eastwick*, and *Bird on a Wire*, among others, his directing career took flight with *Dragon: The Bruce Lee Story*, *Dragonslayer*, *The Fast and the Furious*, and *XXX*.

Stephen Collins earned an Emmy-nomination for his role in the series *Seventh Heaven*, as well as being voted one of the greatest TV Dads of all time by *TV Guide*. He has appeared in *Star Trek: The Motion Picture* and many other films. He has written two novels, *Double Exposure* and *Eye Contact*.

Martha Coolidge, past President of the Directors Guild of America, is known for her excellent directing of Halle Berry in *Introducing Dorothy Dandridge* and Neil Simon's *Lost in Yonkers*.

Roger Corman, though originally known as the King of Low Budget films, has assured his place in film history by his phenomenal ability to spot talent through his mentoring of Francis Ford Coppola, James Cameron, Martin Scorsese, Peter Bogdanovich, and many others. He holds the world record for the shortest feature schedule ever: *Little Shop of Horrors* was completed in two days.

John Cusack, the best known of the equally talented members of the Cusack family, made his feature debut with Rob Lowe in *Class*. His performances in *Say Anything*, *The Grifters*, *Grosse Pointe Blank*, and his father Dick Cusack's screenplay *The Jack Bull* have earned him great respect from critics and audiences alike.

Jan de Bont originally earned fame as a cinematographer. He became a director with the box office hit *Speed*, which he followed with another huge hit, *Twister*.

Richard Donner is an internationally-acclaimed director who has worked on films including *The Omen*, *Superman*, the *Lethal Weapon* series, *Goonies*, *Ladyhawke*, *Maverick*, and *Radio Flyers*.

Richard Dreyfuss' Oscar for his performance in *The Goodbye Girl* is only the tip of the iceberg for this likable and extraordinary talent. His other films include *The Education of Duddy Kravitz*, *Jaws*, *Close Encounters of the Third Kind*, *Whose Life Is It Anyway?*, *Stakeout*, and *Mr. Holland's Opus*.

Jenna Elfman is the Emmy and Golden Globe–nominated star of the TV series *Dharma and Greg* and films including *Obsessed*, *Looney Tunes*, and *Ed TV*.

Robert Forster became known to audiences for his appearance with Marlon Brando in John Huston's *Reflections in a Golden Eye*. He also starred in *Medium Cool*, the cult favorite *Alligator*, and Quentin Tarantino's *Jackie Brown*.

John Frankenheimer, the most famous of the Golden Age of live TV directors, became a major force in American cinema with his clever and controversial film *The Manchurian Candidate*, followed by *Seven Days in May*, *Grand Prix*, *Seconds*, *Black Sunday*, *Ronin*, and his Emmy Award–winning *Against the Wall*.

Mel Gibson was made famous as *Mad Max*. His work in *Gallipoli* won him his second Australian Film Institute award. After appearing in *The Bounty*, he took the role of Martin Riggs in the *Lethal Weapon* series and impressed critics with his starring role in *Hamlet*. He won two Oscars for his direction of *Braveheart*. Against the advice and enmity of all major Hollywood studios he personally financed *The Passion of the Christ*. The film has earned over one billion dollars at the box office.

Dennis Haysbert has appeared as the President of the United States on *24* as well as in films like *Far From Heaven*.

Arthur Hiller, past President of the Directors Guild of America and the Academy of Motion Picture Arts and Sciences, is best known for his Academy Award-nominated direction of *Love Story* and Paddy Chayevsky's *The Hospital*. His comedies *Silver Streak*, *The In-Laws*, and *See No Evil, Hear No Evil* are perpetual favorites.

Peter Hunt is the Tony Award–winning director of the original production of *1776* on Broadway as well as the film of the same name. Well known for his excellent tenure as artistic director of the Williamstown Theatre Festival, his films *Bully* and *Give Em Hell, Harry* demonstrate his great skill with actors.

Peter Hyams began as a journalist and musician, then broke into films by writing and producing *T.R. Baskin* with Candice Bergen. His films of *Busting*, *Capricorn One*, *Outland*, *The Star Chamber*, and *2010* established him as a great action director as well. He is one of the few directors to also photograph and edit his own films.

Jeremy Kagan's film *The Journey of Natty Gann* was the first American Gold Prize winner at the Moscow Film Festival. His films *Heroes*, *The Big Fix*, and *The Chosen* were hits as were his Emmy-winning episode of *Chicago Hope* and his DGA-nominated film *Crown Heights*. He is the chair of the Directing Program at USC Film School.

Randal Kleiser, best known for his direction of *Grease*, *The Blue Lagoon*, *Honey, I Blew Up the Kid*, and *White Fang*, is a pioneer in the use of digital techniques for film.

Frank Langella earned a Tony nomination for *Dracula*. He was a two-time Tony winner for his starring roles in *Seascape* and *Fortune's Fool*, and appeared in the films *Diary of a Mad Housewife*, *Dracula*, *Dave*, *Lolita*, *The Ninth Gate*, *Good Night and Good Luck*, and *Superman Returns*.

Eriq LaSalle, the well-known actor from *ER*, became a director with the acclaimed HBO film, *Rebound*.

David Levinson took home the Emmy for Best Television Series, *The Senator*, in 1971. He followed that as the talented producer of series such as *The Bold Ones*, *Charlie's Angels*, *21 Jump Street*, *The Commish*, *Alfred Hitchcock Presents*, and *The Invisible Man*.

Tom Mankiewicz is the writer of many of the James Bond films including *Diamonds Are Forever*, *Live and Let Die* and *The Man with the Golden Gun*. He directed Tom Hanks and Dan Ackroyd in *Dragnet* and created the TV series *Hart to Hart*.

Michael Mann, four-time Oscar Nominee for *The Insider*, has directed *Collateral*, *Ali*, *Heat*, and *Last of the Mohicans*. He created and produced *Miami Vice* for television.

Penelope Ann Miller, Tony-nominated actress for *Our Town* on Broadway, starred with Marlon Brando in *The Freshman* and Sean Penn in *Carlito's Way*.

Leland Orser often plays deranged characters in films like *Seven*, *The Bone Collector*, *Alien Resurrection*, and *Star Trek Voyager*. He is married to Jeanne Tripplehorn, and has appeared with her in John Badham's *Brother's Keeper*.

Paul Pape broke into films opposite John Travolta in *Saturday Night Fever* and became a major force as a voice-over actor with over 2,500 credits as well as appearing on *Resurrection Blvd.* for Showtime and *The Detective* for Hallmark.

Sydney Pollack is a double Academy Award winner for *Out of Africa*. He was nominated for two Oscars for the films *Tootsie* and *They Shoot Horses, Don't They?* His films include *The Interpreter*, *The Firm*, *The Way We Were*, and *Jeremiah Johnson*. As an actor he co-starred opposite Dustin Hoffman in *Tootsie* and Tom Cruise in *Eyes Wide Shut*.

Judge Reinhold is known for his quirky character work in *Fast Times at Ridgemont High*, the *Beverly Hills Cop* series, *Stripes*, *The Santa Clause*, and John Badham's *Floating Away*.

Mark Rydell was nominated for an Oscar for his film of *On Golden Pond*. His other films include *The Cowboys, The Rose, The Reivers,* and *The Fox*. He received an Emmy nomination for his direction of *James Dean*.

Martin Sheen, Golden Globe and Emmy Award–winning actor for his role as the President on *The West Wing* and dedicated social activist, is well known for his excellent performances in *Apocalypse Now, Wall Street* (opposite his son Charlie Sheen), *JFK, That Certain Summer,* and *The Execution of Private Slovik.*

Brad Silberling, adept at fantasy, comedy and drama, has directed a varied body of films including *City of Angels, Casper,* and *Moonlight Mile.*

Kurtwood Smith's performances in *RoboCop, Dead Poets Society, A Time to Kill, That 70's Show,* among many others, demonstrates his talent for creating memorable characters.

Steven Soderbergh is a multiple Oscar winner for his films *Erin Brockovich* and *Traffic.* His talent for the commercial shown in *Oceans Eleven* and *Twelve* contrasts with his seminal *sex, lies, and videotape.* He is a pioneer in digital video.

Oliver Stone, multiple Oscar winner for his films *JFK, Platoon,* and *Born on the Fourth of July,* continues to rile audiences and critics alike with his controversial approach to any subject he tackles.

Betty Thomas is an Emmy and DGA award–winning director, actress, and producer with the films *Doctor Dolittle, I Spy,* and *28 Days* plus television work in *Hill Street Blues* and *Dream On.*

John Travolta burst upon the movie world with his Oscar-nominated role in *Saturday Night Fever,* followed by the equally big hit *Grease.* Other major hits like *Urban Cowboy,* the *Look Who's Talking* series, *Pulp Fiction, Get Shorty, Face Off,* and *A Civil Action* are only a few of this prolific and talented actor's filmography.

Jeanne Tripplehorn became prominent with her starring role opposite Michael Douglas in *Basic Instinct.* She continued to show a powerful screen presence and talent in *The Firm, Waterworld, Sliding Doors, Mickey Blue Eyes,* and *My Brother's Keeper.*

David Ward, Oscar winner for his screenplay of *The Sting* and Oscar nominated for writing *Sleepless in Seattle,* became a director with his film of

Cannery Row, followed by the *Major League* series, *King Ralph*, *The Program*, and *Down Periscope*. He is the head of the Screenwriting Program at the Dodge College of Film and Media Arts at Chapman University.

James Woods, always exciting, never dull scatological actor, is twice Oscar-nominated for his roles in *Salvador* and *Ghosts of Mississippi*. His performances in *Once Upon a Time in America, Casino, Be Cool, The General's Daughter, Any Given Sunday, Contact, Rudy: The Rudy Giuliani Story*, and John Badham's *The Hard Way*, are only a few of his special performances.

No Day at the Beach

Making a movie can be a first-class blast most days. This is not one of those days. The only blast is coming from the Northeast at 30 miles an hour. It's midnight. I am freezing as I stand on the upper level of the Verrazano Bridge that connects Brooklyn and Staten Island. It is one o'clock in the morning in March 1977. I have a crew of 60 people standing around freezing at 10 degrees above zero. And *we are doing nothing*. We are not shooting. We are not talking. We are supposed to be making "Tribal Rites of the New Saturday Night," fortunately renamed *Saturday Night Fever*. A 22-year-old John Travolta is refusing to do the scene as staged by the director — me. He is shut in his trailer. We still have a big scene to shoot that night and the sun will explode on us at 6 a.m. whether I like it or not. Of course, it must be all my fault. I have to get us shooting — and Travolta won't come out to play. What's a director to do?

Rewind to 1976. Another non-blast day. I am shooting in Macon, Georgia on a baseball diamond in a 100-degree blazing sun with 90% humidity. I have a crew of 60 people standing around melting. And *we are doing nothing*. We are not shooting. We are not talking. My first feature film, *The Bingo Long Traveling All Stars and Motor Kings*, is not traveling anywhere today. This movie, which stars Billy Dee Williams, James Earl Jones, and Richard Pryor, is a very affectionate look at the last days of the Negro Baseball Leagues.

In the hot sun I am looking at a very angry Richard Pryor planted 18 inches from my face, demanding an apology. I allegedly endangered his life the previous day by asking him to drive by the camera. Who knew? Today I have again put him in harm's way by asking him to slide into second base. Pryor is so mad he will fly back to Los Angeles, unless I apologize to him right now. I am young, stubborn, and above all, stupid. I tell myself I've done nothing wrong, so of course I won't apologize. This is why directors die young.

Thank God I'm not the only one who has bad days. Somewhere on location a movie is being made by two first-time directors working as a team on the HBO *Project Greenlight* series. The novice filmmakers have their first full crew, real cameraman, and professional actors, and everybody is rooting for them to succeed. Because it's all been recorded on video we get to watch the filmmakers struggle minute by minute through their shooting days. The series is a huge cinematic lesson for all of us on the perils of filmmaking. It might be easy to make fun of the way their shoot is going if everyone who has ever picked up a camera has not had similar problems. We've been there too and have sympathy for their trial by fire. *Project Greenlight* shows us talented people trying their hardest to make the best film possible. At the same time, the film's communication snafus threaten to cripple the whole movie, not the least of which is the directors' communication with the actors. We see the actors eager to please, eager to adjust in whatever way the directors want. We see the directors, desperate to make the scenes perfect, talking themselves blue.

The creative process often finds rookie directors failing to get the scene they want because of their inexperience talking to actors. The creative process often finds experienced directors failing to get the scene they want because of their lack of skill talking to actors. Talking to actors always seems so easy until the director, no matter how experienced, attempts it. There is a whole language of Actor-Speak. Harder to learn than Hottentot clicks, it can sound very "New Age" or it can be downright brutal and manipulative. Try talking that way to your cinematographer or an assistant director, and you'll get weird looks. What is that secret language? What is that Actor-Speak? Why can't they just do what they are told? The difficulties on *Project Greenlight* are not helped by the fact that the set is awash in kibitzers eager to direct. No matter how well meaning and well attuned to each other the creative team is, the suggestions from the crew are like the story of the blind men describing an elephant. We see the actors melt in confusion. No wonder smart actors learn to defend themselves from incompetent directors.

Jenna Elfman: "I find the most important thing for me is to study acting with a great teacher because sometimes you don't have a director that's going to lead you the way you need to be led, and you have to be able to lead yourself. I love being directed. I always hope to have a great director because I like that dynamic of being directed. One of the greatest experiences I've had being directed was with Ron Howard on *EdTV*."

The more headstrong actors dive into a mode of self-protection. They stop listening to the babble and go for what they think their character should be doing. With luck and talent they may stumble on a good scene, or parts of a good scene. Otherwise they can create a mess that even a talented editor will have trouble sorting out.

Any person who has directed anything, even the Christmas pageant at church, has collided head on with situations like these. There are directors on the planet that stoutly maintain they have *never* had problems with actors. I am thrilled for them, I would envy them but… they are *lying*. Not just through their teeth, but through their eyes, ears, nose, and throat. If there is life on other planets, there are actors out there making directors miserable. It is part and parcel of the often-dubious joy of being a director.

On the flip side, and just as grimly, there are plenty of directors everywhere making life miserable for actors. Some directors seem to do everything they can to alienate, frighten, and intimidate the actor. They rule by fear and yelling. Otto Preminger, Henry Hathaway, and John Ford terrified everyone by their very presence. Some directors like to make life miserable for the crew and the actors in smaller parts. They can't push the star around, so they kick the supporting cast instead.

Steven Soderbergh: "There are some directors that don't like actors, don't understand them, don't want to understand them, and think that they're in the way and that they slow things down."

There are passive-aggressive directors, called "Stealth Directors." They keep a distance from the actors, having little communication with them. The actor is left to creatively sink or swim on his own. Hiding behind television monitors or inside a control booth, these directors leave the actor hung out to dry rather than risk confrontation. Surprisingly, the Stealth director may be more prevalent than those who would emulate the more aggressive directors like John Ford, Roman Polanski, or James Cameron. These war-horses rule their sets with an iron fist, and have excellent movies to show for it.

Stephen Collins: "Few directors know how to talk to actors or do. There seems to be more and more a kind of wall between them and the actors. Mike Nichols said that directors never get to watch each other work.... You can count the number of directors who really, really help you on the fingers of maybe one hand.... If the stories of Hitchcock and William Wyler are true, apparently they didn't know what to say to actors either. But they knew how to do everything else so well."

"Who was the director on that TV show you just did?" I once asked a young actress. (Long pause.) "I don't know... I think he had a beard." I could wallpaper my office with variations on this conversation. It's a predictable one to hear from an actor at a party. They speak proudly of the latest job they've just finished. They tell me how much fun it was, how their agent got calls from the producer saying how good they were. But they don't know the name of the director?! The first six thousand times I heard this I just thought the actors were twits. Then I realized that they might never have had a real conversation with the director. The director had made little if any impression on them.

Betty Thomas: "The first time I remember someone directing me on screen, who really 'directed' me was Bob Butler — who directed the pilot of *Hill Street Blues*. I was supposed to be looking at Veronica Hamel's character Joyce

— Bob wanted to make a specific moment for me. Bob said, 'Your character doesn't like her. Let's show that.' I didn't have any lines, so I said, 'Okay, how are we going to show that?' And he said, 'Well, just think to yourself what your character really thinks of her. Just think it through and I'll do a close-up and we'll have it. That's all you have to do. Don't do anything else.' I said, 'Really? That's it?' He said, 'That's it.' And so he shot it and I did exactly what he said and afterwards he said, 'OK, that was it — I got it.' And he did."

Not so surprisingly, the directors that actors do remember — like Mike Nichols or Sydney Pollack or Martha Coolidge — are known for being good with actors. But do actors remember less well-known directors? You bet. If the director makes an effort to connect with an actor, he or she knows they're being looked out for. That's a lifeline to a drowning person. Actors may have been doing this for years yet still be a bowl of Jell-O inside. When you save somebody's life you have an ally forever. When you let them sink or swim on their own, the makeup artist means more to them than you do. At least they had meaningful contact with her. It's not about the actor remembering your name at a party. You'll make an ally that will do anything to help you make a good movie.

How can a director, young or old, beginning or experienced, talented or not, learn how to survive in these difficult arenas? Every bit of psychology, street smarts, anything that could pass for human relation skills will be called into play in a director's career. The sooner the director learns to confidently cope with the knotty problems that persistently arise, that will *not* go away, the sooner that director will begin to radiate the kind of ease and sureness of direction that make her a leader people want to follow. When Oliver Stone or Mark Rydell, Steven Soderbergh or Steven Spielberg talk on their sets, actors and crew listen. That's not just because they are Big Star directors who intimidate. Far from it. *They are accessible, kind and supportive of their creative partners*, the actors.

Directing students everywhere — USC, the Yale Drama School, the American Film Institute, Chapman University, or NYU — actively seek the answer to the question, "*What do you do when the actor won't do what you want?*" This is something they really, Really, REALLY want to know. A cinematic Holy Grail for aspiring filmmakers.

Sorry, no secrets here. There is no one-sentence answer. To paraphrase the New Testament, it is easier for a camel to pass through the eye of a needle than for a tyro director to understand the inner workings of an actor. Many experienced directors confess their frustrations when they first began trying to communicate with actors. They couldn't find the words to express what they thought. One thing for sure: using the words "more" or "less" or "faster" or "slower" is *not* directing.

How to Hide

Here are some great tools to isolate yourself from the cast so that you will never understand them and they will never know who you are.

1. Video Assist
2. The Camera
3. Lenses
4. Film Stocks and HDTV
5. Lighting
6. Cranes and Grip Equipment
7. Any CGI or Computer Effect

It's lots of fun to learn the workings of the Panavision camera, CGI effects or the Avid editing tools. You can see them; hold them in your hand. You can hide behind them. And best of all: they do what you tell them (theoretically)!

The beginning director can flee behind these wonders of technology, never to be seen again. He says he needs to concentrate on the "visual look" of the film... and the cast... well, the cast will take care of itself. This is nothing more or less than fresh steaming horsepucky. Directors need actors to tell a story, so why would they hide from them?

JB: "Is there anything you wish that directors would do with actors when they are working with them?"

Dennis Haysbert: "Talk to them about their characters. Today what I see with directors is that they are more concerned with the shot, rather than the character that they are shooting. They don't think about who your character is and where you are at this particular moment. In a scene, I'm always looking at where I came from, where I am, and where I'm going. And it helps you get through the scene."

Actors are not machines, actors are creative human beings. Whether they are highly paid professionals or beginning amateurs they have tremendous insecurities. *Just because you are a great actor with an Academy Award, doesn't mean you don't need, and don't really want, all the help and support that a director can give.*

A movie succeeds or fails on three things: the quality of the script, the quality of the actor's performance, and the quality of the director's realization. *If you don't start with a good script, cast, and director, you will not finish with a good movie.* This is not a cliché; this is an eternal truth, inscribed on the Dead Sea Scrolls… or somewhere.

If the director cannot inspire, lead, cajole, or even manipulate his actors to give their greatest talent to the script you will have a mediocre movie. And believe it or not, even a good director can really screw up a good script. All elements of a film have to work together. Mediocrity always lurks under an apple box on the set or an executive's desk, poised to invade. It's our job to make the movie shine, not to let the endless parade of script readers, executives, and producers with their "Notes" turn us into a Stepford Director.

The incidents mentioned earlier on the Verrazano Bridge and in Macon, Georgia are great object lessons about how *not* to work with actors. How *never* to work with actors. My tardy and sincere apology to all the actors I've misdirected or emotionally abused in my years of fumbling to understand their psyche.

In *Saturday Night Fever*, there is a scene towards the end where Tony's friend Bobby C is going to jump from the bridge onto the rocks below. Tony and his friends go out onto an exposed beam to try to grab Bobby C before he jumps.

When we arrived on the set, the temperature was below 30. The wind was 25 knots. The line producer, Mike Hausman, and the stunt coordinator, Paul Nuckles, were worried that the steel beams of the bridge were going to freeze up in the March night air. We needed to make some shots with stunt doubles falling from the bridge before the freezing conditions would make the beams too slippery. Mike Hausman's wise recommendation was that we shoot the stunts first before the beams froze up. Then we could shoot close-ups with the actors in a safe location on the bridge.

While the actors were getting ready, I staged the stuntmen in the positions where I wanted the actors to be during the scene. The cameras and lights were prepped and we shot the stuntmen falling from the bridge.

Now the actors who had been staying warm in the one motor home that the film's $2.5 million budget could afford were called to the set.

And that's where the trouble began.

John Travolta, Barry Miller, and Paul Pape arrive and I show them where they physically have to be, in order to match what the stuntmen have already done. All heads nodded… but one, John Travolta, known as "JT."

The stuntmen had walked out on the beam, standing erect, and then, because they were 300 feet over the water, went on their knees to crawl the last few feet to Bobby C. (It seemed like a sensible idea at the time.) JT looked at me and said that his character wouldn't do it that way. His character would not be a wimp and crawl. His character would be standing upright the whole way. YIKES!

I smiled and said, "But we've already shot it this way with the stuntmen." JT's response was, "Well, you can re-shoot it, right?" "No, the stuntmen have gone home. The scene won't cut together if we don't match the stuntmen's work," I replied. My problem, not his, said JT. With a disgusted look he turned and went back to his trailer.

I was now a leper. Everyone moved away from me. What's a leper director to do? I can't re-shoot the stunt because the stuntmen have gone home. The star won't do what he's told. The producers, Robert Stigwood and Kevin McCormack, won't let us come back tomorrow night. I'm screwed! I would have to eat it and do what JT wanted. The mismatch would be my fault.

So now I have the humiliating job of going to the motor home to see JT and tell him we would do it his way. He nodded grudgingly and we went back to work. We barely got our night's work done and still had to shoot some close-ups faked in a garage a few weeks later.

The editor, Dave Rawlins, had to figure out a way to cut around the mismatch and hide my mistake. If you freeze frame on the DVD you'll see he cuts from the medium shot of Bobby C falling to the extremely wide shot of the fall from below. The size and angle changes are so drastic that an audience's eyes go to the falling figure of Bobby C and not to the kneeling figure of Tony who is supposed to be standing upright. The fact that we got away with it is no excuse.

The Moral of This Tale Is?

Never, never, never stage a scene without the actors' participation up front.

Guaranteed to backfire. I know this; I knew it when it happened. But I did it anyway, duh. If I had taken my competency pills that night I would have staged the scene with the actors *first*, and *then* let the stuntmen match them. Not the other way around. *It was not John Travolta's fault, it was my fault.* Involve the actor when you start staging a scene and uncover simple problems before they become "Nightmare Problems."

Jenna Elfman: "I like rehearsing in the environment that I'm going to be filming in because I'm free to find choices that enhance the story, but if it has already been lit or the director says, 'You're going to sit here and do this and that,' and I say, 'What if I feel the need to walk away during this scene?' It's not allowed because it's already lit and we have no time. That tends to happen a lot. An actor can't necessarily make the choices he would want because it's lit a certain way and there's no time."

It's easy to make lots of mistakes making a movie. You are always under great pressure to "get it done." Any film, no matter how big or small, is forced to be shot in less time than the director really needs. Whether it is *Lord of the Rings*, *The Matrix*, or an episode of *Frasier*, directors always need more time. The first thing in the shooting day, while the actor is in makeup and hair, is usually when directors under pressure screw up. The cameraman needs a camera set-up first thing in the morning. It's an easy scene, you think, so why drag the actors out of makeup? The actor surely won't mind the staging because it's so obviously right. Right? Wrong. The actor arrives, shoots your ideas down, and you look like a fool. And you are a fool because you've lost valuable time.

Richard Donner: "Shooting *Wanted — Dead or Alive*, I get up and I see this hill and I said, 'Good, we'll be up here,' and McQueen drove up in his Jaguar and said, 'Okay, what am I doing?' I said, 'Here's where it is, Steve. The guy is down there and you're up here,' and he said, 'Nope.' I said, 'What do you mean

nope' He said, 'I wouldn't put my back to them. I said, 'Well where would you be? What would you do?' He said, 'You're the director. You figure it out.' And he walked away."

You are thinking, "You're the director, you're in charge. Just tell the actor he *has* to do it!" Ahh, if it were only that easy. You may tell an actor who is only there for one day, to do the scene your way, *but try that with the star and for the rest of the shoot you will have an angry person who believes you can't direct traffic.* Often they will stop listening to you and do what they please.

Novice Director Meets Richard Pryor

The fact that *Bingo Long* was my first feature film is no excuse for what happened in the ill-fated Richard Pryor incident. It appears in the dictionary under "stupid director arrogance." Richard was angry because he believed we had put him in danger the day before in a driving shot. The shot was of James Earl Jones on a motorcycle followed by Billy Dee Williams driving a convertible and Richard driving another convertible behind him.

The shot was in progress when we nearly had a terrible collision. James Earl Jones on his motorcycle and the camera car almost ran into each other. Everybody swerved and screeched to a halt. James Earl was the one who was really in danger of being badly hurt and I ran to him to make sure he was all right. Thank God, he was safe. He laughed it off. Richard was hundreds of feet away from the main part of the incident and was able to stop his car safely. No harm, no foul you think, right? Wrong. The next thing I see is Richard Pryor getting in a car and returning to the hotel. We did the shot again with the stunt coordinator Joffrey Brown doubling Richard. I should have done this in the first place. I thought that Richard would go home and calm down. It seemed like such a petty thing. See it through Richard's eyes however, and petty is the last word you'd choose.

At 6:30 a.m. the next day, I walk out of the hotel to drive to the set. Leaning against my car was Richard Pryor. I said, "Good morning." I somehow could tell "good morning" was not on his mind. Maybe it was the scowl on his face? He looked me in the eye and said, "You owe me an apology." "For what?" I said disingenuously. "You nearly killed me yesterday," he said. "I nearly killed James Earl Jones, but thank God you were alright. I wouldn't endanger you or anyone knowingly." Now I'm patting myself on the back, I'm really standing up to this guy and not letting him push me around.

This is where it gets good (or bad). Richard said that obviously I didn't care about him so he was flying back to Los Angeles right now. Remember how in high school you learned to never show weakness and always have a smart remark? So I looked at Richard and said, "Let me help you out with that. Don't fly out of the Macon Georgia airport, fly out of Atlanta, it's much easier." I got into my car and drove to the set leaving a flummoxed Richard Pryor. Smart move Badham? Not.

My producer and partner Rob Cohen (the wise one) got wind of this dustup and begged Richard to stay and go to work. Richard came to the set where I was trying to shoot the day's work. When it came time for me to show Richard what he should do in the next shot he said, "I'm not doing shit till I get my apology." At that point I was not giving in. I wondered if this would become a fistfight. The thought of me in a fistfight is totally ridiculous. One punch and I'm chipped beef on toast. At my heaviest, I look like I escaped from a concentration camp.

I looked at Richard and saw a sad look in his eyes. Without thinking I said, "I'm sorry that you're so upset by this." There was a long pause where I didn't know what was going to happen. Suddenly Richard nodded his head and went to take his place in the scene.

Billy Dee Williams came over a moment later and said, "Good thing you apologized to him." I was shocked. Oh no! I did what? I stupidly had no intention of apologizing. I guess I would have let the whole movie and my career go to hell over a matter of pride.

Career in the Dumper

Never go to the mat with your cast. You can't win. If you do win they'll get you before it is over. A smarter, more mature director would have found a way to see the situation from Richard Pryor's point of view. Instead of telling him that it was no big deal I should have said something like "It sounds like you're really upset about this. I'll really have to be a lot more careful in the future." That would have solved it right there. All I needed to do was acknowledge his feelings. Nobody wants to be told that his or her problem is meaningless. If your five-year-old falls and bumps her knee and you tell her that it was no big deal, she will just wail all the louder. It works the same way with adults. Just the fact of acknowledging that someone has a problem goes a long way toward being able to talk with each other again. You don't have to be a doormat; you just have to say that you realize that they feel bad. How hard is that?

Mark Rydell: "I had a confrontation with John Wayne. There's a scene in *The Cowboys* where he's hired all of these kids to help herd cattle... and they're about to start the cattle drive. We had 1,500 cattle. Duke (John Wayne) was about 25 yards away... and I was up 30 feet in the air on a Chapman crane. We had eight cameras working on this shot. Now you know, you can't say 'Action' to cattle. You're working with cows that are pretty stupid. I don't mean to say all cows are stupid... just these cows. It takes three minutes at least to get them all moving. So the plan was to wait till the wranglers got the cattle moving. Then we would roll the cameras. If we rolled cameras and then started the cattle we would have run out of film before they got going.

"All of a sudden Wayne decided on his own that it was time to start. He starts riding and yelling 'Move 'em out!' stuff like that. I hadn't said Action. But everyone else started because he started. The wranglers start moving the cattle, the kids start herding them. And we're suddenly in the middle of this giant FUBAR. This was early in the picture, and I had not yet found my ground with him. I also was prejudiced against him. I had heard all of those horrible stories about his bigotry and I was waiting for him to make an anti-Semitic remark, and he's just the most charming guy that I've ever met. I'm up high on the crane and I haven't started rolling the cameras yet. I get the ADs to stop everything, which is no little thing. You have to turn 1500 head of intellectually challenged cattle around and get them back to the start. They haven't read the script and could give a crap. The cattle, not the ADs.

"Wayne rides up... and I start screaming at him from the safety of the crane 'Wait a minute, you stupid jerk.' I'm enraged and I'm yelling at him 'I'll tell you when to go.' I couldn't stop. I was furious. All the pent-up feelings about his political position and everything I was waiting for, it all came out... I'm finished. Even though I'm producing and directing, my career is over.

"It's the end of the day, and that crane comes down slowly. I get off the crane, and the crew lines up to shake my hand to say good-bye. It wasn't congratulations, it was goodbye. I'm thinking I'll get a call from Warner Brothers that Andy McLaughlin is taking over as director. What did I do? I was out of control. There was no excuse for it. It was just terrible. I should never have done it, and I'm sure I'm through. I went back to the production office and there are four calls from Wayne. I finally get up the courage to call him... and he invites me to dinner."

JB: "Fired and a meal, right?"

MR: "We went to a Santa Fe restaurant, Nirvana. Going to a restaurant with Wayne, whose six foot five, hands like ham hocks, there is no experience like it. He met people all over the restaurant. He never turned anybody away. He was the most gracious man. Please meet my mother, and he would get up and go over to say hello. He couldn't have been sweeter. We drank and we drank and we drank. Tequila. He said I reminded him of 'Pappy' [John Ford]. (Ford, a notoriously tough director, cast Wayne in many movies.) He called me Sir from that day on. It was the most amazing thing.

"He went to the john at some point and when he came back one whole side of his pants were soaking wet. He says, 'Would you believe it I'm taking a leak and this guy next to me looks at me and goes, JOHN WAYNE! He turns my way, sticks out his hand. But he never stopped peeing.' I think he probably wet his pants just for a joke, but that's just the kind of guy that he was. It was just an instinctive rage that I experienced that was completely unjustified."

Summary

1. Communicating with actors about their work is a learned skill, difficult to grasp but not impossible.

2. What kind of director are you: the Absolute Dictator who scares people into compliance? The Passive-Aggressive Stealth Director who avoids conflict

and remains anonymous? The Benevolent Director who is friendly and open to other's ideas, using the ones that work and abandoning the ones that don't?

3. A director who hides behind his equipment — video assist, cameras, videos, lighting — and is not communicating with the cast deserves the mediocre movie that will result.

4. Never, never, never stage a scene without involving the actors at the beginning. No exceptions.

5. Never go to the mat with your cast. You *will* lose. Pride and machismo are stupid.

6. You don't have to be a doormat; you just have to recognize your actor's feelings as real, not imagined.

Chapter 2

Dos & Don'ts

This chapter really belongs at the end of this book. But you saw the Table of Contents and can't resist reading this first. So get it out of the way now.

DO make any actor feel at home, in auditions, in wardrobe or on the set.

There is no more important rule than this for a director. When we asked hundreds of actors what they want from a director the answer that comes back like a shot is "I want to feel comfortable on the set."

Penelope Ann Miller: "If a director makes an actor feel insecure, they're not going to do as well. If they feel belittled or patronized or ridiculed or judged in a negative way the actor just gets worse and worse."

Tom Mankiewicz: "The first job of a director is creating an environment where actors can do their best work. Where they feel their Daddy's there. That they're safe, somebody has control and will protect them."

Richard Dreyfuss: "You want to feel that you're being welcomed, that you're not being tolerated. You're here because they like your work, and that's why they're talking to you."

Gary Busey: "Directors have to remember that a lot of players who go in front of the camera are nervous, frightened, insecure, unconfident.... When a director comes to you on a personal level with respect and courage and humor, there's nothing that's better for an actor to hear than that."

Kurtwood Smith: "When you come in, if the director is saying, 'Hi, how are you? Welcome to the set.' If he's in a friendly, good mood, comes down and relaxes you, you feel ready to go to work. If you come on the set and he says, 'Okay, yeah, yeah. Let's just get this. Hurry up.' That's not a good way to start work. You'll get better work from an actor if he's relaxed and comfortable."

Mel Gibson: "Try your hardest to make the actor look as good as possible. The better they look the better you're going to look. If they're any good, they'll figure that out, too. Danny Glover and I got onto that real early. I saw what he was doing with the fumbling, and always being a step behind, and I played on that. I'd run around in circles and try to screw with him to make the guy look good. And he was making me look good. I love actors. You have empathy for them and you really want to make them look as good as possible."

DON'T let your openness make you a doormat.

You decide what works and what to avoid. Don't become some actor's bitch. *Of course* you are interested in their opinion. However, you have the ultimate responsibility for the movie. You have the overall picture in your mind and you have to decide if their idea works or not.

Richard Donner: "It was late at night and we're ready to go and George Maharis says, 'I want a hamburger.' I said, 'What do you mean you want a hamburger?' He said, 'I want a hamburger in this scene. I think I'm hungry.' I said, 'Gee. Can I give you a piece of cheese or something? Maybe the prop man...' He said, 'I want a hamburger.' So we got the prop man to go over to the Universal kitchen, which was closed, and go in the back and get meat and get a hamburger. We're shooting other stuff, obviously. Then we come back and we've got the hamburger and we go into the scene and we go to roll and we're halfway through it and George took the hamburger and took this little pigeon bite. So I said, 'Cut. George, what are you doing?' He said, 'What do you mean?' 'You said you were hungry. This character is down and out and a ballplayer. If you get a hamburger then you eat it. Take a bite. Take a big bite.' He said, 'I can't. I can't talk with food in my mouth.' I said,' Yes, you can. That's the character. That's what you wanted and that's what you're going to do.' He said, 'I'm not going to do it.' I said, 'You've got the fucking hamburger.' And he goes like this and he hits the wall next to me and his hand went through the wall of the set. I looked at him and I went at him with my fist but I missed him on purpose. And I went through the wall with it too. And we stood there and looked at it as his hand is just coming out and he started to laugh. He said, 'Give me the hamburger. Give me the hamburger.' So we did the hamburger. But I had broken a bone in my hand and didn't know it. And I couldn't let on. I'm getting ice when nobody's looking. But it was a confrontation. He wanted that hamburger and damnit we got it for him and he was going to eat it. It's the way you work with actors. He could have not eaten it and then I would have really felt stupid. He had something for his scene that worked for him – then go with it. They're tough. Actors are tough."

DO learn to behave with confidence.

Indecisiveness is the Waterloo of the director. If actors are going to climb up in the rigging for you they need to trust you won't let them fall. You are the captain of the ship. You don't have to answer a question right away, but the longer you wait, the more likely it is that someone else on the set will jump in and fill the vacuum. When a director is indecisive, everybody starts feeling like the ship is drifting with no one at the helm.

Peter Hunt: "The minute one actor thinks you don't know what you're doing, or that he has a good point and you won't listen, it starts anarchy. Actors are terribly insecure in that way. It spreads like a disease across the set. And you can't cure the disease by yelling. If actors believe you understand the film, you understand their part, and you have a point of view, they're terrific. Even the supposedly difficult actors."

Martin Sheen: "If a director is not confident, it spreads like a virus on a set. If one or two of the players start bad-mouthing the maestro, the whole production is in trouble, because it shows a lack of confidence. And it isn't a question of being able to confront somebody on a set. Just like you can't do it in life. If somebody has a lack of confidence, you don't associate with him or her, because you know that you're going to get hurt. If you have a lack of confidence in your pilot, you don't want to get on the plane. And it's the same with a director."

Kurtwood Smith: "The best way to have confidence in your own acting is to have confidence in your director. Peter Weir is a wonderful director who you have great confidence in. He's really watching and paying attention to what you're doing. You have to feel that the director is looking at you and paying attention to what you're doing. A lot of directors don't pay attention to what you're doing, especially in television."

DON'T be afraid to say, "I don't know. Let's figure it out."

Contradiction alert! I just said, "Don't be indecisive." Yes, I am contradicting myself and no, I'm not contradicting myself. The President of the United States cannot possibly know all the answers to the issues he confronts every day. That doesn't mean he is a waffling wimp. If he acts with confidence and asks for help working out a problem, his staff will work with him to solve it. Otherwise chaos ensues. Recognize that there is a big difference between being indecisive all the time and occasionally saying, "I don't know, let's figure it out." A vacillating director is waffling, adrift, and unsure. A confident director doesn't give up the position of leadership; he is asking for input and will make the final decision.

Oliver Stone: "Sometimes I'll go up to the actor and I'll say, 'I don't know, just do it again. I don't know what to say to you.' But he knows I've thought about it and I'm lost. I'm not afraid to tell anybody that I don't know and that I can't follow it. Or sometimes I'll just say, 'Look, I really like it. I'm very happy with it. I think we can live with it. But I think this...'"

Stephen Collins: "I love it when a director honestly says, 'I don't know.' I think that's one of the hardest things for a director to say, given the pressures of filmmaking when the director says, 'Gee, I don't know. Let's talk about this.' Let's think. Then I love it when it's okay not to know, and it's really okay for a director not to know, but most directors don't have the — they're just not built to say that in front of other people."

Jeremy Kagan: "You really do have to know what you want, or you have to be incredibly open and say, 'I don't know what I want,' so that the actor gets that."

DO explain scenes using active verbs.

This is one of the most difficult concepts for all directors, actors, writers, and producers to put into practice. It is so tricky that a large section of Chapter 6 is devoted to it. Briefly, it all comes down to James Woods' bawdy description:

James Woods: "Whenever I have a problem I say, 'Tell me the story again of this scene, just this scene.' She says 'Well, she's been abused by her stepfather.' 'Don't give me all that intellectual crap, just tell me what's going on in the scene. You're coming in to get your money from the guy. He's not giving it to you, so you try to b*** him to get it.' 'Well, I wouldn't say that.' 'But you're seducing him to get the money, right? So seduce him already, what's the problem?'"

DON'T intellectualize scenes.

Acting is about behavior. It is *not* about cosmic themes, it is not about deep meanings. It is about behavior. **It may be *The Matrix* or it may be a Moliere comedy. But it is always about behavior.** It's about what we *do*.

Actors love to intellectualize. Directors love to intellectualize. It is a total waste of time and we all do it.

First thing: Boil the acting moment down to a verb, an active verb (e.g., "seduce"), not a passive one (e.g., "be"). A verb, what we *do*, is actable. Philosophical musings are useless.

In my Directing Fundamentals class at Chapman University one of my students presented a scene from *sex, lies, and videotape*. It was good but unfocussed. The rest of the class then made intellectual suggestions about the terrible childhood of the character, the state of the world, the dramatic thrust of the scene, the mindset of the characters, and so on for 15 minutes.

I finally stopped the student directors and asked, "Yes, but what are the characters *doing* in this scene?" They looked at me as though they understood and then went right back to asking the same intellectual questions.

Finally, I turned to the actors and asked them, "What have we said that you can use when playing this scene again?" The actress thought and then said "Nothing, really." And the actor said "Not much of anything". I asked them, "How about if I tell you that the married woman wants to have sex with her lover and the man wants to find out why she told her sister about them?" Both actors nodded affirmatively. "I can play that," they said.

Now when they played the scene they were focused on what they were trying to *do*, not on unplayable intellectual dribble. Much more on this later.

DO encourage the writers to cross out "emotional stage directions."

What the writer doesn't know is that most actors take stage directions very literally… too literally. If the writer says "angrily," actors will do angry like you've never seen angry. Only instead of being a specific anger it will be a clichéd, generalized anger. It works the same for crying, jealousy, or any emotions. Trust the actor to figure what the emotion is for himself, and see a much more interesting result. And if not, if all else fails, you can always be a lazy slob and just tell them to do it "angrily."

DON'T make the cast say the exact words in the script if they really can't make them work.

If it's Shakespeare, or any great writer, of course we've got to respect the words as written. You want them to try to say the words as written in your screenplay. Often, nothing is wrong with the dialogue, it's just that the actor is too lazy to figure out how to say it believably. But if after a sincere effort they can't make it work it would be dumb to make them say something that sounds terrible. But don't you write it. Make the actor come up with a new line. Or at least try to. Making them struggle to think of a new line is a quick cure for complaining.

Oliver Stone: "The script is not a bible to me. It's a process. I think it's dangerous to be too rigid about the script. Shooting has to be fluid. So I always start by rehearsing with the actors. Ideally, we've already rehearsed that scene before we even go into production. And because the actors have a memory of it, it usually leads to something new."

Robert Forster: "You don't want to hear from a director, 'Say the words exactly as they are written.' It does a terrible thing to the actor. It forces the actor to remember the exact words rather than the meaning of the scene. I'm not talking about big changes. Just a word or phrase change helps an actor roll the thought out of his mouth."

DO make actors answer their own questions.

Remember how a shrink looks at you when you ask, "What should I do about my Mother?" Without taking a beat she comes back with "What do you think you should do?" She's not torturing you, even though it feels like it. She's saying, "You already know the answer, just dig inside yourself and find it."

It works the same with actors. They want your help and approval with some matter. You can give a quick answer. But if you make them work it out themselves, that answer belongs to them. They own it because they thought of it. And possession is nine-tenths, etc. etc. If it disagrees with what you want to do, you can discuss it and work it out so you are both happy.

DON'T ever, ever, ever give line readings.

JB: "How do you really piss an actor off?"

Mark Rydell: "Give them a line reading."

If you want a robotic response from an inexperienced actor, try ignoring this Don't. They will become a drone and give you the phoniest line reading since

"Help, I've fallen and I can't get up!" A really skilled actor will probably be offended but at the same time can decode your terrible line reading and make it work.

The right way to correct a bad reading is to ask the actor two things: 1) What does your character want in the scene and 2) how does your character feel about this moment in the scene. You may have to have them improvise the situation to find their way.

DO put directions in the form of questions.
Instead of saying to an actor, "This next time, move to the door, then turn and say your line," phrase it as a question: "What would happen if you walked to the door and then turned and said your line?"

Why do this? It's simple. Nobody likes being ordered about, especially when they are part of a creative process.

Of course you would get a really weird look if you said to the dolly grip, "What would happen if we were to lay 40 feet of track say, uh, over here?" The dolly grip wants and needs specific instructions. The actor on the other hand is a partner in the creative process. If you don't believe this, try giving orders and watch their resentment and argumentativeness simmer and boil over.

DON'T call out inane things like "OK, give me lots of energy!" or "Have fun with it!"
Stephen Collins: "I have found at least 90% of the time when a director wants more energy, what he's reacting to is a lack of point of view in the scene. Something's wrong with either the way the scene's written or being acted, or the way it's been directed that's causing the actors to hang back and not commit to it. It's never about energy. Energy is what happens to actors when they are specific and do have a point of view. It's used as a kind of catchall by directors who know something's wrong but don't know what it is. Chances are, after you tell them 'More Energy,' the same problem will be there, only it will just be louder."

DO talk to every actor after every take. Even if all you do is walk past them and pat them on the shoulder, they are reassured.
Get out! Do what? Every take? No way, you say.

Way.

When an actor finishes a take, she wants feedback. How did I do? she wants to know. If you're going to do it again, for whatever reason, the actor needs to hear a reason. You may not want to tell them the actual reason but you must say something. Directors who just say, "Let's go again" and roll camera only create confusion among the cast.

It doesn't need to take a lot of time. In the TV series *Blind Justice*, we were under the same time pressure as every other series. Nevertheless, after every take I would walk quickly over to each one of the cast and just give them a nod, a touch on the arm, or some other attaboy. Took only seconds. Then I go to the actors who need help and give them appropriate direction. Now some actors know they are on a good track and others who are given direction know what they need to do. There is always a bit of adjusting and messing around by the crew in between takes. Take advantage of that short time and keep the cast in the loop.

DON'T be afraid to say when a performance isn't good.

The cast wants to hear from you. But find positive ways to phrase your comments. It's a fine line to walk. You can tell an actor anything if you've gained their trust and they know you are supportive of them. Never insult them, or denigrate them in front of the crew or anywhere. You will lose them forever.

Oliver Stone: "Too many directors say, 'That's great, that's great, that's great' to where it doesn't mean anything. What does the actor believe? He doesn't believe anything if the actor is always told, 'You're great.' 'It's good, but...' is a horrible way to start a conversation. I will go right to the point if I can. First of all, I look at the take and really think about it. I might wait three minutes or four minutes. So everybody's shuffling around and the actor wants to hear what you thought. Then I go to them and I say, 'You did this, and I think this is what you did and I think this is what you're trying to do. However... this is what I think we should be doing. I'm not sure. I want you to tell me.' And then we start a debate and that becomes a little bit of a debate. That's fine, because I'm exploring it with him."

Jeremy Kagan: "A well-known actor said to me, you've got to be able to tell me that I stink. Because if you don't, I will stink. I need to be criticized, or I get lazy. This is an actor who knows himself and is saying, 'Direct me this way.' I often do say to certain actors when I'm meeting them; tell me what works with you. We haven't worked together. Tell me what helps."

Betty Thomas: "I worked with Kathy Bates once in *Late Shift,* and the first day of shooting I kept saying, 'Oh, that's good.' Because how could it not be good with Kathy Bates? You know it's good. It was good, but it wasn't the character that she was supposed to be. Her character was based on a real person who was bombastic and rageful. And I never thought it would be so restrained and nice. I was trying to think, 'Can I change everything?' And I let it go for a whole day and that night I was destroyed at my weakness for not saying to Kathy, 'This has to be different.' So the next morning I just went right to her and I said, 'Kathy,' and she said, 'It's not working, is it. What should I do?' I said, 'You have to go for it. You have to go crazy. You have to let her hang out, or this will never, ever work.' She said, 'I knew that was true. I knew it. You're totally right. Let's go back. Let's do it.' And then she did the scene again and it was spectacular. Since then I've tried not to be so affected by great actors or big celebrities."

DO phrase your comments to your actors positively.

"For God's sake honey, you're too slow, pick up your cues!" That's negative in tone and a result-oriented direction. Try something like "What if you tried this next take as if you really have to go to the bathroom now?" or "Try it as though you're about to miss your flight." With a little practice it's so easy to be positive most of the time.

DON'T do extra takes without giving the actors a good reason.

If all an actor hears is "Let's do it again" they think they screwed up. It could have been a sound problem or a camera operator's mistake. But the actor will always think it's about them if you don't tell them. If the camera misses a mark, then tell the actors they were okay but you had a technical problem. (Don't bust the camera operator's chops in front of everyone.)

Michael Caine told Craig Modderno in a *Hollywood Life* interview in 2005: "The thing I hate to hear from a director is 'Let's do it again.' By take three I'm going downhill. I put all my energy into the early takes — otherwise my fellow actors and the crew get bored with me."

Get it right the first time and get on with it was Sinatra's motto. Clint Eastwood, who directs himself, is the same way. He's been performing over forty years and knows what he is going to do. If you're acting opposite him you better be good on take one, because he will often print it and move to the next shot. If Warren Beatty is the star you can do 50 takes before he's happy. Not so with Clint.

Clint was making a film with a young director who always wanted to do lots and lots of takes. Clint tried to work with this for a week or so but he was so used to directing himself and moving very fast that he grew increasingly frustrated. Still, he held his tongue in an effort to be respectful of his director. One day, the number of takes for a scene had gotten up to 12 or 13. After take 13, the director called "Cut." He called out, "Clint, that was perfect… this next time, let's do it more…." But he never got to finish the sentence. Clint was already heading to his trailer. The last words the director heard were, "Kid, perfect is as good as I get."

Dennis Haysbert: "If that was perfect, why do you want one more? Let's not just shoot the hell out of it. And drain everybody to death. I'll give you another one, but, I mean, I've heard that perfect word. What does that leave for you to do? Now, better."

DO be specific about what your actor did right.

After a take, never say "That was great!" It's too vague, too general. Say something like "When you turned at the door and said your line I really believed you." That's specific. An actor will never forget that comment.

DON'T lie to your actors.

Ed Asner: "What do I want from a director? To be honest. I had a prominent director say, 'I want you to do the scene this way.' He treats me like an idiot! I said 'I can't do it that way, because we're on page 65 now, and on page 50, I did this, this and this.' He says, 'Oh great, I see what you mean.' When I saw the picture he had re-cut the scene to be his way. How can you trust somebody when they're two-faced?"

Judge Reinhold: "The actor should never feel he's being manipulated. The director should be creating a trusting environment for you and making you comfortable. If you HAVE to manipulate them, let them know it afterwards and tell them why. Otherwise they'll figure it out on their own and never trust you again."

DON'T hide behind the video-assist monitor.

The video assist monitor is a convenient place for directors to hide. But the actor is performing for you, not some mythical audience in the future. You want to give him appreciation now, not in the future. The very best place to do that is right beside the camera where they can see you. If you have to look at the video assist, then do it during the rehearsal and playback. The cinematographer can watch the monitor for camera mistakes.

DO discuss nudity and any other very special or unusual needs before you cast someone.

Few things are guaranteed in life. This is one of them. *When you have nudity in a scene it won't be a fun day.* Women are uncomfortable with it. Men are uncomfortable with it. Transsexuals are uncomfortable with it. Even a porn star becomes more modest than Queen Elizabeth.

David Ward: "You can be sure you're going to have two very uptight actors, who want to know exactly what you're going to do. How much you're going to show. Most actors really don't like to do sex scenes. Most directors don't either, because it's hard to do them in a way that's really sexy and it's hard to do them in a way that's original."

Martha Coolidge: "I took the actors into my confidence, turned the video monitor around — they were both very nervous about it — showed them their picture and said, 'This is choreography. Love scenes are not real.' Young actors frequently fear that it's going to be real sex, and what they're going to have to do. And you turn around and tell them 'no,' if you don't want to do something or you don't want something seen, we're going to stage it so the camera can't see it."

Even shooting partial nudity, in underwear or bathing suits can be a problem. People hide a lot they don't like about their bodies under their clothes. If a scene calls for them to be in their underwear they can get really uptight about showing whatever "it" is. In one movie I wanted an actress to wear cut-off jeans. "No way," said she. The costume designer whispered to me that the actress hated her legs. That ended that. I am not making somebody wear something they are uncomfortable with.

There is only one way to handle any degree of nudity and/or onscreen sex: Discuss it with the actor frankly and up front. Do this before you hire them, while you still have leverage. If you are going to have resistance better to know it now. Never wait till the last minute. You will have a train wreck.

Go through the scenes with the actor. Tell them what you are planning, how it will be seen onscreen. Get storyboards drawn so they can see what you mean exactly.

Jan de Bont: "In *Basic Instinct* that one famous shot set the whole relationship. Sharon Stone didn't want to do it originally. I had to shoot the shot myself. I said, 'Sharon, you really have to spread your legs a little more, otherwise it's not going to work. I have to see something.' She said, 'But I don't want to see it.' I said, 'Don't worry about it too much. In this scene, we have to get a sense that you're not wearing anything, otherwise the whole scene, we might as well throw away.' That was a matter of just creating a trust with her... Of course she was aware of the fact that it did, because the camera's between your legs, and there's light there. You're not filming shoes."

JB: "Didn't I read somewhere she claimed she was tricked?"

Jan de Bont: "Wait a second, that's impossible."

There are strict Screen Actors Guild rules, which protect actors from having to do any nudity that hasn't been previously discussed with them and agreed to *in writing*.

When you finally do shoot a nude scene/sex scene, only have a skeleton crew on the set. But watch out. Suddenly crews that haven't been on the set in days make up bogus reasons why they have to be there. Don't forget to look up in the rafters. Overweight crew suddenly have to climb 90 steps up to the fly floor to check an electrical connection... and they're just the Teamsters.

DON'T have intimate relations with anybody in your cast, or crew.

In fact, why not just drink Drano instead.

John Frankenheimer: "For a male director to think it's a good idea to have an affair with the female lead is a disaster. In the first place, there are no secrets on a movie set. Everybody knows it, including the leading male actor who feels totally left out of it and feels resentful and who becomes terribly hostile. Usually the affair is over before the movie is over which makes it very, very difficult. I think any type of sexual involvement with any actor working for you is totally wrong."

The same thing goes for two actors working together.

James Woods: "The worst thing you can do is screw your co-star. Because now you've got to listen to her tell you how to play the scene the next day over the pillow. 'Honey, you know in that scene tomorrow? Would you mind if I just took a little longer pause and have a moment,' and all that crap that actors want to do. And now, of course, you're pussy-whipped, so you're going to have to listen to this crap."

DO thank your actors and crew for their work at the end of every shooting day.

At the end of the day a director is often frantically focused on tomorrow's work. The actor is left with little to do but brood. Having finished their work for the day they need active appreciation from you. Never think you don't have to say anything because they were just doing their job.

Elia Kazan: "I often praise an actor openly. They're hanging on you. They can't see themselves. So when they deserve praise I always articulate it. I don't believe in playing cool. One beautiful thing about actors is that they're so exposed. They're not being criticized only for their behavior, but for their legs and breasts, for their double chin; their whole being is exposed to criticism. How can you not embrace them and how can you feel anything but gratitude toward these people."[1]

Finally — DO NOT ALLOW ANYONE TO TALK TO THE ACTORS ABOUT THEIR PERFORMANCES!

This is the proverbial line in the sand. This is where performances get screwed up and confused time after time after time. Getting a performance right is tough enough without having help from everyone standing about on the set.

On a student film *everybody* is a director. Literally. They all work on each other's films as grips, electricians, and cinematographers and know that's the price of getting a crew for their own film. In other words they watch the filming not as a grip trying to do the best grip job possible but as a director who is there to help the director *du jour* with all their "helpful observations."

---

[1] Jeff Young, *Kazan. The Master Director Discusses His Films* (New York: Newmarket Press, 1999), page 106

One award-winning young filmmaker, Stacey Kattman, observed that the set of a student film is such an egalitarian environment that one often can see the script supervisor or an AD piping in with "Gee that was funny when you picked up the toothbrush." Though this may sound harmless, actors are so sensitive to criticism or praise that their whole performance easily can be drastically changed by one casual comment. And the director is standing there, wondering what happened.

Even assuming that everyone means well and isn't out to sabotage the director, it makes no difference. Only the director can control the flow of input to the actor so that they hear a consistent message. Your on-set kibitzer may have exactly the right note to help the actor but will not phrase it the same way as the director. The result is often a confused actor who goes off on the wrong tangent and the director doesn't know why.

On a professional set the crew is well trained to leave the performances to the director. Even if the actor asks the script supervisor or makeup, "How was that?" the answer will be a polite version of "talk to the director." Failure to follow this protocol is justification for getting their ass chewed.

Often, the trouble comes from the *producers*. They feel perfectly free to wade into any situation and hand out comments like M&Ms at Halloween. This is especially epidemic on half-hour comedy shows where the writers are all producers. They have no hesitation in running up to any actor and telling them how to read lines, how to stand, how to smile, whatever. Only the toughest directors will stand up to them and say, "I'll pass on any notes you have to the actors, only please let me do it so we give them a consistent message." If not said with the greatest diplomacy, these remarks can cost that director his next job on the show. The producers are there every week and the director is only there once in a while so it is understandable that they may understand the show and the characters better than the "guest director." However, the guest director is likely to understand how to convey to the actor what the producers want much better than they.

Of course there are exceptions. A stunt coordinator should always talk to the actor about the details of any stunt they are involved with, even if they are only doing a close-up and the stuntman is doing the actual stunt.

Universal Peeves

JB: "Are there things that you can think of that actors do that are irritating?"

Betty Thomas: "Yes, saying 'Cut' themselves. If they make a mistake, you may need the scene to keep going for some other reason: another actor has captured an emotion they may only get one time, or a train is coming by in the background and you want to see it. There's always a reason, that's why the director is the only one who says 'Cut.' And this thing where actors have to put their glasses on or take them off to do a line drives me nuts. No one does that. Did any of us put them on or off during this whole conversation? I just hate all of that glasses crap. I've seen it a million times. If I ever see an actor drumming his fingers on a table or a bar, I usually cut. 'OK. You can't do that. If you had no fingers how would you show me that?'"

JB: "Another acting cliché is when an actor is on the telephone in a scene and the person on the other end hangs up on them. What does a lazy actor do? He looks at the phone. Does any one in real life look at the phone mouthpiece when they're hung up on? No."

Summary

1. DO make any actor feel at home, in auditions, in wardrobe, or on the set.

2. DON'T let your openness make you a doormat.

3. DO behave with confidence.

4. DON'T be afraid to say, "I don't know. Let's figure it out."

5. DO explain scenes using active verbs.

6. DO encourage the writers to cross out "emotional stage directions."

7. DON'T make the cast say the exact words in the script if they really can't make them work.

8. DO make actors answer their own questions.

9. DON'T ever, ever, ever give line readings.

10. DO put directions in the form of questions.

11. DON'T call out inane things like "OK, give me lots of energy," or "Have fun with it!"

12. DO talk to every actor after every take.

13. DO phrase your comments to your actors positively.

14. DON'T do extra takes without giving the actors a good reason.

15. DO be specific about what your actor did right.

16. DON'T lie to your actors.

17. DON'T hide behind the video-assist monitor.

18. DO discuss nudity and any other very special or unusual needs before you cast someone.

19. DON'T have intimate relations with anybody in your cast or crew.

20. DO thank your actors at the end of every shooting day for their work.

21. DON'T allow anyone other than yourself to discuss performance with the actors.

Comfort or Constipate

On the set, directors can hide behind staging, lighting, scenery problems, and alleged failures of the writer. The writer can hide behind the typewriter and the alleged failures of the director. Who can the actor hide behind? The hairdresser?

When a director starts to rehearse actors in front of other people, a jolt of panic rises in even the most experienced actor. Now he is terrified they may not buy into what he is doing. He is putting all his talent and self-image on the line for us to see. What if we hate it? It would be a personal rejection of the actor. And the more he uses his own psyche to build the character, the more vulnerable he becomes. What can we do to be a constructive help to this fragile person? It's very simple.

There is one universal principle about working with actors. It is inviolate. Actors must feel they are in a place where they are totally safe. A place where they can expose their deepest emotions and feel support. A place where they can make mistakes without fear of disdain, mocking, sarcasm, or any kind of negative reaction to their effort.

Frank Langella: "An actor needs a director to make him feel he is the ideal actor for the part he is playing and that his qualities are those the director is looking for in the role. If a director is able to instill that basic belief in the actor right from the beginning, the actor will jump through any hoop necessary to play the part. No matter where the actor is in his work or no matter how young or old he is — he needs the director to communicate unconditional confidence in him (even if he doesn't always feel it). It is a very valuable tool in the director's arsenal."

The rehearsal space must be a playground with a purpose. **If directors want to act like dominating dictators, they can only expect emotional constipation in return.** Even the biggest stars need love. Their egos are just as fragile as the less famous actor. We cannot treat them with anything but love and support if they are to do their best work.

Jan de Bont: "You have to tell an actor what it's about. They're so insecure, actors on the set. They really need something to hold onto, and you're the only person that can give it to them. You and the makeup person."

Gary Busey is one of the most outrageous, free-flowing, and wild actors of our generation, and even he needs constant validation. When Gary worked with me in *Drop Zone* and *The Law,* he would come to me every day asking, "How were the dailies?" Telling him they were good was not enough. He needed to know *how* good he was. He wanted detailed validation. Gary is not alone, not by a long shot. The entire membership of the Screen Actors Guild stands with him, cheek by jowl. Peter Gallagher, an actor who is as steady as a rock and a direct psychological opposite to Gary, looked up at me after a day's rehearsal on *The Last Debate* and said gently, "So how are we doing? Are we even in the ballpark?"

I felt bad because I should have given him feedback *before* he ever had to ask the question. That meant he had been sitting there wanting reassurance so much that he finally had to beg for it. **Every actor needs feedback, even if it is not always positive.** As long as it is constructive feedback he will go overboard to please the director. Our job as directors is to guide this fragile creature who stands before us with his insides exposed for all to see. At any second he believes he will be exposed as a fake and a fraud.

There is a name for this: It is called "The Imposter Syndrome." Almost everyone has it to some extent, but creative people who work freelance are the most vulnerable. That includes me and thousands of others. We feel that our last job was the last one we'll ever do. We'll never work again. We believe we are really frauds who will be exposed soon. Even big stars like Walter Matthau and Gregory Peck freely confessed to their spouses after finishing a movie that nobody would ever hire them again.

Acting for other people's approval may offend some actors. They may believe their goal is reaching a high artistic plane of expression. Acting for others' approval seems like pandering. However, even if this is true, their only indication of how well they are doing comes from the audience. **Remember, the purpose of acting in the first place is communicating a story of some kind to an audience.** If we are not communicating, why do we act? How the actor *feels* about a performance is not relevant. If it communicates the right story and emotions it is right; if it doesn't it is wrong. If an actor says an audience has to take them as they are, they must live with the possibility of having no audience at all.

It is extremely important that the actor get beyond any fears he may have of the audience. Psychologists have found that one of the most frightening events for a human being is speaking in public. It is awful to see someone in the grip of this terror. Their voice quavers, their eyes are cast down, their stomach is aflutter and their whole fight or flight mechanism takes over. They are artistically impaired. Their instrument is bound and gagged. **When all the muscles are bound up, creativity is bound up. But if an actor can get past his fears of the audience, he can free his emotions and his instrument.**

The next time you are in a library or a bookstore, pick up a book on acting technique, any book. Chapter One is usually about relaxation and Chapter Two about imagination. Ridiculously simple ideas, right? Doesn't everybody understand them? A student looking at that acting book in the bookstore will without fail flip past these first two chapters to get to the *real secrets* of acting. Well, guess what, the real secrets were back in Chapters One and Two. **Without being skilled at relaxing and imagining, the actor can't begin to use any of the other techniques that the book is conveying.**

Anne Bancroft: "Relaxation is the key to acting. Most actors will relax if you tell them they are the best thing on God's earth."

Without the freedom that relaxation gives to the mind, imagination cannot flourish. If imagination is dormant, the characters that emerge will be stale, clichéd, uninteresting, boring, and flat. Emotional memories cannot flow; physical qualities such as voice and movement are strangled and stiff. Acting is all about playfulness, openness. To do that we need to create for our actors a comfort zone where they are free to create without fear of failure. Do that, and their imaginations can work and the talent flows.

Peter Fonda gave a terrific performance in *The Limey*, charming and loose yet with an evil undertone. It was much more relaxed than his other work. Steven Soderbergh talks about how he worked with Fonda.

Steven Soderbergh: "We met for lunch before shooting. I had read his book *Don't Tell Dad: A Memoir*, which had just come out. As we chatted I discovered that Peter Fonda is a real Chatty Cathy. He's really funny, loves to tell stories. I remember coming away from lunch saying, 'The most important thing that I have to do on this movie is to figure out how to get Peter to remain Peter.'

"Peter never leaves the set — he's very gregarious and likes to talk to the crew. As we were ready to shoot I'd go, 'Oh Peter, tell them the thing about X' that I'd read about in his book. He would tell the story and as he would wind down, I'd give the crew a sign, 'Here we go,' so that as he wrapped his story up, we were rolling and ready to go and he could go right from finishing that story into doing the scene and never lose his relaxation. Eventually I didn't have to do that as much, because he fell into a rhythm that was really comfortable."

The Magic, Please

A great mistake made in workplaces the world over is to say, "A good job is what we're paying these people for. We don't need to praise them for doing what they're paid to do." What a sorry understanding of human nature. Even the very worst sweatshops in the world would be amazed at how much more productivity they could get by treating people as valued contributors to the effort. People work for many reasons, but only one of them is to earn money and that is not in first place... doing something worthwhile is. What are we to think about our actors? Are we to think that they can work well without personal satisfaction?

Rod Steiger, the Academy Award–winning actor for *In the Heat of the Night*, was often frustrated at how little respect directors had for an actor's talent. How it was treated as easy and disposable. He told Jason Patric and me on the set of *Incognito* a few months before he died, "They spend hours and hours lighting, laying dolly track, fixing the makeup, breaking for lunch. But when it comes time for the actors there is no time left. The director snaps his fingers and says, "The Magic, please!"'

When the film was in first cut I called Steiger to tell him how good it was. "I don't care about that," he grumbled, "How am I?!"

If directors don't give the kind of positive feedback that nurtures actors, what happens? Actors will still try their best. But they are being emotionally starved and will eventually burn out. Any director willing to give them positive reinforcement stokes an actor's creative fires.

Francis Ford Coppola has often spoken of his technique of encouraging actors. **He will look for anything in the actor's performance in a take that he can compliment.** He lets the actors know they are not acting in a vacuum, that somebody is watching and caring about their work. Secondly, the feedback helps them understand what he is seeking.

Summary

1. Actors must feel they are working in a place where they are totally safe.

2. Every actor needs feedback, even if it is not always positive.

3. The purpose of acting is to communicate a story to an audience. How the actor feels about a performance is not relevant. If it communicates the right story and emotions it is right; if it doesn't it is wrong.

4. Tension is the death of creativity. The director must make a relaxed environment.

5. Find things in an actor's performance to compliment. Real things. Blow smoke and you'll get busted.

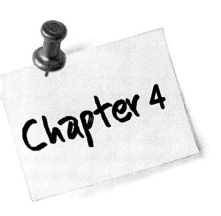

Are Actors Nuts?

Michael Curtiz: "Actors, actors, they want to know everything!"

If the oldest profession is prostitution, what is the second oldest? One cynic said acting. What were prehistoric people supposed to do after dinner anyway? All knowledge was either carried around in people's heads or lost forever. This knowledge extended from the basic needs — where to find water, how to hunt — to knowing what happened in the world before the present moment. Without the ability to write things down, the past could only be related verbally. The person who could remember and relate historical knowledge was a very valued member of the community. Just as today where action films have to get an audience's instant attention, primitive man's accounts of hunting wild animals and fights with other groups of people had to be gripping stories. The person who could bring history and legends to life for an audience was the first actor.

When people began to write things down, the writer could create and relate stories and histories in a more permanent way. But that required that people be able to read what he had written. And up until the last two hundred years only a few people knew how to read. The vast majority of people still relied on actors and performers to bring stories to life.

The actor has always been an interpreter of the written material and a strong participant in the creation of its realization. Of course some multi-talented actors do write their own material, just as many songwriters sing their own songs. But, yesterday as today, the actor is largely dependent on the writer to provide the working material. And the director is the new kid on the block. Until directors came along, actors usually did whatever they thought best. Often the lead actor was also the manager of the group of players and functioned as the director.

The actor's task has always been to interpret and present the story to the audience. In films and most television, the audience won't be present when the performances are created. This can make a big difference in the way the actor performs. Performing for an unseen audience in filmmaking presents challenges to the actor. With a live audience present the actor gets instant feedback. When filming, the actor is dependent on the director for feedback. In either case, good feedback — whether from the audience or the director — is essential to the actor's performance. Just what constitutes good feedback is at the heart of this book. Good taste, artistic vision, and strong people skills are major requirements for a good director.

Michael Chiklis: "That's the perfect director, a director who knows how to speak to actors, knows how to give a direction, is an objective eye in telling the story from the actor's perspective, but also is incredibly adept with camera and knows and has a vision and is there."

The job of the actor and the director is to convey the spirit of the written or unwritten material in a clear, believable, inventive and exciting way. Really good films or theatrical productions have all of these qualities. Take away any one element and the whole thing may implode.

For example, "clear." This innocent little word can contain volumes about good communication. If an actor can't communicate his artistic efforts clearly, we confuse the audience. We are communicators before we are artists. Artistry is something you earn, even if you're born with talent. If we can't communicate we're just playing with ourselves. Since the 1940s there have been misguided students of Constantin Stanislavsky, the great Russian actor and teacher of acting. They have focused on Stanislavsky's techniques of emotional recall and completely ignored his teachings on how to communicate these emotions to an audience. The results have often been mumbling, masturbatory self-indulgence.

James Woods: "The Method killed acting for 50 years, and it's just taken people a while to get out of that nonsense. Everybody's mumbling, 'I love you.' Marcello Mastroianni, I saw him on the *Johnny Carson Show* 20, 30 years ago. He said, 'What is it with these American actors and the Method? They're always mumbling 'I love you.' I have a woman. I don't mumble, 'I love you.' I look her right in the eyes, I grab her around the waist, I bend her over and say as hard as I can right into her lovely face 'I-ah love-ah you.' It works for me.'"

James Whitmore, the lovable gruff character actor, told me how he and his fellow players rehearsed a production of Maxim Gorky's *The Lower Depths*. They rehearsed for eight months. Eight months! I feel lucky to get eight minutes. They finally opened at Royce Hall on the UCLA campus. All the actors in the troupe believed that the most important thing in acting was believable behavior. They were "holding the mirror up to nature," as Hamlet says to the players. If the audience couldn't hear them or see them, that was the audience's problem! The actors were creating "art," not communicating. Whitmore says that by the end of the play the audience had deserted the auditorium. The actors totally lost sight of their job, to communicate the story of human lives and emotions, not just to "live it" onstage.

Lee Strasberg, the leader of the Actor's Studio, taught believability and the importance of a full emotional life for the actors. Later in his teaching he realized that he had short-changed vital communication skills. So Strasberg shifted gears to focus more on communicating the work to the audience. Some of my most fun times at the Los Angeles Actor's Studio were watching Strasberg get on the stage and demonstrate comic techniques. The class loved it. It was about as far as you could get from the grim emotional reality he had taught for decades. "Grab us [the audience] by the throat," he would say. Otherwise, Strasberg would say in his gruff New York accent, "You're wasting our time." Stanislavsky himself was the first to stress that the emotional work that came to be known as "The Method" was not enough by itself. In order to communicate those emotions they have to be passed through the actor's "instrument," his body. The "instrument" has to be trained in voice, movement, mime; all of the skills that facilitate clear communication to the audience.

Most people only read Stanislavsky's first book, *The Actor Prepares*, which lays the foundations for finding a true emotional life. Few read his second book, *Building the Character*, which teaches how to communicate that life. Actors who are unbelievable, unclear, or just plain dull will not last long in their profession. The bars and coffee shops of Hollywood are filled with people who desperately want to be great actors but don't have the right stuff.

If It Looks So Easy, You Try It

When it comes to acting some lucky people are born with great natural talent. Unschooled, they operate on instinct and can't understand why the rest of us find acting so tough. James Cagney, who brought many great gangster characters to life, was supposed to have puzzled, "What's the big deal about acting? Just step on your mark and say the words."

When directing *Blue Thunder* for Columbia Pictures, I learned one of my producers, Phil Feldman, had a not-so-secret yen to act. He had actually appeared in *The Godfather: Part II*. He came to me and asked if he could play the small part of an Air Force colonel. Phil, in addition to being a talented producer, was a good friend. Usually I ask actors to read for the roles they are to play. This time I made an exception… a fatal exception. And the exception again proved the rule: Always audition your actors. An actor who has a great personality off the set won't necessarily keep that personality doing the stressful job of acting in front of people.

On the day that Phil was scheduled to do his part, I was directing Warren Oates, Roy Scheider, and a very impish Malcolm McDowell. I saw Phil approaching the set in his Air Force colonel's uniform. He looked very military, very natty and… very scared. He had that "deer in the headlights" look, that Stage Fright 101 look that directors recognize immediately. It's too late to fire the guy. You just have to live with the consequences. The director's first job is to help any actor relax, to feel at home. Here's a case where major first aid was required.

Roger Corman: "I feel that the biggest thing that I can do for somebody when they come to work is make them feel comfortable. That's the most terrifying thing, coming onto a set. There's something so final about this. When I try to act, I get such a sense of terror and such an appreciation toward the actor, because there I am, absolutely scared shitless, because it's going to be there forever."

A smart director always has a backup plan in case an actor can't relax. Damage control. I spent all the time I could with Phil until we were ready

to shoot his scene. First, I tried to get his mind off the scene. We chatted about playing tennis at his house where his fire-breathing serves aced me every time. We talked about cute girls, baseball, anything. We were not curing cancer; we were just trying to make a movie.

I finally staged the scene with Phil, Scheider, Oates, and McDowell. Instead of relaxing, Phil got more nervous. As we rolled cameras on the first take, he could hardly say his lines. I kept encouraging him, giving him time to relax. Meanwhile, standing to his left was Malcolm McDowell, who had a big wide grin plastered on his face. Though the scene was supposed to be very tense, Malcolm's grin was anything but tense. It resembled that huge maniacal smile on the George Tilyou Steeplechase ride at Coney Island. In between takes I grabbed Malcolm and asked what he was doing. He confessed he was getting gleeful plea-sure out of Phil's obvious discomfort. He said, "We [actors] spend our whole lives learning how to make it [acting] appear easy. Now everybody else thinks they can

do it too. I love the look on their face when they discover how hard it really is." The scene is still in the movie though you'll have to look quickly to find the colonel.

Frank Langella: "It is impossible to explain to anyone who does not step in front of the camera what it's like. However stressful it is for everyone else on a set, it is the actor who must step in front of the lens and make it appear effort-less and in the moment. The director and crew can stand in the dark, but the actor must perform something that he knows will be viewed by others for all time. That is a special burden every young director needs to honor. If you feel you have chosen the right actor and you trust him and his instincts, get the hell out of his way, get it on camera, and take credit for it later."

The best way to begin an understanding of actors is to do some acting yourself. Until you have stood on a stage and felt the fright and terror an actor feels, you will never have true empathy for him. Take an acting class with the best teacher you can find. You cannot just sit in the back of the class and observe, you have to participate. You have to get up on stage and make a scene believable and come alive. By taking a class and actually appearing in some plays, you can learn what actors go through. You will come to understand their language and special ways of communicating that are very different from the way that writers and directors talk.

Mark Rydell: "It should be mandatory that every director act and experience acting. They should go to a class... and get up and try to create real behavior in front of people in an imaginary circumstance. It gives you respect for the actors...."

Richard Donner: "I think it's the best thing anybody can do. Spend a lot of time in an acting class. At least get basics. Because then you know the same fears that the actor has."

Young directors often react to this idea by rolling their eyes, "Yeah right, like I'm gonna do that." It's not just laziness on their part, they are scared. Scared to get up in front of people. Scared to make a fool of themselves. And that's the point. Actors go through that every time they act. I am glad that I had to take acting classes at the Yale Drama School. I use what I learned every day when I'm directing and can empathize with the actors' concerns and fears. Whenever I can find a very small part for myself in a film I'm doing, I take it to remind myself how hard acting really is.

Gary Busey: "Directors should be required to go to psychological classes in college. Understand the commitment that that person on the screen has to have in order to make the story right and correct. And when you approach the actor simply, giving him the worth, understanding the ingredients of that person's work, then you're smacking home runs every time you say action."

Oliver Stone: "When I was a younger director, sometimes I hadn't thought out the ideas completely or satisfactorily enough for the actor, because you're approaching the idea from the director's viewpoint. But, to really make the divide, you have to approach it from the actor's viewpoint. You have to understand what moccasins or what shoes he's walking in. And you take into account his upbringing and his education and his inclinations. I will look at all of the films that he or she has done — or most of them — and I try to see the things that they repeat."

Directors should do whatever they have to do to help the actor. In this sense the director is very much like an athletic coach. Superstar coaches like Bear Bryant or Phil Jackson can train, inspire, cajole, and berate their players to reach levels of performance beyond the player's dreams. The great UCLA basketball coach John Wooden would tell you modestly that he is only as good as the raw material that he has. Every coach seeks out the very best talent he can attract. Even Bear Bryant couldn't take an average quarterback and make him a Heisman trophy winner. Talent cannot be taught. What can be taught is how to maximize the skills that we are born with. A Volkswagen will always be a Volkswagen. It can however be a Volkswagen that outperforms all other Volkswagens because it's been tuned to within an inch of its life. Similarly there are great Ferraris and there are Ferraris out of tune that cough, sputter, and break down. Whatever part we are casting, we want the best we can get. Unfortunately, most of us have Ferrari tastes but Volkswagen budgets. We have to do the best with what is available to us.

Thankfully, actors are not cars. They grow and change as their life goes on. They are not the same at twenty years old as when they were twelve, or when they are fifty. Living in the world, being both blessed and burned by life's experiences, will deepen a person's emotional reservoir. An actor may struggle for years to get established but only start to become really interesting as an actor when he has reached middle age. Life has put its individual stamp on the person. Watching Michael Apted's brilliant series of *Seven Up* documentaries that have followed a group of people since they were children, we can see how people change dramatically as they grow. Some of it is charming, some not very happy. Many qualities can be seen in a seven-year-old child that magnify for better or worse over time. But the point is people grow and change. And thus their talent can also change and grow.

Sydney Lumet, in his book *Making Movies,* tells of working with Paul Newman in *The Verdict,* for which Newman won an Academy Award nomination. After two weeks of rehearsal, Lumet held a run-through of the whole movie. Afterwards, he sent everyone home except Paul Newman. Lumet gently told Newman that his performance was flat and that he hadn't gotten anywhere near the soul of the character. Newman assured him that it was only because he hadn't learned the dialogue thoroughly. Lumet replied that learning the lines wasn't the problem. Newman was going to have to expose the parts of his inner life that connected with the sad and decrepit character he was playing, or risk that the performance would be dull and lifeless. Newman, in his fourth decade of being a major star, was not used to being spoken to this way and he abruptly left the rehearsal.

For the rest of the weekend the two men didn't speak, even though they lived close to each other in Connecticut. Lumet wondered if Newman would even return to work. On Monday morning Lumet anxiously watched the rehearsal room door. The rehearsal was called for ten a.m. and on the stroke of ten Paul Newman walked through the door. He sat at the table and they all began to work. Right away, Lumet says that he saw a fire and a life to Newman's character that had never been there before. Newman had made his peace with the dark and troubled character he was playing and allowed his own inner being to infuse the character with life. Lumet did nothing miraculous, he was not Svengali. But he *was* able to help Newman free up what he already had inside himself. Lumet knows how to speak to actors in a way that lets them know that he is on their side. He knows how hard it is for an actor to reach great heights. He knows how to bring them along without terrorizing, without intimidation, but with firmness. Like a kind parent who nonetheless means business, Lumet has always had a well-deserved reputation as a great director of actors.

Elia Kazan wisely observed that 80% of directing… is good casting. If you cast your actors well, you lift an enormous millstone from your neck. You will not be trying to do all the work. It wouldn't matter anyway. You couldn't do all the work, no matter how much you willed the actor to be good. If you have a less talented actor, you can only get him to do so much. And it doesn't matter if you are Svengali or Spielberg, Sydney Pollack or Ingmar Bergman, you can't get there from here. You can't get your dog to sing Happy Birthday or your cat to do the *New York Times* crossword puzzle.

What a director *can* do is maximize what he has on hand.

Many actors come to rehearsal as out of tune as that Ferrari. For any one of a thousand reasons they are totally out of sync with the script. It is now the task of the director to find ways to tune that actor up. If the director doesn't succeed, he will be saddled with a poor performance in his film. Depending on the size of the actor's role, the film will suffer as a result.

Craziness Clarified

There is no chance that directors will ever learn how to work with actors effectively until we understand their psychology and ways of thinking. To try to work with an actor without an understanding of their inner psyche and a working knowledge of how to talk to them is like trying to fly a plane without taking lessons. It might look easy sitting behind the pilot just watching, but when you are at the controls....

Penelope Ann Miller: "Actors are really sensitive people. I don't think we'd be able to do what we do if we weren't in touch with our emotions. And that's why you hear about so many actors ending up either on drugs or trying to commit suicide. I think it's really hard to balance that. And you need to be emotionally available. I think the thing directors don't always realize is that there's a real vulnerability with what we do. Our faces are up there and we're trying to get into a character. There's a sort of fragility in that. I think it's being sensitive to that process, having understanding and compassion."

Apologies, Penelope, but doesn't this sound like a bunch of touchy-feely crap? Well, yes, but that doesn't mean it's wrong. On a film crew, the director is the Boss, Chairman of the Board, Benevolent Dictator... isn't she? Well... not necessarily. The director may have the title "Director," but to become "The Director" she'll have to earn it. Doesn't a director have the power to hire and fire at will? Like the Red Queen in *Alice in Wonderland*, can't she just say "Off with her Head!"? Well, you can and you can't. If you don't have the respect of your crew and your cast, you are lost. You're just a joke that people have to put up with, an annoyance that people try to get around. Julius Caesar and Benito Mussolini are just two of thousands of supreme dictators who were assassinated because they got no respect. Obedience and respect are two very different items. Saddam Hussein got obedience through fear, but no respect. Supreme dictator directors often have actors and crew whose attitude is, "Fine, I'll do what he's telling me, but that's *all* I'll do. He won't get any initiative or creativity from me. Given a chance, I'll sabotage this bastard."

Why can't actors behave and just do what they're told? Alfred Hitchcock loved to tell people what he said to an actress who asked him, "What's my motivation in this scene?" "Your paycheck," said Hitchcock. This is the same man who said with a smile, "I never said that actors were cattle... I merely said they should be treated like cattle." Funny? Yes. Good tactic? Absolutely not!

Just a Bunch of Children?

Being a child as an adult actor is a good thing, a very good thing. The very qualities that make actors good come from the childish, playful side of their nature. Unless a person is in touch with the child in their soul, they can *never* be a good actor or director.

George Wolfe: "The thing that makes me a good artist is I have this incredible sense of play. As a child I lived in my imagination."[1]

The quality of play that is so much a part of children's lives is the exact same quality that allows the actor to use his imagination and infuse his character with life. He is *playing*. In a playful state, the imagination is given free rein so it can roam the universe. The unplayful actor or director is a person in creative jail: boring, unoriginal, and clichéd. The technical term for this is "untalented."

Actors throughout time have been called "players." They are pretending to be somebody else. They are in a play, or a screenplay. They are *playing* a part. It is no accident that we call children's behavior play and call what actors and playwrights do play-acting and play-writing. Directors don't have the word "play" in their job title, but it is no less true that if they have no play in their soul, they are not directors, they are traffic cops.

Any dingbat can shoot a scene with less than a week's instruction. I said "shoot a scene." That's not the same as "directing a scene." Anybody can just shoot what's in front of them, but a real director puts a special spin on their

---

[1] Robin Pogrebin, "Nothing to Prove, George Wolfe Is Liberated," *New York Times*, August 19, 2002

work. When you hear "He's a really good shooter," know that's a buzz phrase for "all you get from this wing-nut are some cool visuals."

William Shakespeare, himself a talented actor, understood very clearly the actor's strange dilemma. Hamlet hires the players to perform a certain play in order to entrap the King, his stepfather. When he sees an actor in rehearsal weeping profusely over the death of a fictional character, Hecuba, Hamlet says: "Is it not monstrous that this player here... could force his soul so to his own conceit? Tears in his eyes, a broken voice. And all for nothing! For Hecuba. What's Hecuba to him that he should weep for her?"

What he is saying of course is that the actor is only pretending to be upset about the death of Hecuba, who doesn't really exist. It's just a job, isn't it? In fact Hamlet is himself disdainful of these actors and the art of acting. What they do isn't real; it's only a faint imitation of real life.

Some psychiatrists question the value of a person working himself into this sort of pretended emotional state. Robert Redford some years ago supposedly said that acting was not something that real adults did. Was one of the most charismatic and talented actors of our generation uncomfortable about his profession? Was he just tired when he said this? How can that be, when he continues to enrich our lives with his performances and the films he directs? Not to mention that Robert Redford is a visionary who has sunk much of his energy and personal fortune into artistic and humanitarian projects. What Redford was saying was when you are acting, you cannot allow yourself to be an adult. You must be in touch with the child side of you to be an artist.

"Never Act with Dogs or Kids"

So said W. C. Fields. In the history of films, some of our greatest performers found success as children: Judy Garland, Shirley Temple, Patty Duke, Mickey Rooney, Mary Badham, Macaulay Culkin, Anna Paquin, to name just a few. Often these children have little or no experience acting but they seem to have "the gift." And what is that "gift" anyway?

The big trick with children is to cast them properly in the first place. Find a child who has openness to their personality and is not timid or shy. You can't teach a child about the Stanislavsky Method, or how to do sense memory exercises. It's stupid to think you can. Whatever talent the child has is built into their personality at that time in their life. You have to take them as-is.

What do you get for this "good casting" of a child actor that you've done? You get a human being who often lives in fantasy more easily than reality. Children may have all kinds of trouble relating to adults and the real world but they have no trouble living in fantasy. Many of our most talented writers were sickly or handicapped as children and had to create their own reality because they couldn't play with other kids. But in the land of fantasy, you can play with anything you like. If you want to ride a three-headed dragon, you get one. If you want to be king of the world, you are. The *Harry Potter* series lasers to the core of a child's mind. Kids identify with Harry and Hermione and Ron in a heartbeat. Why? Because they get to do all the cool things the kids want to do. For the first time in decades children are reading for pleasure. The author, J. K. Rowling, must be doing something right. She used to be on welfare and now is said to be richer than the Queen of England.

Not only is our "well-cast child" a champ at fantasy, he is hard-wired in his genes to be playful. It is built into their biological being. That's how a child learns the world. Playing with dolls or pretending to be a fireman or a cowboy is all part of preparing for life as an adult. In play, mistakes don't count as failure. Play is nature's way of preparing a child for life. It works the same for animals. Kittens batting a ball, puppies chasing each other are all preparing for their lives as self-sufficient adults.

In my film *My Brother's Keeper,* an eleven-year-old Britt McKillip was cast as the young Jeanne Tripplehorn, fiery and tough. We also needed another girl to be Jeanne's daughter with a completely different personality, shy and withdrawn.

In the casting interviews we could see that Britt was so talented that we hired her to play both parts. I never told the producers what we were doing because they would have freaked. Only after they saw the movie — and still didn't have a clue — did I tell them. And yes, she was paid for both parts.

When the child becomes an adult the need for play is diminished. Real life provides the stimulation. "When I was a child, I spoke as a child, but when I became a man I put away childish things." So the author of First Corinthians knew two thousand years ago that we become more serious as we grow older. We see this in many child actors when they become adults. They may lose the talent and charm they had as children. They no longer let themselves imagine and play. They either give up acting by choice, or no longer being cast, retirement at age 14 is forced upon them. TV specials abound about whatever happened to sweet little Prudence, the child star. Prudence is into drugs, shoplifting, alcohol, and self-destructive behavior. Sometimes they meet an early demise and we read about them in the obituary columns. Without the acclaim, special attention, and applause they got as children, they are often lost.

As far as dogs are concerned, if you're on screen with a dog you're upstaged. Just give it up. Nobody's looking at you. We, the audience, know that the dog is not "acting" and hasn't even read the script. But his natural reality upstages anything a poor *Homo sapiens* actor can do. Did you ever wonder why in animal movies, from *Lassie* to *Babe*, you've never heard of the human actors? It's because the so-called "big stars" don't want to be upstaged by some pig.

Crybabies Too?

Hopefully we now understand the actor's need to fantasize and be playful. But we must also recognize a key element that separates a really talented actor from the journeyman thespian. That quality is one of having easy access to one's emotions. An actor who is not in touch with his feelings is not a very good actor. Whether on stage, on television, or in a film, their feelings are the major tools they use to bring life to their characters. Without access to these feelings actors are no better performers than celebrity athletes who sell sportswear. If you want to be an actor and don't have your emotions right at the surface, you may as well hang it up right now. A career as a barista looms large in your future.

I am not saying if you cry at the drop of a hat or shriek at the sight of a bug you are a talented actor. It just means that you have some of the basic tools to become a good actor. You need to learn to use these tools the right way. Children do it instinctively; most adult actors have to relearn it. So if you see a crazy emotional sort of person come into an audition, don't assume that a great actor is in your presence. They may just be neurotic.

Penelope Ann Miller: "You think of actors like Meryl Streep or Al Pacino or Robert De Niro, and you know them to be really the best actors out there.

The thing that has always really impressed me about them, and obviously why they're so great, it's their passion for what they do. It's not about being a celebrity, it's not about being famous, and it's not about being on magazine covers. It's really about the work, and they love the work. They live and breathe and feed off that. They love their art and they love their craft. They're so committed to it and dedicated."

Conversely, you cannot assume that the shy, sheepish man or woman sitting in the corner of your reception room is a terrible actor. Many great actors are wallflowers in real life. Sir John Gielgud, one of the greatest actors of the twentieth century, was painfully shy; Robert De Niro is the same way. Jodie Foster relates that when she and De Niro were told by Martin Scorsese to get to know each other in preparation for *Taxi Driver*, she would sit with De Niro for hours and he wouldn't say a word.

So how does the shy person go from being a wallflower to a talented actor? The answer is fairly simple: he hides behind the character he is playing. The fact that he is playing a character other than himself gives him permission to come out of his shell. A character is like a defensive armor the actor can put on. Gielgud often started building his characters by getting a false nose. Robert De Niro will gain fifty pounds or shave his head. Orson Welles used noses, hairlines, fat suits, anything that would change the person he was to the character he wanted to portray. Laurence Olivier and Meryl Streep love to hide behind accents. Whatever an actor's method of hiding their "true selves," they feel as though they can release their emotions and sense of play and not feel foolish. The hardest character for many of these people to play might be a character like themselves: nothing to hide behind.

Actors Are Different Than You and Me

Directing Frank Langella in *Dracula* in 1978, I flew to New York to sit with him and discuss the first draft of W.D. Richter's screenplay. I was nervous about his reaction since Frank had played this part on Broadway for eight months, 240 performances. The screenplay deviated from the play, even though both were adapted from the novel by Bram Stoker. The screenplay went where the play could not — the outdoors, the ocean, the castles, and the forests — and introduced many characters not seen in the play.

I found my way to Frank's apartment on the Upper East Side of Manhattan and sat with him in his elegant living room. We chatted for a few minutes and then Frank reached down and took hold of the script. "Now let's get down to our business," he said sonorously. "I have a real problem to discuss," he said. My stomach flip-flopped. "What is this going to be?" I thought.

"It's about my wigs," he said. My wigs!? Here we are discussing the architectural plan of a huge building and he wants to choose the rugs. Frank, who had a head full of hair, thought it might not look very good on film. He wanted to make sure that we used the very best wigs available. The making of a good wig is extremely difficult, and a great art. The slightest misstep and the whole thing looks like an errant beaver.

Frank said there was an even *bigger* problem. "About my capes," said Frank. Capes??!! What's the big deal about capes anyway? You call up Western Costume, order a black velvet cape with a satin lining and you're done. Right? For the average actor maybe, But for Frank to whom average has never applied... Wrong!

I didn't smirk, didn't laugh, as some smart alecks might have done. I knew right away that he was building a character of mythic proportions. Not handled cleverly, the whole character could be ludicrous. He as the actor already knew the *inside* of this character intimately. He now had to design and project the *external* parts of the character too. The British costume designer, Julie Harris, flew to New York to work with Frank to build from scratch the best capes possible. He ultimately used eight completely different capes, some for walking elegantly, some lightweight ones for flying, some "grotty" ones for being in the coffin. A cape for every occasion and an occasion for every cape. And as it turned out, the wigs were not needed because Colin Jameson, the hairstylist, performed magic with Langella's own hair.

Frank Langella as the star had a laser-like focus on his character. He would build it and protect it with an iron will. He was wise enough, and tough enough, to resist requests from me or Walter Mirisch, the producer, to use fangs or wolf's eyes. He knew he didn't need these silly props. He could project Dracula with his talent, and he wanted a Gothic, Romantic Dracula: subtle, intense, and honest.

Martha Coolidge was preparing a movie with Walter Matthau and Jack Lemmon, *Out to Sea*. They play two men who take jobs as hosts on a cruise, dancing with old ladies.

Martha Coolidge: "I had the nightmare of meeting Walter Matthau, who had to play a dancer in this movie and he's not a dancer. Walter said to me, 'Martha, I will not dance. I do not dance. I cannot dance. I will not be dancing in this movie.' And of course the big key scene was Walter dancing. Big physical comedy scene, so I thought about this particular question and how I was going to deal with this since basically this was the second time I had ever met him. I went out and found myself the cutest, most darling female choreographer I could find. And it worked. And he danced. And he was great — just great. Walter had a natural opposition to everything so I would just not get upset about it. I would say, 'Walter, could you do it this way?' and he would say 'No,' and he would do it the other way. But if you just left him alone and didn't complain, two takes later he'd do it your way."

Richard Donner is one of the cleverest directors I know. A combination of Type A charm and a great sense of humor give him fabulous rapport with actors. But even he has had moments. As was said earlier someone who says they've never had problems with a cast member... is lying.

Richard Donner: "I said to Gene Hackman at our initial meeting in Los Angeles for *Superman*, 'Look, Lex Luthor is bald and a skull cap is a pain in the ass and it's going to be hot. Would you consider shaving your head for the picture?' He said, 'No, I'm not shaving my head and I'm not going to wear a skull cap.' And I said, 'But Lex Luthor is bald.' He said, 'That's your problem.' So I said, 'The mustache? You'd shave your mustache, wouldn't you? At least that?' He said, 'No, the mustache stays.' And that was kind of it. 'Good luck. Nice meeting you.' Two months later I was over in London when he arrived. I had figured out what to do with the hair: we would present him as a bald guy who wore wigs. On Gene's first day of shooting I asked the makeup man Stuart Freeborn, one of the really great makeup men. I said, 'Stuart, does he still have a mustache?'

He said, 'Yes.' I said, 'Come on down to my office and bring your mustache kit.' And Stuart came down and I said, 'I want you to put the best mustache on me you can possibly do. I don't want to see the lace and I don't want to see the glue.' He said, 'Why?' I said, just do it. Okay, so he did it. And then he left and I went up to makeup. Gene was there and I said, 'The wig idea for the hair is going to work.' He said, 'Yeah, it's a good idea.' 'Do you like your wardrobe?' He said, 'Yeah, it's going to be great.' I said, 'Gene, the mustache — it's got to go.' He said, 'No, the mustache stays.' I said, 'Look, we're getting by with the hair and everything but we'll never get by with the mustache.' I said, 'Come on. You shave yours off and I'll take mine off.' First he said no. Then he looked at me and said, 'Alright, but you do it right now.' I said, 'While you're sitting there, let Stuart take yours off first.' I said, 'Stuart, take off Mr. Hackman's mustache.' Stuart started to shake. He knew now what was going down. And it wasn't going to be pretty. And he shaves off Gene's mustache. He said, 'Okay, sit down. You're next.' I said, 'I don't have to,' and I peeled the fake mustache off. Hackman looked at me and his neck went four sizes bigger and the veins in his temple started to throb. He's a big mother, I knew he was going to knock me through the wall. Gradually a smile came to his face and he laughed and he said, 'I see what this picture is going to be like, but I owe you one.' And from there on in he was a doll. He was a doll on the set with ideas. He was easy to work with. We broke the problem. He had put the chip on his shoulder and I knocked it off and I didn't get hurt, and he became one of the dear friends of my life."

Peter Hyams is a talented, tough-minded writer/director who has written and directed *Outland, Running Scared, 2010, The Presidio, End of Days,* among others, talks about working with Steve McQueen, who was said to be a director killer.

Peter Hyams: "All of my friends said, 'He's going to kill you.' I kept saying, 'No, he thinks I'm terrific.' McQueen and I would sit at Alice's Restaurant in Malibu. We'd chew tobacco. He had a drinking glass, and he would spit tobacco juice into this clear drinking glass, and it would be half full. In the middle of a conversation, he'd say, 'I could flick your eyes out if I wanted to.' I said, 'I hope you don't want to.' During the writing of the screenplay, he got tougher, crazier, and nuttier and nuttier. I visited him on the set of *Tom Horne*, and he shot a chair next to me with a gun. Remember that expression about somebody having you for breakfast? — I was a cocktail weenie. So David Picker, who was Vice-Chairman at Paramount and my brother-in-law, said, 'Go talk to Richard Brooks down the hall. You can ask him for advice.' Richard Brooks is one of the greatest writer/directors ever. He wrote and directed *In Cold Blood, Lord Jim, Looking for Mr. Goodbar, The Professionals, Elmer Gantry.* He's also the angriest man that ever walked the earth. Richard Brooks woke up each morning in a state of abject fury, and then got progressively more pissed off as the day went on. The story goes that once long ago he had a great idea stolen and made into a big hit. After that he never gave anybody a script to read. He kept his scripts in the safe. David Picker, when he was Vice-Chairman at Paramount, had to read *Looking for Mr. Goodbar* in Brooks' office. Most of the actors didn't get the script either. They would only get pages for that day's shooting. Never the whole thing.

"So I go to Brooks' office. His assistant stands up and opens the door to his office, and basically stuck her foot in the middle of my back, and closed the door. She had no desire to go into that office. It was like Darth Vader in there: a dark office with a track of down-lights way at the end of the office where he sat in his desk behind this semi-circular pipe rack. The door closes behind me. Richard had about seven teeth left in his mouth. They were kind of yellow and green teeth, and the rest of his mouth had big spaces. He was a pipe smoker. I stand there in the shadow. He's cleaning a pipe. Nothing. I cleared my throat. Nothing. I walked forward. Nothing. I stand there. Nothing. Finally, while he's cleaning the pipe, he said, 'Picker sent you?' I said, 'Yes.' He said, 'What's your problem?' So I inhaled. Then for 20 minutes non-stop, I was talking to him about every koo-koo mean thing Steve McQueen was doing. Finally, I got tired or I needed air. I stopped. He never looked up. He's still with the pipe. He said, 'Are you done?' I said, 'Yes, sir.' He said, 'I'm going to tell you this once. So listen and listen good.... The business of making movies with movie stars is the business of eating shit. Now get out of here.'

"The door closed. I'm down the hall. I suddenly heard this choir of angels singing, and a shaft of light came down. I thought, 'Oh my God. Richard Brooks eats shit.' The worst part of eating shit is you think you're the only shit eater. If Richard Brooks eats shit, I can certainly eat shit. I became like Bubba in *Forrest Gump*. I said, 'I'll have shit on a stick. I'll have barbecue shit.' It was the most liberating thing that was ever said to me. That moment when you are eating shit, which is a daily occurrence in film, and that moment when the sweat is pouring down, the worst part of it is you think you're alone."

OK. So now are you thoroughly confused? First we say that you have to make a comfortable environment and be nurturing to your actors. Then we say be strong-minded, not a doormat. Now we are saying you have to eat it! Well, what is it? Baby it or eat it? If you are really confused, you are starting to become a director. If you think directors can just be dictators, you either haven't directed very much or are overdue for one hell of a wake-up call... day after day after day. Did I ever say this was easy?

Try an image from football. The quarterback runs the team. He's got to inch his team along the field, down by down. There are always obstacles and setbacks but he keeps on working with the game as it develops. Yelling and stamping his feet only gets him laughed at. Giving up and letting the other team have its way only gets him fired. He's got a game plan but he changes it from play to play.

Summary

1. Acting is way harder than it looks. Good actors make it look easy.

2. We can never understand actors unless we learn to get inside their heads.

3. Take acting classes. Do some acting yourself to understand how tough it is. If you're inclined to blow this suggestion off, you will regret it later.

4. Clear communication of the emotions in a scene is more important than what the actor feels inside. However the actor gets there is OK, whether it's the Method or some external device like a false nose.

5. Look in an actor's eyes on the shooting day. If you see or sense fear, you have your work cut out. Help that actor relax and become a child again, not a terrified robot who can't walk and say lines at the same time.

6. 80% of directing is casting.

7. Talent is not teachable. Maximizing someone's talent is. As people grow and mature their talent will change for the better, or sometimes for the worse.

8. Actors must be in touch with their child side to be an artist. They are not children, but they must to be playful like children. An actor who is not in touch with his feelings is not a very good actor.

9. Children and animals teach us that natural playfulness and relaxation are powerful tools for effectiveness on screen.

10. Just because an actor is emotional does not mean he is talented. Just because an actor is painfully shy does not mean he is not talented.

11. Actors prepare characters in unusual, illogical ways. Logic is not important, emotion is.

12. When you are working with an actor, give them the room to express their thoughts and concepts about their character. Many stars are strong-willed and must be heard. A director who is not open-minded and clever will get run over in the process.

13. The emotion that comes from talented actors may also exist in their real life. It doesn't shut off like a tap at the end of a take or even the end of a day. This is where it gets fun. The actor is great on the set, that night they go to their hotel and throw a telephone at the desk clerk.

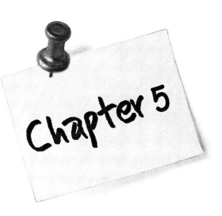

Chapter 5

A Lazy Way to Success— Casting

I can really save you a lot of time. There is no need for you to read this chapter. You are an expert in casting. In fact *everyone* is an expert in casting. Right now in the middle of Papua, New Guinea is a cannibal and his wife watching a movie on an old Sylvania black-and-white TV. The cannibal turns to his wife and says of the lead actor, "What a wombat. I wouldn't eat this guy with a ten foot spear." So you can skip ahead if you want.

But before you do, read what Michael Caine told Craig Modderno in an interview for *Hollywood Life*: "John Huston told me that the key to being a great director is casting. If you get the right actor, you can just stand back and they'll do it."

If you don't know an actor from an acorn you can succeed as a director by casting great actors. This has saved more directors' bacons than the Directors Guild wants known. Actors were here long before directors and will be around long after the last shooter calls "Wrap."

Casting, of course, emanates from the script. Doesn't it? Well, no. Not always. In the ideal world it's said that "In the beginning there was the Word, and the Word was God." In the real world the first question is "Who the hell's in it?" And that leads us to Star Power. Whether it's a mega-movie or an episode of

Friends, the moguls of the moment will try their best to shoehorn in some star names whether they fit the parts or not. When the star is genuine like Julia Roberts it's easy to understand, but often the names designated as "stars" are no more well-known than a hobo from Hoboken.

One of Mark Rydell's most interesting films is *The Rose*. Today a studio would go kicking and screaming before letting the unknown, inexperienced Bette Midler star in a film. Rydell talked about how she was cast.

Mark Rydell: "Natalie Wood came to me with the Janis Joplin story twenty years before *The Rose* was done. Because I knew Bette, I said, there's only one person who can play this, Bette Midler, or I'm not interested. They wanted the girl who played Lenny Bruce's wife, Valerie Perrine, and I said, I'm not going to do that. Every time I see somebody lip-synching, it leaves a kind of visceral emptiness that is unavoidable, so I left. They had John Schlesinger on it and eight or ten other directors on it over a period of ten to fifteen years, until they finally realized that I was right. They called and said, 'We're ready to use Bette Midler now.' That's the way it went down. She's a freak of nature. She could do anything you ask of her immediately, if she has your trust. She turned herself inside out for me."

We know that people often show up/tune-in to see their favorite stars, even when they *know* the picture is a stinker. They just *have to see* Tom Cruise, Julia Roberts, Jim Carrey, or whoever. "Angelina Jolie is *naked?* I'm going!" But more often than not the audience has a sixth sense about stinkers. The stars can appear on Letterman and Leno, press their hands in the cement at Mann's Chinese Theatre, millions are spent on TV commercials, and still the movie doesn't open! Why? Because the script is way more important than moguls want to admit. If the story is weak, the biggest stars can't draw flies.

When the audience gets a sense that the story stinks... THEY STAY HOME! Film exhibitors liken it to a person from California phoning a stranger in Iowa and saying, "You don't know me, but whatever you do, don't go see *Gigli!*"

Stupid Casting Trick #1

At some point the director has to get down to the business of casting the other parts in the movie. Here are some good ways to really screw up your casting:

Cast smaller parts before casting the lead character. All films and plays are like pyramids, only built from the top down. At the very apex of the pyramid is the lead character or characters. You cannot assemble the secondary roles until you know who is going to play the lead.

Every character is connected to the other in some way in the screenplay. Otherwise, why are they there? Unlike life, where random people show up, the writer has created the characters for a specific purpose. Since the characters react and respond to one another, they are related in a way that forces us to recognize that the actions of one cause a response from another. They do not exist in isolated jewel boxes. If Mel Gibson is cast as Hamlet, his performance and personal qualities will be different from Kenneth Branagh's *Hamlet*. That means that the Queen Mother Gertrude will need to be thought of in terms of either Branagh or Gibson. You can't just say, "Let's cast Glenn Close" and let it go at that. Even if she is available and begging to do the part. You have to know how she will fit with Mel Gibson. Is there any chemistry there?

One of the reasons that critics thought Sidney Lumet's film *Family Business* didn't work was that audiences never bought Matthew Broderick, All-American Wasp, as the son of Jewish Dustin Hoffman, who was playing the son of Scotsman Sean Connery.

Of course, you will be considering other actors for the secondary roles at the same time you are working on the leads. But you don't make final choices until the leads are set. Avoid the obvious traps of two actors who look like each other. Or two actors with the same rhythms. Dynamite combinations like Spencer Tracy and Katherine Hepburn or Dean Martin and Jerry Lewis succeeded because of the differences between the actors. Those differences made the chemistry that enchanted and amused us on screen. One of the biggest mistakes we make in casting is to cast two people who have the same energy, tempo, and rhythms. Put two high-energy actors like Richard Dreyfuss and Danny de Vito or two low-key actors like Candice Bergen and Jason Patric together and the result would be a mess. The high-key actors would become annoying and the low-key ones would put us to sleep. We absolutely need the distinct differences between people to keep the scenes interesting and dynamic.

Stupid Casting Trick #2

Don't meet or read your potential cast. Just have them show up on the day. Sure, we'll find Osama bin Laden or Atlantis before we get Robert De Niro to come in and audition for our movie. But we at least want to *talk* to De Niro. We have to know if he sees the role in the same way we do. We do want to sit down with him, have lunch, chat, get to know each other, etc. If we're not on the same page we won't be on the same stage. This is a critical, critical step in casting.

Jeremy Kagan: "The directability of the actor becomes an essential issue in the casting process for me. So I often want to have the person read, even if they only want to talk. I find it important to have readings. I know many incredibly skilled directors who don't do it and don't have readings. Quentin Tarantino, he'll have lunch meetings with these actors. He'll spend an hour with an actor talking about all kinds of stuff, and never having a reading, in order to be able to get a sense of who the guy is and who she is, and that's going to be the basis on which the choice is going to be made. I like his work, so it works for him. I still need to have a chance to see if I can actually direct the actor, so that's very important."

There's another reason to meet with your cast. How have they changed since you last saw them? How much older, balder, fatter, thinner, etc., etc., etc. are they now? If you don't look at them face-to-face you could expect anything to arrive on the set. Francis Ford Coppola hired his friend Marlon Brando to appear in *Apocalypse Now*. Coppola had totally revived Brando's then-moribund career by tricking Paramount into hiring Brando for *The Godfather*. Brando gave an astounding performance and was deservedly back on top of the acting world. Everyone was delighted when Coppola landed Brando for the role of Colonel Kurtz. Even if he did have to pay him $3 million, in the days when $3 million was a lot of money.

Flash forward to Coppola in the Philippines shooting *Apocalypse Now* under the worst of conditions in the monsoon season. He is personally mortgaged to the hilt, including his house, to finance the movie and it is going very badly. His first leading man Harvey Keitel has left the picture; his replacement Martin Sheen has had a heart attack. Typhoons have destroyed the sets. Awful. Finally Brando appears on the location and Coppola is horrified. Brando weighed some three hundred pounds and looked terrible.

Pretty bad, right? Wait, it gets worse. Brando now tells Coppola that he thinks the character of Kurtz should *never be seen*. He tells Coppola, Kurtz should always be in the shadows. While Coppola digests this bombshell, Brando drops another one: he thinks that his own voice shouldn't be used either. And when Coppola reasonably asked why they needed him at all, Brando just shrugged. It took a lot of discussion before Coppola brought Brando around to a reasonable position. As it is, in the final picture you can barely see or hear Kurtz. He is almost always in shadow.

In 20/20 hindsight, wouldn't it have been better if they could have met and spoken in detail *before* Brando arrived? Before he had the power to sink the ship. Of course Coppola could have fired him once he arrived, but then he would have had to pay Brando the full salary.

The time you spend with an actor before you shoot is invaluable. It's not about rehearsing the lines. At this stage the lines are the last things to think about. It's about bonding with the actor, establishing a trust. **Spending time with them is about learning the way the actor's psyche works.** What does he like, what does he hate? What does he fear? Who does he respect? What are his opinions about anything and everything? When you understand all this you will understand how to work with them. Actors are not machines, they are individuals. **They are not robots programmed to appear and do what we want.** We cannot expect them to just show up on the set and have them go to work the way that we expect a camera or a light to work.

Brad Silberling: "What I would always make a point of doing when I was shooting a TV series was to get in as early as I could and prepare. I tried to spend a little time with the regular cast; maybe grab a cup of coffee or lunch, and just ask them questions to get to know their characters. And of course, you learn about what they're going to be like as actors. You can get a real quick sense of someone's process by asking a few questions about how they like to work. In television, for me, some of the most constructive times that I ever had to direct the actor was at the audition, where you have a somewhat calm place to sit and make adjustments with them and really see what they're like as an actor. When they show up on the set, I could say, 'Hey, do you remember the work that we were doing? Keep going that way.' So you use your casting time as directing time. I find that even happens with costume fittings. I'll make sure that I drop by at costume fittings so we can keep talking about the character and the scenes. Use any moment you can. Because, otherwise you may not get any other rehearsal time."

Marlon Brando loved to play practical jokes on people. He liked to test the director on the first day of shooting. Brando would do a very honest, specific, well-acted take. Then one that was fairly mediocre where he would just indicate the necessary emotions. He waited to see which take the director printed. Then he knew if the director shared his taste or not. If not, Brando would just write him off and do as he pleased for the rest of the film.

When Richard Donner cast Brando as Jor-El in the first *Superman* movie, he met Brando at his house in Los Angeles.

Richard Donner: "We sit down and for one hour he mesmerized us with all of this great conversation — wonderful. Marlon Brando about life and about this and that. One of the things he talked about was his son. He said, 'You know, the kids today are so bright. I was telling my son a story about the quick brown fox that jumped over the wall and went around the log and the kid said, 'No, Daddy, he jumped over the *log* and went around the *wall*.' You can't fool them.' Then finally he said, 'You know, that's not the reason that you're here — to hear my stories. You're here to show me my wardrobe and what I'm going to do. Before you do, let me give you an idea, I think I should be a bagel. I said, 'What do you mean, a bagel?' He said, 'Well this is Krypton; maybe everybody looks like bagels up there. But because I'm sending my son to Earth, I create him in the image of the Earth people?' And he's really convincing me that Krypton is another planet and maybe they look like bagels. And I'm really stuck. I said, 'You know, Marlon, you told us about your kid and the fox jumped over the wall thing and you said you can't fool them. Kids have known what Jor-El looks like since 1936. And you can't disappoint those kids, because they're adults today.' He looked at me and he said, 'I talk too much, don't I? I talked myself out of it, didn't I?'"

Stupid Casting Trick #3

When interviewing actors, always be aloof and show how cool you are. Put yourself in an actor's shoes. You get a call from your agent that you are up for a role in a TV series. The audition is tomorrow. What do you do? Well, if you're a smart actor you know you have a lot of work ahead.

First, you'll find out what kind of part and what kind of movie it is. You have to know something about the character. So you ask your agent, you ask anyone who might know something. Get a copy of the script; go to the producer's office if you have to and ask to read it there. You run all this through your trained actor's mind and construct a character, decide on some appropriate wardrobe so you will look the part, rehearse it with your acting partner, your coach, your mother, or by yourself. Then you'll Google the director's name and the producer's. Find out what kind of things they might like. Anything to give you a clue what kind of lion's den you're walking into.

Word of warning to actors: *Never* accept as true what your agent tells you about the character or what the director wants. Nine times out of ten they screw it up. They're making 50 phone calls an hour and information runs together in their brain like a septic tank. So their assistant makes the call instead. The assistant has to make 100 phone calls an hour and all he hears from the agent is "Call Badham and tell him to go to Steve Bochco's at 10 a.m. tomorrow for a teacher part." This is almost no help at all. First of all, what kind of teacher: a second-grade math teacher or a college professor? A football coach or a ski instructor? A good guy or a pedophile? See what I mean? You can show up wearing totally the wrong stuff and with the wrong mindset. Get the script yourself and make your own decisions.

Jenna Elfman: "When I would go out and audition before I had my own show, I would make sure I was familiar with that show. It's like going to someone's house. You want to know what type of house they have because it tells you what kind of housewarming gift to bring. When I book a job, I look to see what I did in the audition that was successful. When I don't get one, I look to see what I did that was not successful, even if it had nothing to do with me. Maybe they just were not sure what they wanted, and they were bringing in lots of people, and then I'd find out who did get it. If it were someone similar to me, I'd think, 'All right. What do they have that I didn't bring?' Or I didn't prepare as much or I brought totally wrong energy to the audition because that's not the energy of the show. So I learned a lot by my own observations. Also, you have to be willing not to get the job because you're not going to get every job."

On the morning of the audition you get ready, trying to look right for the part. You travel halfway across town in the heat; hit traffic, panic that you'll be late. You reach the audition and fight for somewhere to park and wind up having to walk six blocks through the summer scorcher. By the time you get to the audition you are pretty well stressed and soaked. Sitting in the waiting room you see... ten clones of *you*. The same wardrobe, the same hair, the same body type, and all with resumes thick enough to start a bonfire.

You wait and you wait and you wait, getting more anxious by the minute. You vow to kill your agent for sending you here. You are inferior to all these other people. Your choices for your wardrobe seem stupid. And finally you begin to think of going back home to Boise and taking a nice job selling time-share condos to prairie dogs.

Cut to the Audition

Inside are half a dozen fatigued, bored, Type A producer and director know-it-alls there who just want to get this over with. They have been seeing people since ten this morning, and they have hours to go. The casting assistant calls your name. The other waiting actors look at you like "Who dressed you today?" And you walk into the audition sweating bullets.

This sounds like a bad dream. It is. And it happens thousands of times a day in casting offices everywhere. Actors go through this every day when they walk into an audition. And we wonder why they are nervous, hostile, stressed.

Gary Busey: "Jimmy Best was my teacher. He was in my back pocket. He wouldn't let me down. We were at his class sometimes, 4 o'clock in the morning. I would be in tears, and he'd just be giving me the information I needed. He's a master at teaching cold readings. He gives you a script and five minutes to study it. You go out and you read it twenty times. You read your line out loud, and you read the line that's being given to you silently. And you do that twenty times in a row with no emotions. So when I come into a real audition room, I put the script down. I look for something that looks pretty special. One time, for example, I went over to a picture on the wall and said, 'This is really neat. What is this?' And the director said, 'That's a Father's Day gift from my son.' And Lynn Stalmaster, the casting director, says, 'Are you ready, Gary, to read the scene?' And I whipped around and hit him with the first line, and just walked around the room doing the scene. I had the job before I was finished reading."

Here's the point: When an actor walks in to see you, you may be tired, you may be bored, you may have twenty-five other things on your mind; you may look at the actor walking in and *know* that they are totally wrong for the part. None of this matters! The only thing that matters is that actor who just walked in the door. You get up from your chair, greet him warmly, shake his hand, tell him he looks nice, and tell him *anything* to put him at ease. You are facing a nervous wreck, a wreck that needs the job, needs the validation, and who has spent a lot of time creating a character for your film. Tell yourself: "Underneath all this could be hiding a fabulous idea."

Steven Soderbergh: "The most glaring example that I can think of probably in my career is Andie MacDowell. I had written *sex, lies, and videotape* with Elizabeth McGovern in mind. Her agent read it and hated it so much that she didn't tell Elizabeth that it was submitted. And I couldn't get to her, because I was nobody. In the meantime, I had gotten a call from one of my producers saying, 'Andie wants to come in and read.' I only knew her as a model and the sort of notorious story about her voice being replaced in *Greystoke* by Glenn Close. So there weren't a lot of incentives for me initially to see her. But my producer said, 'I really need you to do this.' She came in and was amazing. It was just she and I in a room. She made some choices that were very unusual and not in the text, but that totally worked. Absolutely worked. I never would have thought of doing it that way and she really delivered."

You owe it to the actors and to yourself to treat them as civilly as you can. If you can put them at their ease you will get a better audition, a much better audition. No actor can do a good job if they are terrified. *What if you miss a really good actor because you didn't care enough to make them feel comfortable?*

Jeremy Kagan: "When I meet someone, my initial effort is to relax him or her immediately in whatever way I can and have a conversation about something intimate right away."

Free Rehearsal

From any reading, even a bad one, you are getting a free rehearsal. Actors who come in are giving you the benefit of their instincts regarding the role. Even a poor actor may have a good idea that you can use. Listen carefully for interesting choices that never occurred to you. **Even if you are the smartest person on the planet, even if your talent exceeds all comprehension, other people will also have good ideas.** The ideas may not work for your movie but don't discard them just because you didn't think of it. From any good actor, interesting creative possibilities are uncovered. You may see things in the scene you never saw before. You will often see opportunities for added business, new dialogue, and character insights. And all that can come from someone who is not right for what you want.

When you get those good insights from actors, thank them for their idea. Don't hesitate to ask, "Would you mind if we use that idea?" Of course they won't mind. They are flattered. Thrilled to be validated, to have their ideas taken seriously. Even if they don't get the part they will feel good about the interview and about you. If somewhere down the line that actor becomes the star of a TV series and approves the directors, you could be very glad you had that meeting.

If you work with the actor in the audition you learn quickly how directable they are. It's a good idea to ask the actor to do it again slightly differently and see how they respond. Sometimes nothing happens. Sometimes you'll see a miraculous transformation. Very telling. Don't just say "do it differently," that's too vague. Give them something specifically different to play. Give them something that is "actable." Give them an "as-if" direction. Examples: "Do it again *as if* you have to go to the bathroom right away." "Do it *as if* you detest the person you are talking to." "Do it *as if* you are woozy on pain medication but you don't want the other person to know that." "Do it *as if* you are late for your train and it's the last one tonight."

If, after reading a few people for a part, you notice that they are all making the same mistakes in the scene and either overplaying certain moments or missing the point altogether, stop and look at the scene itself to see if there is something in the scene that is throwing them.

Very often an actor will come in having taken the stage directions in the script literally, too literally. If the script says the character is "angry," you'll see angry like you've never seen angry. The actor will often make very obvious choices. He thinks to himself "They said it should be *angry* so I'll go for that." You'll know it's the script that's causing this because most of the actors reading for that part will make the same mistake. The cure is simple. Ask them to play the opposite emotion. Happy instead of angry. The results will be surprisingly good. It may not be quite right for the scene but it will tell you how much range the actor has and how directable he is. And the very best part: You get some really good ideas how else to play the scene. After the auditions grab the script and cross out the misleading stage directions. Give them some credit for figuring out the scene themselves. There are virtually no stage directions in Shakespeare's plays because he had more confidence in the actor's intelligence than we do.

Jeremy Kagan: "Sissy Spacek. She comes in and she is absolutely brilliant in her read and takes direction fabulously, and she's got this nice, thick eastern Texas accent. I sit with myself and I say, Okay, what do I do? Do I take the actress who is terrific for the role and rework the role for her, or do I just pass on her? Immediately I made the decision that this was the girl. If I had wanted black and fat, I've gotten white and skinny. That's what I'm taking, because she's the best person and she's going to make the role. And I regard that as always true that the actor is more important than what's on the page. So if I find a great actor for a part and there's something that doesn't work in the part for that actor, then I'm going to change the part for that actor."

Many directors prefer to read from the script the exact dialogue that will be shot. Others like to improvise the situation in the script or some other imaginary situation to see how the actor handles himself, what kind of personality emerges when he's set free. Any way that works for you is fine. **You have to satisfy yourself that your choice of actor will deliver on the day.** Robert Altman, Woody Allen and David Mamet are directors that often use the same actors in their films. There is a great level of comfort in that. When you have worked with the actor before, both parties feel comfortable with the other.

Cast at Last

When we decide to use a Panavision camera or an Arriflex camera or a Moviecam we want to know everything about the capabilities of that camera. Why don't we take the same care with actors? **Once you've decided on your cast, call each one up and congratulate them.** Spend time, a half hour, an hour, whatever, to take the relationship to another level. Now that they know they have the part they will be more excited and will open up even more to you.

Paul Mazursky said that he'll ask his new cast to go to dinner, go to the movies or take them all ice-skating. He doesn't want them meeting on the set and saying, "How do you do, I'm going to play your husband."

It is another opportunity to get your thoughts across on the character and most importantly, to listen to what they are saying. You may hear some things that are different from what you had in mind. The actor may have mentioned them in the initial audition. You may have dismissed it as a poor idea that would go away. Guess what? Those ideas don't go away.

Elia Kazan talked about meeting James Dean when he was casting *East of Eden*. He knew right away he had a tiger by the tail. Kazan called John Steinbeck, the author, and had them meet. After Steinbeck talked to Dean, he called Kazan back. Steinbeck hated Dean and called him a real pain in the ass. Then he admitted that Dean was perfect for the role of Cal. Kazan said he was willing to work with Dean because he was so special it was worth the trouble that he might cause.

Elia Kazan: "As a director, I do one good thing right at the outset. Before I start with anybody in any important role, I talk to him or her for a long time. I make it sound like chatter. Everybody will talk to you about their most intimate problems if you give them a chance. They're dying to tell you that they tried to kill their brother once. They're eager to tell you their problems with their father. An actor will tell you anything in five minutes — if you listen. You're storing it away. You're getting your material. By the time you start with an actor, you know everything about him, where to go, what to reach for, what to summon up, what associations to make for him."[1]

However James Dean behaved on the set of *East of Eden* has been forgotten. The performance however, lasts forever. In order for Kazan to have a chance at controlling this diamond in the rough, this loose cannon, this emotional firecracker, he had to understand Dean at the deepest levels possible. So he spent as much time as possible with him at dinner, on the weekends, whenever, to bond and form a trust. Was he manipulating Dean throughout the filming? Probably. Is the film great? Yes. Is Dean's performance heart-stopping? Yes. Is there anything else that matters? No.

Mark Rydell: "You spend time. You walk around, and have lunch, and talk, and you find some kind of common ground... how willing they are to expose their private vulnerabilities. I suspect, whenever you see some great moment, it's because some actor has allowed you to peek into something really personal and private that they've injected into the material. Your eyes pop open the minute that you see that because it's immediately recognizable. Some private and personal revelation has filled a moment... it's nothing predictable. You can nurture it into existence if the actor trusts you. That's probably the most important aspect of the director's craft, which is to provide an environment in which people can flourish. Everybody can flourish. You're interested in their ideas, and once they feel that they'll give you anything."

---

[1] *Kazan*, page 20

Videotape — Blessing and Curse

In the Stone Age before videotape there were only three ways to judge an actor's work: from the audition itself, from film excerpts which had to be run in expensive projection rooms, or from personal knowledge of the actor's work.

Videotape allowed the casting director to keep a record of the audition so that at the end of the process you could review all the actors up for the role. A blessing and a curse. A blessing if you've seen a ton of actors and they all run together in your brain. A curse because today's TV execs are micro-managers, more politely known as control freaks. They want to see tape on every single role right down to the one-line nurse who says, "This way, Doctor."

When a lazy director realizes that he or she doesn't have to be present at every reading it gets worse. With no one there to guide them the performances are all over the place. The casting director becomes the director *pro-tem*. How good are they at directing? Just because they are great at casting doesn't mean they are good at directing actors.

When you receive the tapes of those auditions you don't know what the actors have been told or not told about the role. They may have come in with a wrong interpretation of the role or been led astray by bad stage directions, bad directions from the agent or the casting director. If a real director is present, all that can be corrected.

If you have never met or worked with the actor in person and only have the tape to go by, how can you know what they are capable of? It is legendary that Al Pacino's audition for *The Godfather* was so bad that Paramount and Robert Evans turned him down. Francis Ford Coppola believed in him so strongly, however, that he forced the issue and put his own job on the line in order to get Pacino the part.

The lessons are several: A. Be at all the auditions. B. Don't rely solely on the audition videotapes. C. Know the actor's work by looking at their reel. D. Many terrific actors are *terrible* auditioners. If you know their work you can cut them slack. Your audition tapes are always slapdash. What is on their reel was done under decent circumstances with proper photography, makeup, wardrobe, and music. Still no substitute for seeing the actor in person, and working with them.

Professionals vs. Amateurs

There is certainly no agreement among filmmakers concerning experienced actors vs. amateurs or real people picked off the street. We all would love to have Robert De Niro and Meryl Streep in our film. But we can't get them. So we readjust our horizons to those we can get. Many a new star gets created when all the obvious choices have been tried. This is especially true when it comes to young actors and children. But it can also be true with older actors. Richard Farnsworth, Lee Strasberg, John Houseman, G.D. Spradlin, and Wilford Brimley became important actors late in life. Many directors only want experienced actors while others like John Cassavetes, Paul Mazursky, Betty Thomas, and Michael Mann have had great success mixing both kinds.

In *Thief*, Michael Mann had police playing police, and thieves playing thieves. It was very unique. This was inner-city Chicago. They all grew up in the same neighborhood. They all knew each other. Some were even married to each other's cousins. It wasn't two alien cultures. The self-consciousness would be eliminated if they were playing their opposite. So if Mann had Dennis Farina playing a cop he would have been as good as if he were playing a Mob boss. The reverse is also true. Mann had a guy named Brown who, along with John Santuchi, was one of the two best professional thieves operating at the time. *Thief* is based on John Santuchi. Mann said they didn't have to buy any props in *Thief*. They just used John's tools.

Paul Mazursky told me that he needed a cab driver in *Harry and Tonto* and was having trouble casting the part. One day he was in a taxi on the way to casting and this lady cab driver started talking to him. She was a very funny, one-of-a-kind person. When they got to the casting session he asked her, "How would you like to be in a movie?" She went in and read, and he gave her the part. And it was a big part. She never blew a line, she did take after take, perfectly, brilliantly for two days.

There definitely are reasons why these actors worked as well as they did. They were playing themselves or someone really close to themselves and doing what they do all day long. In *Saturday Night Fever* we cast a young woman cook who worked in a White Castle diner in Brooklyn to play a young woman cook who worked in a White Castle diner in Brooklyn. She had never thought about acting till ten minutes before shooting when I asked her to be in the movie. In the scene she had to cook and assemble a dozen White Castle hamburgers in seconds. When the camera rolled, her hands were shaking so badly the crew was making book on how many takes this would be. "Action" was called. Her shaking hands wobbled toward the hamburgers on the grill. Suddenly the hands became rock steady and performed a virtuoso display of hamburger assemblage.

If one of the actors had been picked to do the job we might still be shooting that scene. Our cook could do it because that's what she did all day long. Paul Mazursky's cab driver did what she did all day long.

One thing to note is that Paul Mazursky made his cab driver read for the part. If the character has much dialogue, you have to be sure that they can walk and chew gum at the same time. The White Castle woman had no dialogue; Michael Mann's cops had very little, and what they did say they said all day long anyway. It's not okay to cast somebody just because they are friends or we want to do someone a favor. Professional actors have worked hard their whole life to be able to do what they do. It's not right for us to put professionals out of work without a really good reason.

Train Wreck #1: Cast the Producer's Girlfriend

Disaster! If you don't believe in an actor's talent and you agree to work with them, you might as well have surgery without anesthesia. We're not talking about their personality; that you can live with. We're talking about their talent. First off, you are resentful of having your arm twisted. Secondly, how in God's name are you going to direct them? Everything they do will look terrible to you.

I am not saying that you are right. An actor could be terrific and you don't get it. But that's not the point. They need guidance and help to fit into the film as a whole and you hate what they do? How bad is that? Better that you don't do the film at all. Either that or learn to appreciate that actor on their own terms. Run every film they've done. Try to become a fan. Pretend you're their uncle or aunt who loves them no matter what. If all that doesn't work, you are in an untenable situation and you're better off taking a hike.

In 1976, when I was casting *The Bingo Long Traveling All-Stars & Motor Kings*, I went to see *The Wiz* several times. (Not the New York electronics store.) It was the most popular musical playing on Broadway, *The Wizard of Oz* done from an African-American point of view. The concept was brilliant, the music was terrific, and Geoffrey Holder's costumes and choreography were delightfully clever. The cast was to die for: Stephanie Mills as Dorothy, Ted Ross won a Tony as the Cowardly Lion, Mabel King won a Tony as the Wicked Witch, Andre de Shields was the flamboyant Wiz. The show earned all the praise and Tony Awards that New York could muster. After a slightly shaky start, *The Wiz* became the most popular show on Broadway.

My producer Rob Cohen and I were convinced we could make a great movie of *The Wiz*. With the backing of Motown and Universal Pictures, the rights were purchased. The screenplay adaptation placed the movie in the Sea Islands of Georgia where people still lived a very simple life. Modern civilization had not invaded. One could imagine a little girl like Dorothy growing up with strong echoes of African and Haitian influences, that still exist, in dark corners of the islands. A perfect setting for this story. In the original

L. Frank Baum books Dorothy was only six years old. That explains the appearance of characters like the Cowardly Lion, the Tin Man, and the Scarecrow. To a six-year-old, they are wonderful and scary at the same time. To an adult they may be charming but we don't believe in them any more than chocolate Klingons.

So it was an amazing day when Rob Cohen came back from a meeting with then Universal Pictures President Ned Tanen. Mr. Tanen and Berry Gordy, the founder of Motown Records, thought that the role of six-year-old Dorothy should be played by none other than Diana Ross. Diana Ross, an extremely beautiful woman, the leader of the Supremes, the most talented black actress and singer of the time. Her Academy Award–nominated performance in *Lady Sings the Blues* was stunning. A movie of *The Wiz* would cost $7 million (dirt cheap for a musical) and needed a big star to carry it to success at the box office, they said. They hadn't forgotten that the show on Broadway had nearly failed until African-American audiences made it a hit.

I should have been happy, right? I was not happy, I was crazed. I was distraught. Diana Ross was almost 30 years old. Though she might have a little child residing inside her soul, on the outside she was a grown woman. Hollywood movie magic can do many things, but it cannot make us believe a grown woman is an innocent six-year-old. Even in the original *Wizard of Oz*, sixteen-year-old Judy Garland had her breasts bound down so she wouldn't look too old.

The story and the script dictate the casting, not the other way around. This story is about a little girl who is lost from home and enlists the help of a Lion, a Tin Man, a Scarecrow, and a bogus Wizard to get home again. To believe a grown woman as Dorothy we would have to believe she was mentally retarded.

I met with the Universal executives; I reasoned with them, I pleaded with them. They listened politely and nodded understandingly. And at the end of every conversation they would say, "But you know we have to protect our $7 million investment. We have to have a big star."

Why couldn't we cast the other roles with big African-American stars to give Universal the star power they needed? Bill Cosby loved the idea, as did Richard Pryor and Lena Horne. But their names would not pacify Universal, who would only be happy when they had Diana Ross. One night at 2 a.m., she woke Berry Gordy to tell him she dreamed that she was Dorothy. At 3 a.m. he woke up Ned Tanen, who then woke up the hapless Rob Cohen an hour later. They couldn't wake me because I turn the phone off at night. By dawn, everyone but me was in a tizzy.

You get the picture. The pressure was on. On me. They held all the cards. I was just a punk director with one minimally successful movie, *Bingo Long*, and all the clout of a plucked chicken at KFC.

What was I going to say to Diana Ross on the set? How could I explain the thinking of a six-year-old? How could I guide her when I didn't believe in her in the first place? I would spend every day of the next year during painfully intense filmmaking trying to make sense of a decision I didn't believe in.

I couldn't just quit. I had to get fired! Fired with a capital F. If I quit they wouldn't have to pay me a dime. I had already worked for free for six months and my wife's checks were bouncing all over L.A. So I couldn't quit. Universal had to fire me.

I requested a meeting. Ned Tanen, Thom Mount, his Senior VP, and Rob Cohen (representing Motown) gathered in Ned's office. They were all stressed to the tips of their Gucci loafers. I told them I too had a dream, a vision. I now knew how to make this work. How Diana Ross could play Dorothy. How her singing, dancing, and acting would light up the movie and thrill audiences all over the world.

The assembled group visibly relaxed. They had come expecting some big confrontation but now they could see that the kid director was going to fold. They would just wait while I saved face.

I continued. "You remember that Robert Montgomery made a fabulous movie a few years ago, *The Lady in the Lake*. It was all shot from the point of view of the leading character. You never saw him. Since *The Wiz* is about what Dorothy experiences on her travels, we only need to see it from her point of view."

Thom Mount, who ultimately succeeded Ned Tanen as President of Universal, asked in his polite Southern way, "So John, that sounds like a wonderful idea. We will see Diana, of course, won't we?"

"Oh, no," I disingenuously replied. "That would spoil everything. The only way we see her is if she looks down at her shoes or her dress. There are no mirrors in Oz so she wouldn't see herself. That's the beauty part. We get Diana Ross's amazing talent, without having to see the one part of her that is wrong for the role, her face and body."

The room temperature suddenly dropped sixty degrees. No one looked at me. I had just died. Nobody said a word. The meeting broke up and everyone vanished into the chilly November evening.

The next morning my eternally patient agent Sam Adams called to tell me Universal had fired me. My father, a General in the US Air Force, pleaded with me to change my mind. He didn't care about the artistic principles; he knew I was burning career bridges. The "common wisdom" around Hollywood was that I had blown a huge opportunity and would never recover. Sam Adams settled with Universal for a small portion of my salary. Better than nothing, we said.

So why did I commit career hari-kari? Very simple. How can you show up to direct a movie, when you don't believe in the basic premise? If you don't believe in it you *will* screw it up. As bad as dropping out could be for my career, the damage to my self-esteem would be many times worse. Universal could not have paid me enough to direct the movie now. I literally took a job with my father-in-law remodeling his shoe store in Lancaster, California.

Postscript: Sidney Lumet took over the directing and Joel Schumacher the writing of *The Wiz*. The movie was made for $26 million, nearly four times the original $7 million budget. Diana Ross played Dorothy. The home of the Wizard of Oz? The World Trade Center.

Three months after being fired, I was asked to take over the directing of *Saturday Night Fever*. The budget was 3.5 million dollars.

Summary

1. You can succeed as a director by casting great actors.

2. Cast your lead before anyone else. Then adjust the rest of the casting to blend with the lead.

3. Never cast two people who have the same energy, tempo, and rhythm.

4. Always meet with every cast member before committing to them. Do they see the part the same way you do? Are they fatter, balder, drunker than you expect?

5. Bond with as many of the cast as possible. Take them out for meals, coffee. Encourage them to talk about themselves. Gain insight into the way they think and what pushes their buttons.

6. Be open and accepting in auditions. Don't play "Director!" Remember how tense the actor is and relax him or her.

7. Auditions are also free rehearsals where the actor is very open-minded.

8. Don't rely on audition tapes unless you directed the actor at the time. Who knows why their performance is good or bad?

9. Casting non-actors is most successful when they are playing a character very close to what they are in real life: a fireman playing a fireman, a cab driver playing a cab driver.

10. Don't cast anyone you don't believe in. It's better to quit the job than have someone who makes you look bad. And you will look bad.

Rehearsal –
Panacea or Pain?

Want to start an argument? Go to a Directors Guild affair or a student film-maker event and bring up an innocent-sounding topic: Rehearsal: good idea or bad idea? You can get a good dust-up going in a heartbeat.

Bunch One says that rehearsals are critical. Preparation ahead of shooting saves time, money, and conflict on the set. Most actors *love* rehearsal, they say. They will work for free, on their own time, whatever. Why? Actors don't want to look like a fool in front of the camera.

Bunch Two counters, who needs rehearsals? Actors should be spontaneous. When you rehearse you take out all the life.

Let's bounce on both sides of this fracas.

Bunch 1 – Must Have It

Robert Forster: "Now the first day is the most important day of all. It's the day you get to hear other actors. It's the day you get to feel what the set is going to be like and what the director does and all that. That's always helpful. I consider the rehearsal to be wonderful for actors."

Penelope Ann Miller: "A lot of the times, when you're trying to work out a scene, a director sees it one way, and sometimes your instincts are, 'Well, I don't feel like sitting here right now. It just doesn't feel right.' You want to have a chance to be able to discuss it in an environment where people aren't sitting around like the grips and the DP and the AD looking at his watch saying, 'Can we just get on with it?'"

If it takes everyone behind the camera a good amount of time to get familiar with the film to be made, why shouldn't the actor get the same chance? Casting nearly always happens at the last minute. The lead actors may get a head start but usually everyone else is scrambling to catch up. And it is much more than just learning lines. Learning lines is the easiest part of acting.

Michael Chiklis: "Memorizing lines comes really easy to me because my focus when I'm doing my script work is what the story is. If you fully understand the story you're about to shoot, scene by scene, the lines come to you because they make sense. The actors who sit at home and learn the words by rote, they're just memorizing words. They don't have any understanding of the depth and gravity of a scene.... So they're just talking heads saying words."

The actor needs time to get inside the imaginary skin of their character. If acting were just learning lines we would all be stars. "The prop girl knows the lines, let her go on for the star." Director Busby Berkeley must have had a good laugh in 1935 when this line was spoken in *42nd Street*.

Jenna Elfman: "In sitcoms when I rehearse, I run it, I run it, but I'm not fully living it yet. I'm in my head but not in a bad way. I'm looking, I'm testing, and I'm sniffing out my possibilities. I do a lot of sniffing. With a line here, I'll think of a possible moment and then I'll try something else. Every now and then, I'll try a bold move, just to hook me in. Then during the run-through, I fully live it, taking stock. But I really light up when the audience comes in and the cameras start rolling. That's when I connect and I exude energy. That's my rehearsal process for the television format."

Good actors are good because they bring an original life and special quality to their roles, not because they know their lines. Without that special quality there is little hope that a movie will succeed. When a character's humanity is lacking or tired and clichéd, we the audience cannot get involved with the characters. If they don't care about the characters, they won't care about the plot. So what is left? Does anybody come out of the theatre humming the special effects? If that were true, *Catwoman* would have been a hit. On the contrary, reviewers for *Spider-Man* were astonished that it is possible to have interesting characters in an action movie.

Directors can have all the fancy camera moves, special effects, etc., but if the actors and their characters are not intriguing, the movie *will* be boring.

Jeremy Kagan: "I believe intensely in rehearsal. I think rehearsal is a magical time. I think it's incredibly exciting and nerve-racking, and I love it. I love it for three aspects. I love it in terms of hearing the script as a whole. I love it because you can really work a scene and discover what a scene is about. And I love it because you can do Improvisational work that has nothing to do with the scene itself that will give a history to the scene that makes all the difference.

"Working with Jonathan Silverman and Bernadette Peters, two days before shooting, we have rehearsal. They're supposed to be brother and sister in the movie. I say to them, 'I want you to go out and spend $20 gambling. And I want you to write a song and come back and perform it for me.' The next day, they go and perform this song. They take three or four hours and they've got the song and they've got the body movement. So then when they're on the set, they've got a reference. They've got a little history. That's what that rehearsal time gives you, that improvisation time, and I think it makes all of the difference in the world."

Oliver Stone: "I like to rehearse long in advance, if possible, because rehearsal is a great chance to get together and make it work. If it works in rehearsal in some way, that's wonderful. Now that doesn't mean it's going to work the same way on the floor If something is just not working — it's the actor, the script, or I'm not sure — that's when I've really got to do my homework and prepare. So I don't want to be surprised on the day with the first rehearsal on the set where nothing works. That's horrifying, because you've got the whole crew waiting. And when I hear about these young directors not rehearsing?"

Bunch 2 – Who Needs It?

Sydney Pollack: "Now actors don't like to hear this, and every time I say it I get in an argument with actors. I personally prefer a slightly nervous actor who isn't quite so set. It's easier to transplant a tree where the roots haven't set down. I often work without any rehearsal which makes the actors terribly dependent on me and on the other actors, and uncomfortable, in a way. But it produces very good results if you can handle it properly. What you don't want is an actor whose nerves are jangling coming into the performance. That's not what you want. But a slight level of freshness, where they don't know precisely what the next moment is, can sometimes be marvelous. It's a far worse thing to see a great moment in a rehearsal and never get it again on film, than it is to waste ten takes by shooting too early. I'll always roll camera one or two rehearsals earlier than I should. And I do the rehearsals that day when I'm shooting. I don't say this is the only way to work. I just say this is my way to work. I see great movies all the time done another way."

Every actor has a different way of working. There is no way of working that is better or more right than another *if* the result is interesting and truthful. James Woods would rather come onto a set and just do the scene the first take. He talks about his first scene in *The General's Daughter*.

James Woods: "And Simon West said, 'Okay. Perhaps you come in...' I said, 'Simon, can I just say something? I'm never going to move from that desk. I'm just going to sit there, like a spider in a web. And he'll come in and I'll make him dangle from the end of my fine silken string. That's what this scene's really about.' He said 'Well, let's rehearse it.' I said, 'Let's just shoot it.' So I had never said those words aloud. They put up two cameras, tight and loose.

"I did the entire scene with John reading it off-camera, because he doesn't like to learn his lines until he does his half of the scene, I don't mean that pejoratively, it's the way he likes to work, he likes to be fresh."

Woody Allen loves to throw highly skilled actors into a scene with very little rehearsal. He wants to keep it raw, unexpected, to get the kind of reactions and actions that come from working without a net. Alan Alda told me that Allen's scenes are so under-rehearsed that every actor but Woody Allen is in a panic when the cameras roll. How does this work? First of all Woody Allen works with the most talented of actors, who are so talented and skilled that they can be spontaneous without effort. They are relaxed and their funny side is readily available to them. Not to mention, comedy can easily be ruined if over-rehearsed. **In a comedic scene or a highly emotional scene there is a great advantage to spontaneity.** Even the funniest actors can only keep a comic scene fresh for a short time. Even the most talented dramatic actors only have so much emotion in them.

When it comes to emotional scenes what we are seeking is very fleeting and has to be captured on film before it dries up. Spontaneity is key. **In a highly emotional scene the best technique for capturing the emotion when it happens is to shoot the close-up before shooting wider shots.** If it takes the actor a few takes to get to the emotion that is right for the scene, it's OK. The readiness is all. The camera must be there when it happens. If we were to start with a wide shot, then a two-shot and work our way in to the character, by the time we get to the close-up the actor very likely will have dried up. They may be able to fake the emotion for us but it certainly won't be as good as what they gave early on.

There are always two sides to every story and it is dangerous to take a position that there is only one right way to do something. John Frankenheimer confronted this head-on when starting to work with Frank Sinatra on *The Manchurian Candidate*. Sinatra refused to rehearse… at all. He would arrive on the set and expect to just walk on and shoot it.

John Frankenheimer: "I had a long talk with Frank Sinatra before we ever started about the movie [*The Manchurian Candidate*] and about the character. I said to him, 'Frank, we have a couple of big problems here. One is that you have this reputation of being continually late and keeping everybody waiting, and I don't handle that really well.' He said, 'Well, I'm an insomniac. I can't get to sleep until 5 o'clock in the morning.' He said, 'If you could, not on exteriors but on interiors, if you could begin filming like the French do at noon having had lunch and shoot till 8 o'clock at night, I assure you that I'll be there promptly every day and work right through.' I said, 'You've got it.' We did that. I said, 'The second thing is this business of you doing only one take. I can't do that.' He said, 'John, let me tell you something. I'm an entertainer. I'm not an actor. It's very difficult for me to repeat myself. If you could find some way where we did it, and I know your shots are very complicated, but if there's some way we could technically not screw it up on the first take.' I said, 'There is. What I need first of all is two weeks of rehearsal. I'll have the camera crew in for the last week, and they'll run this stuff so that they really get to know it. The second thing is that before we do the shot, we do a couple of really intensive rehearsals. I'm not saying you have to get to the level you're going to get to when you're acting. The moves have to be that way. In other words, if you're going to move across a room, I don't want you to do it in slow motion, and suddenly we get on camera and you go like a shot out of a cannon because we're going to miss the shot. If you do that, I think I can pretty well guarantee you we won't screw it up technically.' That's what we did. And Sinatra and I liked each other. I think a director owes it to himself and an actor to try and have as many meetings and as many encounters as possible before you start filming so that there is some kind of relationship when you walk on the set. You should never take this foolish approach that everything's going to be fine, and we're going to get along. I think if during the preproduction process you find that you don't get along, you have to make one of three choices. You have to either pay to have the actor replaced, or walk away from the movie, or know that you're in for a terrible bumpy ride."

Why was Frank Sinatra able to work that way when other actors have to rehearse for a long time to be ready to shoot a scene? Because Sinatra, a superb musician who sang every day of his life, was born rehearsed. He was supremely confident in his skills and could deliver every time. He had no patience with people who wanted to fiddle around with a song or a scene.

Laurence Fishburne: "I love rehearsal on the stage, but film; no. On film I like to swing, just put me on the street and let me go."

The actor that feels this way is often a highly skilled, highly experienced artist like Laurence Fishburne. **They also play characters that are either close to what they have played in the past or close to their own personality.** That means, in effect, that they have rehearsed a role extensively before. This applies also to actors who work in television series or soap operas. They know their character so well that rehearsal is not a big deal. I can't imagine Tobey Maguire staying up nights worrying about his character in *Spider-Man* either. He knows it backwards and forwards because he developed it in rehearsal and performance for the first film.

Dennis Haysbert: "As I get more comfortable with my character I start thinking about my lines in terms of how the character thinks about them instead of an actor thinking about it, then putting the character on top of it, and then trying to execute it."

When Dennis Haysbert comes on the set of *24* playing the President of the United States, he needs very little rehearsal; he knows his character inside and out. He is so relaxed playing that character that his emotions flow easily and he can concentrate on the two key elements of acting: listening and reacting.

But take Dennis or any actor out of their comfort zone, give them a different character to portray, and they will have to build that character from scratch. If they are lazy they may just ignore all that and play the new character in exactly the same way that they play other things. Wilfred Hyde-White, the charming English character actor from *My Fair Lady*, was working with me on the television series *Cool Million* years ago. He told me he had to finish shooting that day because he started a new film the next day. When I asked him if that was difficult since he had no time to prepare, he gave me his famous elfin grin and said: "They think they're getting a whole new character from me, but I'm just giving them the same old thing I always do." He was honest at least. If that was the character that everybody wanted that was what everybody was going to get. It's the McDonald's approach to acting: a Happy Meal tastes the same in Baghdad as it does in Birmingham.

However, when Laurence Fishburne played *Othello* for Oliver Parker in 1995, it's unlikely that he just showed up on the set and started to speak Shakespearean iambic pentameter. He had to retrain his voice and his body to accommodate the character, Othello, who is so distant from the modern characters that Fishburne normally plays.

Rehearsals Are for Wimps?

The iconic American playwright Arthur Miller wrote of the early rehearsals of *Death of a Salesman*. He didn't like Elia Kazan's choice of Lee J. Cobb as the lead character, Willy Loman. Miller visualized Loman as a small, mousy man in his late fifties. Cobb was only thirty-seven at the time and a bear of a man. Miller watched the first few days of rehearsal with growing unease. While the other actors fit quickly into their characters and moved around the rehearsal set with confidence, Lee J. Cobb stayed planted in a broken down chair center stage, mumbling Miller's great dialogue. He couldn't be heard five feet away.

Miller's rising panic told him that they had a lox for Loman. Miller went over to director Elia Kazan in the rehearsal hall. Kazan waved him off saying, "Yes, yes, I know. He'll be fine. Don't worry." Miller probably thought Kazan was sleeping with Cobb. And still Cobb mumbled on. The only way the cast knew when to speak was by watching Cobb's lips. When he stopped moving his lips it must be time for the next line. Arthur Miller had visions of being tarred and feathered on Times Square by New York theatre critics.

Ten days of rehearsal passed. Things got no better. Every actor in the cast was on their feet, and bringing the play alive. Everyone except Lee J. Cobb.

One day after lunch on the stage of the New Amsterdam Theatre, the rehearsal seemed to drone on. A shaft of light cut from the skylights above the stage through the dust giving an eerie mood to the day. Miller was sunk low in his seat when he was roused by a clacking noise. He looked up and saw Lee J. Cobb rocking back and forth, his chair threatening to break apart any second. Cobb's voice began to rise in volume, and an intensity grew inside him that Miller had never seen before. Miller froze in his seat. Slowly Cobb lurched to his feet knocking over the chair and looked at Mildred Dunnock, playing his wife. And then he said in a full voice that echoed in the rafters, "I am not a dime a dozen. I am Willy Loman!"

Arthur Miller writes, "And the theatre vanished, the stage vanished. A new creature was being born before our eyes... made real by an act of will by an artist summing up all of his memories and intelligence... He had altered the stance of his body, no longer that of the thirty-seven-year-old Cobb but that of a sixty-year-old salesman." And at that moment Willy Loman was born.[1]

Lee J. Cobb's performance is one of the greatest of twentieth century theatre. **Greatness does not come when ordered. It comes when it is ready, when the ground is prepared, when the foundation has been laid.** Cobb wouldn't rise from his seat or speak aloud until he had a solid grasp on this character that was so different from Cobb's persona. But spontaneously? Not likely. The good actor makes acting look so easy we can be fooled into thinking there is nothing to it. Don't ever believe it.

Here's the critical point about rehearsal. **When we start to shoot, an actor must be comfortable in his character's shoes.** He needs to have his acting feet on solid ground in order to be spontaneous. Sounds contradictory but it's not.

Don't forget that our most talented actors make it look easy, but there is a lifetime of preparation and talent behind that ease. Even Jack Nicholson, the king of laid back, works really hard to prepare for a shoot. The rest of us have to work even harder to be relaxed and spontaneous.

"Nicholson takes up *The Witches of Eastwick* screenplay to show how he breaks down a script. Nicholson has affixed numbers from 1 to 4 along the margins of this particular page; each number represents a single 'beat.' He explains that the first thing he does with a script is divide it up into 'beats,' or moments of response, and measures — a measure being a sequence of beats in a scene — to get to the fundamental rhythm of the part before playing it in rehearsals."[2]

When we say "actors are comfortable in their character's shoes," we mean that they know the history and background of the character, know their physical quirks and emotional fears. They don't just "know" it in the sense that they read about it, they *know* it internally; they make it part of their being. When they combine this character with the special circumstances of the scene that is being shot we get the unique result that we call a performance.

[1] Arthur Miller, "The Magic of the Theatre." *Holiday Magazine*, 1954.
[2] "The Devil and the Details." Interview with Jack Nicholson in *The Secret Parts of Fortune* by Ron Rosenbaum (New York: Random House, 2000).

Many actors, like Sean Penn, for example, stay in character the whole time they are shooting a film. They don't just turn the character on and off in-between takes. We may make fun of this, but if it works for them we should shut up.

Rehearsal comes in many forms. It is not just sitting around a table reading and discussing the script. It is not just blocking the scenes on the set. It is not just the director and actors having dinner or the actor developing the character alone. It is all of the above. It is whatever works for the script, the actors and the directors involved.

Sydney Pollack actually does like to rehearse. It's just a different kind of rehearsal. He prefers to have intense personal discussions alone with each individual actor. He wants to make sure they are comfortable with the script and understand it the way he does. On the day of shooting they are somewhat anxious. The anxiety comes from not having worked the scene with the other actor. Pollack believes that gives a freshness to the performance.

Sydney Pollack: "I think that there's an approach to film-making where you solve all of the problems before you ever go on a set and then you film what you've solved. It's the way we used to do live shows, where you taped the sets on the floor and you rehearse and rehearse and work out all the cameras and work out the staging. It's the way Sidney Lumet works."

Sidney Lumet rehearses for four weeks on his films with the entire cast. When shooting begins they already know how they will approach a scene in the broadest of strokes. However on the day they will still be nervous and let their spontaneity come through.

Sydney Pollack: "You cannot have an actor so unsure that it creates tension. All you're doing is trying to prevent an actor from going out of habit and repetition to where it's planned for them to go. They have to be open enough to see where the scene is making them go. That's all you're trying to do. You have to do enough preparation, and a lot of that is done just by spending time — dinners, conferences, going through the script."

Ultimately it is a very personal choice of the director and the actor as to what works best for them.

Train for Spontaneity

Imagine a football team going into the Super Bowl with the attitude, "We know what we're doing — who needs practice?"

Why does a baseball team have spring practice? Just to work on their tans? Not only are they getting their bodies in shape for the job before them, they are getting their minds in shape too. They will meet different players this year. They will encounter different strategies. They will learn new techniques. All so that when they are on the playing field in a real game they will *spontaneously* be ready for whatever comes up. Because they have worked hard through many possible plays and strategies they can feel comfortable as they face their opponents. And most importantly they can *improvise* when faced with new situations that come up constantly in any good sporting event. If they hadn't practiced endlessly they would be unsure of their moves. But now they own the field and are more comfortable playing with their peers.

Don't tell me that sports are different from making movies. I know that. Any skill, especially a new one or a strong variation on an old one, needs to be learned, practiced, kept sharp by making the athlete, the Army Ranger, the Navy Seal, and yes, even the actor, so skilled at his job that he has the ability to be relaxed and spontaneous in any situation. They don't have time to be thinking about their bodies or their minds when they are performing their tasks. They have to be so at ease with what they do that they can be totally spontaneous. The terrific "Inner" series of books — *Inner Tennis, Inner Skiing,* etc. — show how this Zen approach to sports can work in any situation.

Too many directors worry about spontaneity being lost with too much rehearsal. That would be true on the day of shooting. But if a scene has been rehearsed days or weeks before, the actor comes to it on the shooting day with a fresh mind.

Oliver Stone: "I don't think a good actor would just take his rehearsal, freeze it in a refrigerator like food and come back and say, 'Okay, here it is.' Who'd play an old moment? You're looking for the new one. Rehearsal really helps to lay a base. Two or three rehearsals help. A tough scene I'd like to rehearse three times or four times. Not too much. You know, you don't necessarily have to get the result. You have to get the feeling."

Jeremy Kagan: "Mozart said, 'Be spontaneous, but inevitable.' Inevitable, meaning that this is what the character wants. This is what is supposed to be accomplished in this scene. There is a purpose to this scene. But, the way it's being done should feel like it's spontaneous. That's the goal. And I feel if you say a lot of 'nos,' that kills spontaneity. That comes from my understanding of one of the basic principles of improvisation: You never deny. So if I say, 'You know, I really love you,' then the other actor can't say, 'Oh, no you don't,' because that ends the improvisation. The other actor has to deal with it. Say something positive, 'Oh yeah, well prove it.' Just saying 'no' suddenly ends the improvisation. And kills the spontaneity."

Just think. The writer spends months alone in a room working very hard to make a script good, then more time with directors and producers developing it further. The production designer works tirelessly on the sets. The director spends months preparing his vision of the film. **None of these people show up on the job without preparation and just start to be spontaneous.** Everybody prepares extensively for their jobs before we are ready to be spontaneous.

Gary Busey: "I love to improvise. Some of the best things I've done in movies are called mistakes or accidents. But there are no mistakes or accidents; it's just something that's going with the truth of the endeavor. You keep that truth going by being stable, focused, and paying great respect to the director and to everybody in the crew."

There's No Time to Rehearse

This is just an excuse. It doesn't matter if we are talking about an episode of *ER*, a student short, or a big epic film, there is always *some* time available. Producers always say there is "no money for rehearsal." Yet without arguing or raising a fuss any clever director can get some rehearsal. **Any rehearsal is better than no rehearsal.**

You can rehearse with actors the day before shooting, or on the morning of shooting, or off to the side on the set while lighting setups are going on. There is always time on a set. Even a fast-moving episodic TV series has to light, lay dolly track, and get props ready. And during that time, look around. What do you see? Actors are hanging around the craft service food table or relaxing in their dressing rooms. You see the director talking to people about last night's Lakers game or some movie. What would happen if they took this time to go over the lines? Even for five minutes. What a concept. **There is always time if you look for it, steal it, create it, force it to happen.**

Michael Caine, in his book *Acting in Film*, makes a big point of what he does while the crew is setting up a shot. He works in his trailer preparing the upcoming scene. He hears other actors on their cell phones talking to their friends or their agents. Acting to them seems like some annoyance that gets in the way of having fun. Caine says when he steps on that set he wants to make it look totally effortless and he does this by knowing the scene inside and out so he never has to think about the lines, they are just there when he needs them.

Jean Tripplehorn and her husband Leland Orser working on a television film, *Her Brother's Keeper*, observed:

Leland Orser: "The rehearsal week, or the dinners that you have in advance, establish a parallel vision with the director, and establish a vocabulary and a language that you will understand throughout the film. The arc of your character. You can turn to each other at 6:30 in the morning and say, 'All right, we're here on Day 10. We had this happen and we're going here.' To keep the timeline and the original mission intact is something that's extremely important. If you don't have a director that you trust, that's maybe where you have to rely entirely on yourself and your own."

Jean Tripplehorn: "But even if you do have somebody you trust you're still on your own, in terms of figuring it out. Unless you get some of that valuable rehearsal at the very beginning."

There's a big temptation for everyone to relax while the cinematographer is lighting. When I direct an episode of *The Shield* or *Blind Justice* I'm lucky to get much of any rehearsal between camera setups. But even when things are the most rushed, I find moments to work with the cast. I actually save time by working with the cast on the sidelines. I will even start rehearsing the next scene to come up before we finish the current one. Once I've got the master shot and we are doing coverage, the actors are relatively comfortable with what they are doing and it's easy to start to discuss the next scene. This means the minute we finish one scene we can show the crew a rehearsal for the upcoming one. This always results in a better picture. The cast has just been kept one step ahead of the crew instead of sitting around discussing the weekend box office.

Organic Valium

An entire cast and crew just stands around while you and the actor deal with a problem? On the schedules that 99% of directors have to work with, this is catastrophic. The actor is using up precious time in a schedule that is already cruelly short. You may solve the problem but use valuable time in doing it. Directors of television episodes at Universal Studios who went over schedule would often be fired on the spot in the middle of the day. **Rehearsals in advance will set the cast and yourself at ease.** Actors who can be temperamental, nervous, unsure, quixotic will feel more comfortable. **With rehearsal you will have done yourself and the cast the greatest favor possible: you will have given the actors peace of mind.**

Penelope Ann Miller: "I find it very hard to be creatively collaborative when you feel pressure. You feel like people on the technical side of things don't understand the process. And you really want to have the opportunity to get comfortable with it. Even if they say, 'Well I really need you to do this,' or 'The shot won't work if you do that,' you say, 'Let me try it a few times so I can get comfortable with it.' Or 'Let's see if there's another way we can work it out.' I think that having that little time alone can be time-efficient as well. Then you can bring in the crew, and say, this is the scene that we're going to do. It's much better when you map it out beforehand and have that chance to do it privately."

Many problems with scenes will be unearthed that can be solved in rehearsal well in advance of shooting. On the day, the pressure to perform quickly is so great that there is little time for discussion. If problems come up, and they *will* come up, the director has to generate solutions quickly. If there is a problem with a scene, or an actor has problems with their character or another actor, you must calm the waters to get on with the shoot. **If you have had any rehearsal, you will already have uncovered many of these problems. In rehearsal, you can solve them much more easily than in the high-pressure environment of the shoot.** If you have not dealt with these problems before, you *will* deal with them on the day. Only now you will not have the luxury of time.

Roger Corman: "What I do is talk to the actors in advance of shooting and just discuss the character in general. What kind of person the character is, what his relationship is to the other people, his motivation, that great old word. It's a cliché, but it's important. What does the character want out of this scene, or out of the picture? The important thing to me was that the actor understood, before the picture started, what his or her character was."

Jan de Bont: "Directors have so much to do that's just listening. Just listening to what the actor has to say and what they feel. Address their insecurities and address their concerns and things like that. The most important thing is that you show them your passion. If you show them your passion, and they feel your enthusiasm and excitement, then you have a very good chance that it will transfer to them."

Take the time *now* to work through any issue with an actor. Be open-minded. It could be a very good idea that just takes getting used to. But whether it's an issue or an idea, it's crucial to resolve it before stepping on the set. Or else it *will* resurface there and it *will* be harder to deal with. If you insist on doing it your way, you may get cooperation, but it will be reluctant cooperation, which is almost as bad as no cooperation. Imagine an actor doing a scene or a moment in a scene under protest. He bites his lip and gives in to the director. What kind of performance is this going to be? Not to mention that you may have several more days to shoot with this actor. And they won't be fun days.

Thinking about problems I've had with actors over the years I see that many issues were right in front of me from the time of casting onwards. If I'd only had the sense to pay attention to them instead of ducking them, I could have saved myself a lot of grief.

What kind of issues? They could range from something petty such as the wardrobe or the actor's makeup, to something major, like his interpretation of the character. The petty issues can become as serious as the major ones. If an actor won't come on set because he doesn't feel comfortable in his wardrobe, a giant overhead taxi meter starts ticking ominously. A major studio film costs an average of $450,000 per day. That's $37,000 an hour. $600 a minute. Costly, right? All over some petty crap that could have been resolved in rehearsal.

Betty Thomas: "They could be right about hating their costume. They're not going to say, 'I hate the costume.' So it might be the costume that's causing them to say, 'This isn't right.' So I have to look everywhere. It might be that their agent is on the set, which I don't like. There could be a million things, but in general there's something off about the scene. So the job is for me to find out what that is. And with good actors, it's always about the scene. And it's always something that I should be paying attention to — that I had forgotten or that I misinterpreted or that I made an assumption about and didn't make that assumption clear to the actors."

The late William Ball, longtime director of the American Conservatory Theatre in San Francisco, wrote in his book *A Sense of Direction*:

William Ball: "When an actor says, 'Can I talk to you about my costume?' the director must become super-sensitive. He must stop whatever he is doing and give the actor his full attention… it is not really a request to talk about the costume."[3]

The director has to focus all his attention on uncovering what is really bothering the actor who needs to feel that he is on the right path. His problem could be anything except his costume. That's just the excuse to start a conversation. The problem may be with the scene, or another actor, with a piece of business that feels awkward. Whatever it is, take him aside in private and sincerely hear him out. If you don't you will soon have a gloomy and resentful actor on your set.

So where do we wind up on this rehearsal business? Like everything else in creative work, "you pays your money and you takes your choice" as the man said. There are so many ways to get ready to shoot a scene and different directors use different techniques. But if you ask me, I say rehearse it every time. Whether it is a full scale Sidney Lumet rehearsal or a minimal Sydney Pollack discussion of the scene alone with the individual actor — do something. Ignore it at your peril.

Summary

1. Any rehearsal is better than no rehearsal.

2. Rehearsal is a learning time, a discovery time, for the actor and the director.

3. Rehearsal is a problem solving time. Nobody sees a script the same way as anyone else.

4. An actor playing a new character very definitely needs experimentation time.

5. Directors may come to rehearsal very prepared, actors often have not spent much time thinking about the script. They need time to catch up.

6. Just because a good actor makes acting look easy, does not mean that it is. A less experienced actor needs time to learn.

7. Never fear losing spontaneity. It is repeatable when there is a bit of time in between.

8. When an actor comes to you with some minor problem, stop, look and listen. Very likely there are deeper problems to be discovered.

9. If you deal with actor's problems beforehand you may not solve them totally but you will save major aggravation on the set.

---

[3] William Ball, *A Sense of Direction* (New York: Drama Book Publishers, 1984), page 52

Rehearsal – Day One

Rehearsal spaces always seem to be horrible, dingy caverns on dirty sound stages, in smelly conference or hotel rooms. Thankfully, this isn't very important. What *is* important is a sense of comfort and welcome.

When the actor arrives at a rehearsal, you are the host. You called the rehearsal, you are the leader. Welcome every actor, even the producer's cousin, stripper "Jaybird Leno," who you cast as a favor. **Make them feel at home.** You'll have simple things to drink and to eat. Everyone is there to work, but a relaxed atmosphere must prevail.

George Wolfe: "You can't bully people, because if you bully people, they're going to freeze and lock up."[1]

You are creating a team of players to work together, support you, and support the script. Let them know you will all work together as a team to make the best film possible.

They need to know how passionate you are about this script and what drew you to it in the first place. Of course there will be problems, long hours, tedious times, short tempers, etc. But when they occur, go back to the original script to remember why you wanted to make this film. Eyes on the prize. Keeping focus on what is really important makes the tough times worthwhile and memorable. It's ironic that we laugh at shooting catastrophes later on. We were really alive then, horrible as it might have been at the time.

---

[1] Pogrebin, "Nothing to Prove"

The fat paychecks the press loves to wave around are beside the point. Mel Gibson, who makes huge fees for his films, didn't work any the less hard in *Braveheart* or *The Passion of the Christ* where he worked for SAG and DGA scale. His talent didn't change because his paycheck was small. He didn't give us scale acting or directing. No actor or director with a shred of integrity ever does.

First Readthrough

Tell the actors *not* to act. They aren't ready to act. They've read the script once or twice but haven't really focused on it till now. They mustn't try to act their role, but get to know the other characters. It is fatal to try to perform at that point. Remember Lee J. Cobb in the *Death of a Salesman* rehearsals. His slow, methodical, probably irritating approach was a way to discover his character without committing to an approach too early.

Actors have two simple jobs in a first reading: to listen to the other actors' characters and to talk to them. Look for the simple human feelings that will start to emerge. This job is much harder than it sounds. The actor often has many things on his mind, the least of which is the other characters.

Perhaps they are thinking of how they look and sound to the producers. Can they do this job? Will they get fired? How will they spend their paycheck? That has to change. And it will change if you make a relaxing environment for them. A good performance comes not only from the individual characters, but also from the *interaction* between the characters. As an actor you want to listen carefully to what other characters are saying to you. Your response is based on that. If the two actors just say their lines as they rehearsed them at home there will be a total disconnect on film. The actors have to begin a process of listening and interacting with each other.

Gary Cooper: "I'm not a very good actor, I'm just a good listener."

Jodie Foster: "If the actors don't listen to each other, it's really, really annoying. For example, you'll be doing a scene with somebody and you haven't even finished your line of dialogue, but they are darting their eyes around getting ready to say their line. It makes me want to say the wrong line just to bug them. Sometimes you tell them to listen, and then sometimes you have to make sure that you are going to be able to cut in some listening pauses in the cutting room."[2]

---

[2] Jon Stevens, *Actors Turned Directors* (New York: Silman-James Press, 1997), page 59

An actor has to be ready to respond to what the other actor is giving them. If the other player says a line differently than before, the first actor has to respond freshly, not just return what they did before. That means staying in the scene from moment to moment.

John Frankenheimer: "Look at Robert De Niro. Just watch him. What he does better than anybody else is he listens. His concentration is tremendous. You never have to say anything twice to Robert De Niro. That quality comes across on the screen too. He listens. I think that so much of acting is reacting. It's listening.

Their second job is to talk. Talk to each other. Not make speeches. Not say lines. Talk, in the sense of speaking as conversationally as possible. They should never try to put feeling into their readings at this point. They are not ready. They must avoid committing to any kind of line readings for as long as possible. When they start acting too soon they start unconsciously committing to the choices and line readings they are making at the time. When that happens they stop exploring the role and it may never change. An actor can *never stop* exploring a role or he grows stale, dull, tired, and unprofitable.

On the first day of rehearsal of *Bird on a Wire* in Vancouver, I was in a rehearsal room with Mel Gibson, Goldie Hawn, David Carradine, Bill Duke, and Joan Severence. Mel Gibson seemed to have no more interest in reading the script than acting in hemorrhoid commercials. I *think* he was reading because I saw his lips move. Maybe it was just peanut butter stuck to the roof of his mouth.

Mel Gibson: "I hate rehearsals. I hate them. I was never a big rehearsal guy. Even in drama school, I found the rehearsal process really draining. I'm not saying it's not necessary. I probably need to pay more attention. I just get so bored by it that I just wanted to shoot it now."

JB: "At the end of the day, after rehearsal, we were on Robson Street walking back to our hotel. I was depressed, thinking, 'Is this the performance we're going to get?' You came over to me, and you said..."

MG: "I remember. I said something like, 'Don't worry, I'll be there on the day.'"

Of course Mel was right. He was wonderful in the film, bringing a whimsical charm to his character. When we would shoot a scene I saw that he would hold back until the camera rolled. On take one he would come alive, not only doing the scene beautifully as written but also adding ad-libs and jokes that improved the scene tremendously.

Mel Gibson: "I like when they turn the camera on. In fact, there's no need to get hot and bothered until they say, 'Action,' when there's film going through the gate. That's it. I hear that noise and nothing hurts anymore. They could pound nails through me and I wouldn't feel it. I've had terrible injuries in the middle of a take, and not felt them until they say, 'Cut,' and I fell over. I had a guy kick me and not feel it. It's a weird high."

Martha Coolidge: "In a comedy, I don't particularly like a full-out rehearsal on set before shooting. I like to walk through it, block it. I don't like to blow it out before and lose the spontaneity of the moment. If the actors are good, if they're prepared, then most actors are really good the first take. I don't like to go on and on and on with take after take, especially in a movie with Lemmon and Matthau. Forget it. They get bored and not interested."

That Means No Rehearsal... Right?

Just because some brilliant actors feel comfortable not rehearsing does not mean that all actors feel that way. The vast majority of actors are extremely insecure and want, no, they *need* time to prepare. They *need* to work with their scene partners. They *need* time to discover the possibilities of the scenes. They *need* to get over the very real anxiety of doing new material. Very, very few people can do that without rehearsal.

Psychologists say public speaking is one of our greatest fears in life. Actors — and the rest of us — want to feel comfortable with what we are doing before we get in front of people and make a fool out of ourselves. Creativity is no bed of roses.

Actors are creative artists. Creativity does not happen on demand. As much as some producers and some very shortsighted directors want actors to be machines that can be creative on demand, it takes time to find the best, most creative approach to a scene. Some take more time than others.

There are no one-size-fits-all rules that will work for every actor. Find out the comfort level of the actor before committing them to rehearsal or no rehearsal. You will always have a cast with very different rehearsal needs. Candice Bergen, Dustin Hoffman, and Hal Holbrook are all actors who really, really want to know what they are doing before they step on the stage. They can still be spontaneous, they can still improvise, but the rehearsal gives them a comfort level that they need. Mel Gibson and Frank Sinatra are just different animals. Directors have to discover what they are dealing with.

Never Invite Guests to the First Reading

Not even the producers, or your spouse, or your agent? Why? Because the reading will be *terrible*! What did you expect? The actors won't be acting. You'll tell them not to.

Sydney Pollack bluntly says, "I never rehearse in front of anybody, not even my dog." If you have to invite the writer, caution him not to panic. It won't do much good… he'll panic anyway. Hearing a first reading takes a strong heart. The actors are just feeling their way through the script. If there is an audience present they feel compelled to *act* for them. They may be scared they'll be fired if they don't go all out. But remember we're trying to get them to immerse themselves in the whole script, not just their own part.

David Foster, who has produced many wonderful films from *McCabe and Mrs. Miller* to *The Mask of Zorro* as well as *Short Circuit*, rang me one day. Would I direct a reading of a script that MGM was considering? Michael Nathanson, MGM's President, liked to hear good actors read a script aloud before he decided to green light the movie or not. His casting director, Mali Finn, is a genius at getting excellent actors to come in for these readings. The plan was to gather the actors one afternoon to read through the script once. The next morning it would be read again. Then Nathanson would come in after lunch to hear it. At the first reading Jason Alexander, Christopher Lloyd, Julie Warner, Jeff Corey, Mary Mara, and several other really talented actors gathered around the table. David Foster promised he would stay away. Giving these actors the instruction not to act, just talk and listen, the reading began. After a few minutes the door slid open quietly and Foster, ever the maverick, slipped into the room. He just couldn't stay away.

At the halfway point there was a bathroom break. Foster grabbed me in the men's room. "This is *terrible*! They're not putting any feeling into it. I can't understand anything they're saying. You're ruining this. Why did I hire you?"

I looked at him with a grin, "David, you didn't hire me, I'm ruining this for free." David struck his forehead, "Ohmigod, jokes, I'm dying and he starts with the jokes."

"David, I know you are worried, but please, let us rehearse. Come back in the morning and you will see a miracle. I promise." Looking like he had just bought 1,000 shares of Enron he nodded and promptly threw up. Well, not really… but it would have been funny if he had.

The next morning, the second reading began, everyone feeling the pressure of that afternoon's performance. Again David slipped into the room and listened.

At the break, David drags me into the men's room. "This is *great!* WOW. What did you do? What a change. If Nathanson doesn't go for this, I'll eat my Porsche!" Classic David Foster hyperbole. "Thank you," I replied. "I'm thrilled that you're happy. The actors have done it by themselves. I just get out of their way."

The reading for Michael Nathanson went well. The room full of assembled executives were laughing and smiling the whole time. At the end Nathanson stands up and applauds followed by the rest of the execs. He comes over and shakes our hands. "Boy, this is great. You guys have really made this script come alive so much better than I thought." He paused, "But this is a movie about baseball." David looked puzzled. "Yes, it always has been, Michael." "You're right," Nathanson, replied, "I just forgot. Baseball movies never work, you know. After *Bad News Bears* and *Pride of the Yankees*, that's it; the rest... straight in the toilet. But hey, you guys did a great job."

He walked jauntily back to his office... and David threw up all over again. The movie was never made.

When *Do* You Direct?

Wait as long as possible before saying a word to your cast. You've been studying this material for a long time and they are just coming to grips with it. They need time to internalize the script, make it organic. Give them the time to work it out. Give them some credit for intelligence. Don't start jumping around like some idiotic caricature of a director yelling "No, no, no!"

Elia Kazan: "One thing a director has to know Is when to keep his mouth shut, to wait and see what the actor does instinctively, personally, without trying to fill any preconceived patterns. [In *Viva Zapata*] there's a scene between two people who love each other. Brando... did something with his face. Then he brought Quinn's dead hands up to his own face. That was all Brando, unprompted by me. Only if you're not getting what you want do you start giving directions."[3]

As a student director at the Yale Drama School I felt frustrated. I would rehearse scenes for my directing class and I would want the actors to be

---

[3] *Kazan*, page 99

good *instantly*. They were doing so many things wrong that I had no idea where to start helping them. A hopeless task. I asked my professor, Nikos Psacharopoulos, the brilliant artistic founder and director of the Williamstown Theatre Festival, what to do. In his heavy Greek accent Nikos answered, "Just give them a chance to play with it. Leave them alone. They'll work it out."

This didn't sound right. Wasn't I supposed to be the "all-seeing, all-knowing director" who would tell them everything? "But, but," I started. Nikos, intuitive as always, continued. "That's all you need to know, do it." "But you just told me to do nothing!" I replied. Too late, Nikos was off down the hall to another class.

Anne Bancroft expresses for all actors the frustration of not being allowed to discover things on their own and do their job.

Anne Bancroft: "Don't give me results before I have failed!"

Steven Soderbergh: "I've learned the hard way, that when actors seem to be onto something, shut up and stay out of the way. If you've cast properly, and the scene basically works in its construction, you shouldn't be bugging them a lot. Don't get them in their heads, don't get them thinking, and never call attention to something specific that they're doing that's great, because it will never be great again. I've also learned that the hard way. Never say, 'I loved how you picked up the such and such,' because you'll never love it again."

Contradiction Alert: Soderbergh's approach to compliments differs from Francis Ford Coppola's. Coppola advocates specific compliments to the actor and Soderbergh believes it's dangerous. I personally tend to follow Coppola's advice but at the same time I know that Soderbergh is often right. What he means is that a compliment about a specific moment to an actor can cause the actor to jump on that moment with both feet the next time the scene is done. It will be performed with "quotation marks" around that moment and it may be a take or two before it settles back to some level of believability. On the flip side however, if the actor is doing something terrific at a moment they may not be aware how well it works and stop doing it. Then it can get lost forever. It is a curious dilemma.

When asked how he got the Oscar-nominated performance from Mary Badham in *To Kill a Mockingbird*, Bob Mulligan said, "I didn't do anything. I just set up a playful environment for Mary, Phillip Alford, and Johnny Megna and turned them loose. If we did something well it was to cast the right kids in the first place." Bob was being modest, his films speak for themselves. He

knew enough to let the actors run with the situation, even if they were nine years old.

Peter Bogdanovich, talking about his work with Tatum O'Neal on *Paper Moon*, said when he was directing children he treated them like they were forty years old. Unless one is a literalist, one can see that these two approaches are not contradictory, they complement each other. It is possible to treat them like adults yet be playful at the same time. The child knows when he is being talked down to and really likes being treated like a grown-up. At the same time they are still children and need to be playful. Bob Mulligan said he found the children were always fascinated with the process of filmmaking and he would involve them by letting them look through the camera, listen on headphones and so on.

Oliver Stone: "I trust most actors to do their homework and to prepare well. Of course you send them books, you send them movies, you send them documentaries, and you start to put them in the atmosphere. You have lunches and meetings with them occasionally, because often they're working on other films or they're doing other things. You establish a respectful, mutual relationship, if you can. And then you talk about characteristics. Each actor is different. In Cruise's case, I introduced him and spent a lot of time with him and Ron Kovic, and then I left them alone, because Ron is such a dramatic individual. And Tom could learn a lot from just being with him. So they would go out together in wheelchairs and spin around the shopping malls of Southern California.

"When working with Anthony Hopkins on *Nixon*, there was no Richard Nixon alive, but Anthony looked at a ton of material. There was a lot of documentation of Nixon. And Anthony worked a lot from the outside in. The script provided the inside out or at least an attempt at it. The outside in, by which I mean body posture. Anthony was a believer in body posture and in imitating the accent as much as possible, but above all the mannerisms. And the mannerisms would free him up. It would free up his mind in a strange way to start to crawl inside the character. And Anthony claimed to have read the script 100 times or plus. He was one of these people who said he couldn't get enough of reading it and re-reading it and re-reading it. That was the way he learned lines. It was very hard to believe that he could read that script 100 times. You know, it's an extraordinary amount of work to put in. I said, 'Why wouldn't he read it and then just concentrate on the lines?' He's re-reading and re-reading. And then you would see him in the makeup room and it's there. It was always around him."

Improvisation

When actors are working to get an understanding of the dramatic thrust and the emotional life of a scene, it can be extremely helpful to have them play the scene making up their own dialogue as they go. If the language is unusual, as in Shakespeare, this may be the only way for the actor to dig underneath the more flowery language and get a handle on the scene. Certainly if the actor doesn't understand the text we cannot hope for the performance to be any good or for the audience to follow the story. If the character is foreign to the actor, this is a way to gain understanding of the character's psychology.

The techniques of improvisation are easy to learn. **The main point is to keep focus on the dramatic direction of the scene.** Keep it simple. What does each character want? Stay away from intellectualizing! What's the simplest active verb that each actor can play? A sense of freedom is important so that actors don't suppress their instincts.

Roger Corman: "I always like improvisation, and the beauty of it is, you don't have to use it. If they improvise a scene and it's no good, you don't have to use it. You don't even have to print it."

There are certainly pitfalls to improvising during the takes. If the actors are not really similar to the characters in real life, their improvs can be bumbling and false. If on the other hand Michael Mann is using a real cop to play a cop, improvisation might be the very thing to relax the cop turned actor and to help him sound believable. Joe Pytka, the highly successful commercial director, is very good at getting performances from real people in his Budweiser or Coke commercials. He does this by having them improvise the situations that the commercial calls for.

On the other hand, actors that are good at it can bring an amazing quality of truth to the screen. Mark Rydell, who directed Steve McQueen in *The Reivers*, comments.

Mark Rydell: "McQueen had a magical improvisational sense. He wouldn't look at the script. He'd say, show me the scene right before we start. He didn't want to rehearse on the set. He wanted it to be fresh and improvisational. He just had a way of living in the moment that was startling. He really was a star. Everyone talks about, what is it that makes someone a star? No one can define it, but Steve McQueen had it. You knew it, just like you knew James Dean was a star. It's like a light that they have. A personality or a behavior that's just attractive. Very attractive. They can also be horrible people."

Since relaxation is such a key to creativity, and since improvisation is pure creativity, I work hard constantly to relax my actors. I always tell them failure is OK. Some of their ideas will be terrible and some will be great. That's OK. As long as they are honestly trying to explore and learn, they have the safety net of knowing that they won't be yelled at or embarrassed. They know they are free to try anything that comes to mind.

Repeated improvisations will deepen the actor's control of the scene and their character. **It's a good idea to record any improvs so the actors can remember when they did something really good.** The writer can also take advantage of any good ideas that emerge from the improvisation. When Roy Scheider utters the now classic line of dialogue in *Jaws*, "We're gonna need a bigger boat," co-screenwriter Carl Gottlieb got the credit, but admits happily that the line was ad-libbed by Scheider.

Sydney Pollack: "You find the behavior and then you drop the text in on top of it. That's why people do improvisations. But don't start with the actual words in the screenplay because if you try to create meaning with the words alone you strain emotional muscles. It's like trying to load the text with meaning, and it's just the opposite. The behavior is what you find first and the text follows quite easily, unless you've got bad text."

Before starting any improv the director and the actor have to be totally clear what the objective is for the scene. It's not important that the actor achieve that objective in the improvisation, what's important is that they continue to try different ways to achieve their goal. **Ignore the written dialogue.** The scene can't be internalized as well if the actor falls back on the writer's words. The first time an improv is tried it can be painfully bad. Don't look for it to solve all the problems in one try. Like anything it profits from repetition, which can help the actor relax. **It profits from the feedback given by the director to the cast.** Keep the focus on the objective. Keep them looking for various ways to achieve it. Most scenes in films are short but the improvisation can be as long as the actor's imagination can sustain. If the scene is very serious, the improv does not have to be serious. Humor creeps into every situation. Humorous scenes do not always have to be funny.

Improvisation is exploring, experimenting and by so doing, finding a different perspective than on the written page.

Staging During Rehearsal

In a play where the actors will be seen for the entire performance, staging is a critical part of the play. Consequently, it should be extensively rehearsed and perfected. However, in a film the staging of the dialogue scenes can be done very late in the process. First of all, we often don't know the locations for the scenes until the last minute. Second, we may not have enough rehearsal time to explore the characters *and* stage the scene too. Third, since the scenes are relatively short, a few pages at once, the actors can quickly learn whatever staging is needed.

Steven Soderbergh: "I'm not a big rehearsal person as opposed to when I started. And now, I like getting people together, and we talk about the script in general and try and see if there are any red flags, but I'm not big on seeing it anymore before we're on the set. I've taken the more Fellini approach, which is a big, long dinner with lots of wine and stuff and everybody sort of just hanging out. And it's because I'm really afraid of getting in their way. And so, what I really want from them in the rehearsal process is, how do they want to be talked to? Who are they, for one? I'm going to be in a trench with this person for ten or twelve weeks. Who are they? Where did they come from? How do they talk? How do they carry themselves? So I'd rather spend more time seeing them in a non-performance mode at this point so that I have a sense of who they are than seeing them perform."

Of course if you have the time in rehearsal you can lay out ground plans of the various sets, bring in furniture and rehearsal props and be very thorough. In the best of circumstances you may be able to rehearse on the actual sets you'll use in the movie. **You'll want to allow a great deal of experimentation on the part of the actors. There is much to be gained from the process of exploration of the scenes in a rehearsal environment.** Stay very open-minded and you will discover lots of interesting ideas.

Oliver Stone: "Okay, I'm Joan Allen and I'm doing this scene with Anthony Hopkins in a small room and I have two pages of dialogue. It's academically boring. It's the hardest thing to shoot, as you know. How do you shoot two pages of dialogue? Well, I think I'm going to circle the whole room. I just have a feeling, and my hunch says that I'm going to circle the whole room and they're going to be moving. And she's going to chase him. Because that was the nature of the scene. So if you look closely at the scene, they do circle the room in fits and starts, but they never break the pattern. And she pursues him and he backs away, until he comes to a place where he has to take a stand and he says something rather radical and illuminating. That's the way I think the scene should go. But I'm not going to tell that to the actor right upfront. It's like telling them what I want — my result. So I'm faced with an issue. Okay, they've rehearsed the scene. We rehearse the scene in the studio, outside, in the office weeks before. We come in to set. New scene, and we rehearse alone — me and the actors. Not even the script girl is there. I don't want anybody there. Mistakes have to be made. They need to be made quietly, privately, and not embarrassingly. So we rehearse and we rehearse. And sometimes the crew will sit there for an hour or two hours, if necessary, if it's a tough scene. And you rehearse it and you've talked to them and now you go. And you often let them do it the way they are inclined to do it the first time or the second time, and often it becomes sticky. It may not always work the first time. You work it. You say, 'Now pursue him.' It doesn't feel comfortable. 'Do me a favor. Just run after him right now.' So what I'm saying is sometimes by just forcing the action — not always — but forcing the action does bring out a thing in the actor's head that wasn't there. They often get stuck. Even if the two actors sometimes have worked together before. And it's fine with me. And they can work it out in their trailer. But generally speaking, it reveals itself. You don't have to be smart and say, 'I told you that didn't work.' It comes out. Mistakes come out. They feel something is wrong. Every actor will do a scene in rehearsal, and no matter what, when it's over most of them will say, 'That sucked.' Very rarely do I have an actor say, 'That was great. Let's do it that way.' Or they'll say, 'I'm not sure about that.' Every scene has its series of problems. So you identify them in a semi-intellectual way and sometimes in a very visceral way, because you have to talk to the actor's visceral side. Intellectual doesn't work for the actor. It's very hard to play an intellectual thing. Kazan said, 'You play the action. You have to give an action.' And life is action."

How Much Rehearsal?

Rehearsal time varies from picture to picture. *Dog Day Afternoon* director Sidney Lumet and *Panic Room* director David Fincher will take a month to rehearse. At the end of Lumet's rehearsals he shows a polished run-through to his crew. His films rarely shoot more than thirty days, as opposed to other major feature directors who often take fifty days or more for a similar story. Those thirty days of rehearsals cost a tiny fraction of thirty days of shooting.

Here's how Lumet schedules a two-week rehearsal period, as described in his book *Making Movies*:

1st day   Read and discuss

2nd day   Discuss

3rd day   Read again

4th day   Staging on taped areas

6th day   Work through staging

9th day   Cameraman run-through

10th day   Run-through once or twice

Randall Kleiser said of his rehearsals preparing *Grease*:

Randal Kleiser: "We rehearsed *Grease* for five weeks. Pat Birch, the choreographer, would have the actors doing the musical numbers on one sound stage, and I would have them doing the dialogue scenes on the other sound stage. The cameraman was present, and we were able to figure out the way to shoot the scenes and musical numbers. It was a great way of working."

If the rehearsal time is short, spend most of it around the rehearsal table. The actors can learn a great deal from just reading over the scenes and getting used to each other. They will have many questions about the scenes that can be addressed right there. This is where rehearsal time is the most valuable. You can spend hours in rehearsal working out a problem. If you do that on the set with a full crew standing around waiting to film, you will shoot yourself in the foot.

In rehearsal, first concentrate on helping actors understand their character and their role in the overall story. Any good actor will relish this opportunity to explore new ways of playing things. And if they are too lazy to think, you have to challenge them. Give them homework: write a biography of the character, detailing his background, his physical characteristics, his likes and dislikes, and his goals. This is a critical part of the actor's homework.

After Rehearsal

It's hard not to say this too many times: *actors need validation*. They need to know they are on the right track. At the end of rehearsals, especially the early ones, go to every actor in turn and talk to him or her about what they are doing. They would like to hear good things, but more importantly they want to know if they are on the right track. In the words of psychologists, they need to be positively reinforced.

Karen Pryor: "Watching sports on TV we can see the beautifully timed rein-forcers that players receive again and again. As a touchdown is made or a home run hit, the roar of the crowd signals unalloyed approval. It is quite different for actors. Except for occasional response from a director or camera operator or grip there is not timely reinforcement; fan letters and good reviews are pallid compared with all of Yankee Stadium going berserk at the moment of success."[1]

We don't have to treat them like delicate flowers or children whose self-esteem can't be endangered by negativity. Go to each actor and give them positive feedback on the things they are doing right. When it gets to the things which can be improved, never use the word "don't." "Don't" is an automatic roadblock. Right away the actor gets defensive because "don't" is the beginning of criticism. She must have done something wrong. Instead of "don't," use "and" or "what if" or "how about." Always use the most positive approach you can think of.

John Travolta couldn't come to work the day we shot the opening scene in *Saturday Night Fever* where he walks down the street swinging a paint can. His fiancée, Diana Hyland, had just died of cancer and he had traveled to California from New York for the funeral. So I had to work with his stand-in Joey since we would only see his feet. I asked him to walk in time to the music of "Staying Alive" which we were playing loudly on the street. His first tries were very stiff. I could have gone to him and said, "Come on, Joey, don't be so stiff when you walk. Loosen it up." Instead, I said in a positive way, "Good, you've got the rhythm down. Now what if we add some bounce, to your step?"

Very slight change, right? **If people were computers, it would make no difference how we talk to them.** But, because we are emotional beings, we don't always react rationally. Our backs stiffen when our parents start telling us what to do. Works the same with directors, teachers, and ski

---

[1] *Don't Shoot the Dog!* by Karen Pryor (Bantam Books, 1999), page 9.

instructors. The good tennis coach doesn't say what he's really thinking about your rotten playing, but finds ways to make positive suggestions: "Try hitting the ball on the rise" as opposed to "Don't hit it so late." The good ski instructor doesn't fall down laughing at your spastic skiing, but says, "Try leaning down the hill," never "Don't lean back like that."

Postscript on Travolta. When he returned to work we went back on the street to shoot the missing parts of the scene. We showed him a playback of the walk that had been shot so far. His reaction was not enthusiastic. "That's not the way Tony walks," he said. Travolta was protecting his character, which is the actor's job. And like the earlier incident on the Verrazano Bridge, he stood his ground. And like that incident, we didn't have time for re-shoots. We shot what we had time for with Travolta walking the way he wanted. If you are a connoisseur of walks you will be able to spot the two different walks in that sequence.

I did a remake of John Ford's classic Western *Three Godfathers* with Jack Palance and Keith Carradine, who was then twenty-four years old. Keith was playing an arrogant and overbearing young Confederate lieutenant. Keith's first readings in rehearsal were coming from a character that was formal, stiff, and arrogant. Plus he was doing a Southern accent from hell. Carradine is extremely kind and charming, but he had a cardboard cutout idea of this lieutenant. My first reaction was it's slit my wrists time.

After a sleepless night, I told him: Your character is a new lieutenant. They are always insecure in front of their men. He wants to look like he knows what he is doing so he uses big words and tries to sound authoritative. This makes it easy for you Keith as an actor because the words themselves are so pompous that you don't have to emphasize them. Just say the words as conversationally as possible and they will still sound pompous but the difference will be that the words will sound natural. The second thing I said was, "Let's use your natural California accent for now until you feel totally comfortable with the character. Accents have a nasty way of getting in the way of truthful acting. When you feel you have the character under control you can start to use a Southern accent."

So, now I've skirted around the "you were terrible" sand trap and "that accent is for dog-doo" land mine. Was Keith bamboozled by this avoidance of negativity? *Absolutely not!* Was he willing to work with the suggestions? *Absolutely yes!* Even though he knew I was saying there were problems with what he was doing, he could tell I was on his side and pulling for him to do well. With that confidence he could relax and try the different things I suggested. Overnight he got a good handle on the character and was excellent in the movie. I did nothing miraculous. I just gave him the comfort he needed to try a new approach.

Summary

1. Welcome the cast to the first rehearsal. Let them know your passion for the script and your belief in them as members of a team.

2. Let them know you don't intend to be a cruel dictator. At worst, you are a benevolent one who wants to hear ideas and problems and solutions from everyone.

3. Don't let the cast "act" at the first reading. They must just say their words and listen to others. Talk and listen, don't *act*.

4. If they "perform" too early they commit to a performance that will only be half realized.

5. Different actors need different amounts of rehearsal. There is no rule how much. It is totally dependent on the individual actor. Mel Gibson wants to jump in and just do it, Robert De Niro wants to explore lots of options.

6. Keep guests away from the first reading. Even the producer. Let them come to the second one. The pressure to perform is too great the first time through.

7. Wait as long as possible before saying a word to your cast. Give them plenty of time to discover problems and solutions on their own.

8. Allow a lot of experimentation by the actors. It's how they discover what works and what doesn't.

9. When improvising, be totally clear with the actors about the dramatic point of the scene.

10. Record an improvisation if possible. Good discoveries can be remembered and incorporated into the scenes.

11. Validate your actors after rehearsals. Let them know what's good and what's problematic about their work. They want to hear from you.

Chapter 8

Killing Acting

Intellectual discussions about scenes and character are the death of good acting and directing. It is wasted time that produces no good results. Acting is about behavior. Whether it's *The Matrix* or *The Miser*, it's always about behavior. It is *not* about cosmic themes. It is not about deep meanings. It is about what we *do*. *What is the character doing in the scene?* If you can't answer that question with an active verb, you don't know what the scene is about. You only think you know.

Directors everywhere have the hardest time expressing a character's behavior in active verbs. Too many English Lit classes have trained us to look at the bigger thematic pictures. This gets everyone hopelessly lost in psychobabble and pretentious cosmic themes. As far as acting is concerned, we must look strictly at the *behavior* on the page.

Everything we do in the world is an action. Every action is for a reason. Even if we do nothing, that itself is an action, a choice. The choice may be ours or it may be forced upon us. For example: **Action.** We go to sleep at night as an active choice, *to get rest*. If we can't sleep there is some reason: We are upset, we had coffee after dinner, we feel ill, etc. We react to this in some way: We try to force sleep, we toss and turn, or take pills. Whatever we do, we *act* in some way. And we have a *feeling* about what we are doing.

We never do things without some end in mind. If a branch falls off a tree and hits us, we are acted upon. We may be knocked down involuntarily but our body *reacts* to stabilize itself. So we have action, and reaction, then reaction to the reaction and so forth and so forth. The great acting teacher Sanford Meisner said acting is very simple: It is "Pinch", followed by "Ouch!" Action, reaction. Keep it simple.

Sydney Pollack: "Everything happens from wanting something, from having an objective, a goal. All your behavior, right now, everything you're doing, even your pauses in chewing, is because you want to listen to what I'm saying. You have a real reason to want it. Even your nodding and smiling. It's all happening automatically. You don't have to think about it. The minute these circumstances begin to be imaginary it's a little tougher to believe in it, but you have to make yourself."

Let's get technical briefly so that we can all be speaking the same language in terms of objectives, actions, and adjustments. Everyone uses them slightly differently but the principles are fairly uniform. Some of the other phrases in common use are: intentions, beats, arcs, journey, given circumstances. It really doesn't matter what words we use, they are all about understanding a character's behavior.

Conflict is the basic foundation of drama. Conflict between characters leads to the sequence of action-reaction, "pinch-ouch." **No conflict, no drama!** Another word for conflict is obstacle. In a good scene, every major objective needs an obstacle to remain interesting. No obstacle = boring!

If you can't break a dramatic scene down into actable objectives that can be described by strong actable verbs, the scene is no good. It has no place in the movie or the play. You may shoot it anyway but it will always stop the movie cold. It contributes little or nothing to the overall story.

This is why the first twenty minutes of a movie is always such a tricky challenge for the filmmaker. **A film has to set up many things at the beginning: the characters, the location, and the world of the movie. Conflict gets temporarily lost in the melee.** A film's preview audience often complains that the beginning of the movie is slow. What they are really saying is that they are not yet involved or invested in either the characters or the plot. Once they find out that the characters are supposed to travel across the battlefields of World War II to find one soldier, as in *Saving Private Ryan*, the audience knows where the movie is going and will follow it. But up to that point in the movie they could lose interest while all the characters and plot points are set up. director Steven Spielberg's opening to *Saving Private Ryan* brilliantly handles that challenge. It is so traumatizing and horrifying that we are instantly ripped out of our comfortable worlds and immersed in the violent universe of World War II.

The same goes for the characters. **A good movie gets you invested quickly in the characters. If we present clichéd characters that everyone's seen a thousand times, the audience goes right to sleep.** *Patton* and *The Godfather* both seize the audience in a vise-like grip in the first few seconds because of the strength of the characters. This kind of character grip is invariably stronger than big explosions, CGI monsters, and car chases. If we want our movies to work well, we must humanize the characters. Our favorite television shows succeed on a character level. *The Sopranos*, *The Shield*, and *The West Wing*, for example, don't present stories that many other movies and TV shows haven't already done *ad nauseam*. However, when we get involved with the characters and are anxious to see what happens to Tony Soprano or Vic Mackey or President Bartlett, the show will very likely be a big hit.

Dennis Haysbert: "Nobody goes to see a movie for the shots. They go because they like the people. There never was a movie where people said, 'Oh, honey, there are some great shots there, let's go see it.'"

Given Circumstances are all the things a character brings to a scene with them. It is all their physical state, their mental state, and their past history, as well as what is going on around them. Given Circumstances are part of the homework that the actor has to do for himself. He has to understand the entire life and psychology of the character he is playing. That understanding affects how he will perform the action called for in the script.

John Frankenheimer: "The intention of each character in every scene in the movie? There's a real intention and there's the intention that's being played. Now, what can I do to find a way for an actor to play a scene so it's not on the nose, not obvious? What is the actor/character coming into the scene with [Given Circumstances]? In other words, if I say to you, 'John, I want to have lunch with you,' and if I'm coming into this lunch with, 'John, I want to have lunch with you, because I want to borrow $100,000 because I desperately need it.' Or, 'John, it's great to see you, but I'd have to tell you that maybe it's the last time we're ever going to see each other because I'm moving to Europe and just wanted to have lunch with you to say good-bye,' my attitude during the lunch is completely different. My body language is completely different. The way I order from the menu is completely different. Everything I do is completely different, including the way I dress.... Everything depends on what you, as the actor, are coming into the scene with and who you are and what your circumstances are. There are hundreds of ways to walk into this restaurant, depending on what you come in with. Somebody from East L.A. is going to walk into this restaurant completely differently than someone who is from Montecito... So you have to be able to know those things. What the past is, what the psychological and economic breakdown of every character is. You have to know that. You have to be prepared to give that to the actor, which is why I love rehearsal. I have extensive notes as to what every character is — who and what they want and why they're in the play or the script."

Objective: Each character in each scene has an objective: what they want to do at that very moment. There is no such thing as no objective. When a character achieves or changes their objective they immediately have a new objective, even if the objective is to do nothing or take a break.

Adjustments, the magic As-If: How does one perform an action? A professional baseball pitcher throws a ball one way. A Little League reject throws it another way entirely. A new mother feeds her baby one way, a mother with six children another. A man angry with his boss acts differently from when he has just gotten a raise. Stanislavsky taught that the approach to an adjustment is to perform the objective "as-if." Throw the ball "as-if" you were an uncoordinated kid. Feed the baby "as-if" you were scared you would choke him. Walk into your boss's office "as-if" you want to punch him, but you can't let him know it.

Action: What the character does in that moment. The pitcher *throws* the ball. The mother *feeds* the baby. The man *enters* his boss' office.

Reaction: The result of the action. The batter swings. The baby eats. The boss looks up.

So the combination of these elements leads to how an Action is performed. Given Circumstances + Objective + Adjustment = Action → Reaction

Let's make up a mini-drama of a woman coming home at the end of the day. The character's given circumstances are she is a lawyer with a six-month-old baby. She has had a good but long day at work.

Her objective: "I want to get into my house"
Her adjustment: "I'm relaxing, coming home."
Her action: "Put the key in the lock."

Watch what can happen to the woman who wants to get into her house. **Reaction:** The key doesn't work. The **Given Circumstances** are the same. The **Objective** stays the same. The **Adjustment** changes to "irritated with the stupid locksmith who made the key." The **Action** changes to "trying the key more forcefully."

Reaction: The door still doesn't open. The **Objective** is still the same but the **Adjustment** becomes "Concerned. Somebody better be home!" The **Action** changes to "Ring the doorbell and knock on the door harder."

Reaction: No one answers. Objective: She wants to get in the house. Her Adjustment is growing anxiety: "Is there's a problem inside the house?" She takes a new Action, "go around to the back door quickly."

She walks quickly around the house. Action: A baby is heard screaming. Her Adjustment changes to one of "need to act now." Her Objective is still "get in the house." Her Action becomes "break through the back window."

The Shifting Sands of Objectives

When two or more characters are involved the timing of objectives, intentions, and adjustments gets more interesting. As I'm sitting here in Carmel writing, my Westies, Barkley and Fanny, are nagging me to take them to the beach. This is a complete little story, with beginning, middle, and end. This little story is a Beat.

Dogs' Objective: Go for a walk. Action 1: Scratch at Dad's ankle get his attention. Adjustment: Give me the message patiently.

My Objective: Keep writing. Adjustment: As-if I don't hear them. Action 1: Ignore them.

Dogs' Reaction 2: Impatience. Adjustment 2: Turn up the heat. Action 2: Scratch harder.

My Reaction 3: Put them off. Action 3: Mollify them, tell them to be patient.

Dogs' Reaction 4: Annoyed. Action 4: Snap their jaws and start barking.

My Reaction 5: Resignation. Action 5: Get up and put their leashes on.

Here we see all characters thinking and reacting at different times. Our adjustments change at different times, rarely simultaneously. **It's very important that each actor understand what their own individual objectives are. They don't necessarily need to know what the other character's objectives are. If** they are actually listening and reacting to the other actor in the moment they can respond the way they choose.

Dennis Haysbert: "I consider every character their own lead character for whatever movie they do. I'm not saying that you should try to steal the scene if you're just delivering a package to the boss. Take what that means to you, delivering the package to the boss, what will this boss do to you if you fall and trip and break what's in this package? What would the boss do to you if you were late with this package? The guy is the boss so that's the way your mind should be operating. Or if your character is an assassin, how do you react? Is your gun clean? Are you going to aim it or are you going to just point it in a general direction? How do you feel about the person you have to kill?"

Non-Actable Directions

Suppose for example that a woman has come across a very young intruder in her house at night. She overpowers him and gets him locked in a closet till the police arrive. Now *the intruder wants to escape.* That's his over-all objective for the scene. How does he do it? First, *he looks around to see if he can escape from the closet physically.* That doesn't work. He has to choose a new way. So he tells her his parents will kill him when they find out. The new adjustment is (escape by) *making her feel sorry for him.* When she won't listen to him because her objective is *protect herself from danger,* he has to choose another adjustment. So he tells her he is claustrophobic and having a panic attack. It's the same objective (*escape*) now he heightens the stakes *to really make her feel sorry for him.* For the moment suppose she is dumb enough to fall for this and starts to soften her attitude. Her adjustment is changing: "*I'm getting confused.*"

I'm getting confused is **not a good playable adjustment.** Why? It is very general and non-specific. It is playable, but only in the most general way, which is boring. It is just **indicating,** an emotion which looks fake. A better name for indicating is bad acting. A more specific adjustment would be to act as if she had people screaming different commands at her from all directions. *Keep him locked up? No, help him now? Don't do that! What do I do?* If she plays these specifics instead of a general "confusion" we will see it on camera.

Active Action Verbs

When we are trying to sleep and can't because our stomach is upset, we are not symbolizing man's torturous balance with nature. We are "trying to get comfortable." We get up and take an antacid. We go back to bed and try again. Then we feel ill and run to throw up. Rinse out our mouth and go back to bed. This is all action and reaction. And each moment of this sequence of actions and reactions has a clear intention, something that we want to accomplish. We cannot act this in a scene unless we understand what that intention is. You're running to the toilet so you don't mess up the floor.

Whatever the reason, we can always express it in a verb. A verb describes action and there is always a verb for our actions.

Jeanne Tripplehorn: "Give me a verb. I love to be given verbs. Give me a verb to play, give me an action, and I'm yours. I love a director who can speak in action, in terms of using verbs. To say, 'In this scene, you want to seduce him.' Really clarify, give me a purpose."

If we are going to help actors we must, must, must learn to explain a scene to them in verbs. If you try to explain a scene to an actor in grandiose terms you are only confusing matters. You must pick verbs to describe the action of the character. **And not just any verbs. Pick strong ones, active ones, ones that create a powerful picture.** Which is stronger, "He spoke to the group" or "He implored the group"? Imploring is much a much more active, interesting intention than just speaking. Stanley Kubrick observed that real is good, but interesting is better. We want our audiences to be involved in the story, not bored.

Steven Soderbergh: "Don't tell an actor what to think. Tell them what to do. Give them things to do. Less and less I'm telling them what to think, because I don't want them thinking. I want them doing. I want them behaving. Instead of saying, 'You know, he's a guy who in school was a nerd.' It's better to say to the actor, 'Don't walk like an athlete. You walk now like somebody who has an athletic background. That's not that guy. Find another way to carry yourself, because you look too physically comfortable.'"

Judith Weston's superb book *Directing Actors* lists pages of terrific usable verbs for acting. Strongly recommended, it shows what a single verb can do for an actor's approach to a scene.

Rehearsing Emotional Scenes

Directors disagree on many things: whether to have rehearsal or not, should we cast real people or real actors, etc., etc. One thing good directors all seem to agree upon is how to work with emotional scenes: **With emotions like grief, sadness, or loss, always treat the actor's ability to respond as a precious, finite resource.** It is like a well with only so much water. Many female actors can cry on demand. Males learn to hide their softer emotions. Even with much stronger emotions such as irritation, anger, or rage that seem easier to perform, it is wise to tread lightly around them when rehearsing.

Jodie Foster: "I only rehearse emotional scenes for blocking and for impact and for what we are trying to talk about. I never, ever, blow an emotion on a rehearsal."[1]

Always protect the actor's emotions from being drained before it is time to commit them to film. Work right up to the emotional points of the scene and then either mark through them or avoid them altogether until it is time to shoot. We want the freshest response possible from the actor. Over-rehearsing beforehand will dry up emotion in a New York minute.

Elia Kazan: "As far as rehearsing the emotion, you never do that with any actor in any scene. Shoot the rehearsal. You stay away from him, don't talk too much, and pray for a miracle."[2]

When we save emotion for the first take we are setting the stage for the actors to work at a performance level for the first time. Their responses to each other will be genuine and more likely to evoke fresh emotional responses.

Richard Dreyfuss: "The story of rehearsal is that the first time you read it, it's great. You have all the instincts and your blood is up. Then you begin to break things down while you work it. Then you put things back together, and then you can perform it. If you rehearse in a movie all you do is get to the breakdown stage."

This goes not only for the obvious delicate emotions like crying but very importantly also for the stronger ones like rage. Acting rage may seem easy. Easy until we watch some of the reality TV shows like *COPS* where we can see the real emotion — which is like a fireworks display with ups and downs. We can see a person in a bar fight have an initial burst of rage, calm down a bit, then re-explode more violently than initially. It is hard to take your eyes away from the screen. That's what we are trying to get on film and faking it just doesn't cut it. It comes across as nothing more than screaming and shouting.

I was shooting an episode of *The Senator* with Hal Holbrook dealing with welfare reform. There were half a dozen quick "documentary interviews" with "real people" giving their thoughts on welfare both pro and con. The actors were instructed not to learn the dialogue exactly but just to understand the essence of it and then improvise on camera. It was never rehearsed. The results were excitingly real. One young "black militant" grew so enraged as he spoke that he literally got to where he couldn't speak. He could only stand there and bluster. This was not a comic bluster; it was a boiling rage that gave a terrifying insight into the mind of oppressed peoples everywhere. Another actor

---

[1] *Actors Turned Directors*, page 60

[2] *Kazan*, page 100

working on a lathe in a factory
spoke so eloquently of the values
of working versus taking welfare
that the crew was moved to
applaud and the editors had a
tough job cutting it down to the
time available for it in the show.

**There is a favorite technique
among directors: Shoot the
close-ups first.** If you want to
get an emotion while it's fresh
you better be right in there
where you can capture it. How frustrating would it be to shoot a master, some
over shoulders and then finally get to the close-up and find out your actor has
dried up? Frank Pierson told how he shot Barbra Streisand's songs for *A Star
is Born*. The songs were pre-recorded by Streisand in the studio in the tradi-
tional manner. But on the set Frank would bring crowds of people to react to
Barbra singing. He would shoot her close-up before shooting anything else.
He knew that she would respond strongly to a live audience. Her "close-up
soundtrack" would always be so much more alive than the prerecorded one
done in a sterile studio environment that it would become the new "playback"
track. The first playback track was only a safety back-up in case she was not
in good voice that day.

Does this emotional coddling take too much time on a TV series? Not at all.
The set and the actors still have to be lit. And you get from the actor a sparkling
diamond, not a cubic zirconium. In a TV film about the Watergate scandal,
Martin Sheen played John Dean, one of the convicted aides to President
Nixon. Dean was a pure WASP who had never done anything really bad in
his whole life, and now here he is in the penitentiary. Sheen relates:

Martin Sheen: "I had to walk in, walk the length of the cell, get to the back wall,
turn around, and break up. That's what John Dean told me he did. He said, 'I
just wept uncontrollably. My whole life was over and I realized it.'

"The director, George Schaefer, said, 'It's very simple. You just walk in to the
back of the cell and turn around, and then I'll dolly into a head close-up. Give
us whatever you can give us.' I said, 'Okay, George.' And so I was standing there
looking at the set and I was fatigued and I'm thinking, 'What do I do? How am
I going to do this?'

"There's a set decorator writing graffiti on the walls with a big thick marking pen, marking up the whole set. Then it hit me. I went up to him and I said, 'Could I use your pen?' I went up to the back wall and I wrote 'Ramón Estevez.' I gave him back the pen; I went off and I just sat in my trailer and waited for the call. When they were ready I said to George Schaefer, 'George, I'm only going to be able to do this once, so please, if you have any focus problems can we make sure they're OK?' We walked through it once without any emotion. George was looking at me. 'Are you alright, Martin?' I said, 'Yeah, I'm fine. Let's go.' We started the scene. I walked to the end of the cell, the camera is moving in, I turned around and I totally lost it. Boom, it ended.

"When my father died I had to go to New York to be with my sister who was extremely ill. I had to miss my dad's funeral. I never mourned him. And that was in 1976. This movie we were shooting in '79. So for three years, I had not mourned my father. Why the 'Ramón Estevez?' Because my Dad was the only one that ever called me Ramón, and that was my real name. And so that's it. That's the depth and that's the place you go. That's part of the place you dwell, but you cannot go there by accident or just casually. You have to go there with confidence and you have to have a director who says, 'Fine.' And they know something happens here. You know when an actor is ready to shoot an emotional scene. You know when they're not."

If an actor goes into a scene saying "I have to cry" or "get mad" they are very likely to start to push to get to a preconceived ending. When they push, they indicate. When they indicate they look fake. And even my eight-year-old niece Lindsey can spot it.

This is because we put the emotional cart before the horse, as it were. In real life we don't go around adjusting our emotions in advance of situations. It is the other way around. What we *do* creates feelings

Penelope Ann Miller: "It's only actors who want to cry. Ordinary people don't want to cry. Whenever you think, I should cry here, and you try to force it, it never works. But if you see somebody fighting an emotion, and they can't help but tear up or choke up, that to me is so much more effective. Then an audience can relate to it, and then can feel for that person. I'm always saying to myself, fight it. Fight the emotion. And then of course it becomes like a waterworks you cry so hard."

Every few years in Southern California brush fires rage through the hills destroying thousands of homes. The TV stations have a feeding frenzy interviewing homeowners who have just seen their lives go up in smoke. I can't help being amazed at how people confront horrific situations. Often they seem strangely rational as they relate what happened to their home. As they talk, they go through a transformation. All their repressed and stunned emotions burst into the open before our eyes. Here we see a situation create their feelings. The house burning created fear, terror, panic. Now that the fire is out, there is numbness on the surface that fragments as soon as the person starts to talk about what happened.

Steven Soderbergh: "The reality show *COPS*, was a huge influence on *Full Frontal*. My whole idea was imagining scenes from a marriage shot like an episode of *COPS* where you're just chasing people or pursuing them, that it would be an interesting combination. I watch that show all of the time. I find it fascinating that the people never behave the way that you think you would; how people behave under these extraordinary pressurized situations."

There are always specific things that we do or have done to us that cause our emotions to arise or change. We can wake up angry or sad. A man wrongly imprisoned can have his anger re-ignited by almost anything that happens to him. A woman who has PMS can easily be irritated by small things. These emotions fall under the heading of Given Circumstances or Back-Story. These Given Circumstances are the state of our body, well-being, and emotions at the beginning of any scene. But they do not dictate how we will be at the end of the scene. **Even if we are irritable we seldom head into a situation knowing we are going to cry or get mad or whatever. It is what *happens* during the encounter that affects our state of mind.** There are certainly plenty of times where we go into a situation thinking we will react one way only to have our emotions take us in a totally different direction. Modern Nightmare: we get on the phone with a computer tech-support person. We're already irritated, thinking we'll get some idiot unhelping us. Then, mysteriously, the planets align and a knowledgeable and helpful person comes on the line. As we cheer our good fortune, our emotions change without any help from us. We hang up the phone and the day suddenly looks much brighter than an hour ago. The emotions were changed by actions.

Lesson learned: Don't let an actor focus on *emotions* going into a scene. Let them get the Given Circumstances clear for themselves and then focus on what happens moment to moment in the scene itself. If you don't get something terrific you can always spray fake tears in their eyes.

Sydney Pollack: "Barbra Streisand in *The Way We Were* had a strong emotional scene to do. She's been horribly embarrassed in a class and comes outside where she breaks down. Howard Koch Jr., the assistant director, comes up and tells Sydney Pollack, the director, that Barbra could not cry. 'She can't cry, and she's going to think about this.' I said, 'What are you talking about?' He said,

'Well, she's got this thing that she can't cry. She was very embarrassed. So she doesn't like you to look when the guy blows the camphor in your eyes and puts the tears in.' I said, 'I don't believe she can't cry. If she can sing the way she sings, she can cry.' So I said, 'You stay here by the camera. I'll wave for you to roll the camera.' I went behind the tree, and I sent the guy with the camphor away. She said, 'What are you doing? What are you doing?' I said, 'Shh.' I went over and put my arms around her. She started to cry. I just put my arms around her and held her for a minute, and she just started to sob like a little baby. I told them to roll the camera and pushed her out. It unlocked her for the rest of the movie. She cried in every scene. Now that's not anything to do with saying anything. That has to do with seeing that she is full of emotion and she's stopping it with tension. She just was tense. Something about being held touched her. It triggered it. It just let it loose. I don't think that I knew that. I think that I was trying to make her feel protected first."

This'll Shut 'Em Up

How to stop actors from bugging you with ideas: Just make fun of them. Sarcasm, that's the ticket, always good for shutting someone down. Oh, and by the way, it works best when you do it in front of the whole crew. Guaranteed you'll never hear from that actor again or from most of the crew either. **Sarcasm may be fun at the moment, but it breeds fear and deep resentment every time.** No one likes to be humiliated, in public or otherwise. These are traumatic events for people and will always stand between you and the actor. When Bob Fosse was making *All That Jazz* in 1978, he originally cast Richard Dreyfuss in the role that Roy Scheider played. Dreyfuss worked for a week in rehearsals and suddenly resigned from the movie. The grapevine had it that Fosse was a tyrant to his actors. Fosse, a brilliant choreographer before he was a brilliant director, was used to being extremely tough and sarcastic with his dancers. That attitude carried over to his actors. Richard Dreyfuss, no shrinking violet, chose to quit a fabulous role in a fabulous movie rather than work that way. Your actor may not quit and still work for you, but his attitude will have completely changed. He will think, "Fine, you rotten s.o.b., just tell me what to do," and you no longer have an actor but a meat puppet.

David Ward: "What you don't want to do is discourage your actors. You really don't want to break their spirit by being too controlling, too critical. When you are critical, you have to be critical in a positive way. They feel that you are still enthusiastic and you're really excited about where the scene is going and the performance is going, they will hook into that. If you're not, they will sense it, right away. They have real radar for that."

Napoleon's One-Minute Manager

Napoleon Bonaparte grew sick of his officers coming to him asking questions about every little thing. He decreed that no one could come to him with a problem unless they had at least three solutions to choose from and could articulate which one they would choose themselves and why. This works just as well for a director as it did for Napoleon. Use this with the actor, the wardrobe person or the sound mixer. Remember, you don't have to have every answer to be in control of a set. Forget your pride. Remember, you get to choose which of their three solutions to use. Or you can send them back to the drawing board, or come up with one yourself. **When people come up with solutions they are much more invested in the film you are making and think more carefully about what is right for the film.** Not to mention the amount of time you save this way. You won't find people coming to you willy-nilly without having thought about something.

People love to make fun of actors who fret about their work. Hitchcock's reply, "Your paycheck," to the actress who wanted to know her motivation may be a funny line, but she still had a legitimate question. **The problem is the actress should have worked this out on her own before coming to work.** If she's truly stuck, that's one thing, but if she's lazy and wants the director to do her work for her that's another and directors shouldn't reinforce it. As a rule, the answer to this question should always be, "What do you think your motivation is?" They have to discover the answer themselves for it to really mean anything to them. **If they have to solve it themselves they will own it. If you solve it for them they will just be following orders.**

Phantom Kibitzers

Behind the scenes of many movies is an unseen force acting on the film. Many actors who don't feel secure about their work and about the director have gotten in the habit of working privately with an acting coach. This is someone who discusses their character in depth with them and who guides them in what they think is the best direction. The good news/bad news is they are a security blanket for the actor, a source of creative ideas, but a potential pain in the patooty for the director. Strange performances appear out of nowhere that have nothing to do with the rest of the movie or the play.

Christopher Reeve was appearing in a stage production of *Death Takes A Holiday* at the Williamstown Theatre Festival. The director, Peter Hunt, was very pleased with the work that Reeve was doing in rehearsal. One day Reeve comes into rehearsal and has a weird approach to a scene they had done several times. Peter let it go for a while, not saying anything. When it continued, he took Reeve aside and asked him about this odd new approach.

Reeve said he had been talking to his acting coach who was in New Orleans, a thousand miles away. The coach had suggested that Reeve play it in this new way, which Hunt thought didn't work at all. Since Hunt and Reeve were old friends Hunt spoke frankly. "If you want to have a coach, that's fine," he said. "But he can't coach you long distance from New Orleans. He has to come here to Massachusetts to see how everyone else is playing. Your work has to fit in with theirs."

After some tense moments things settled down. Chris Reeve's coach stepped back, Peter helped Chris blend in with the cast and he gave a wonderful, well-reviewed performance.

There is no way to stop an actor from consulting with mothers, coaches, and gurus if they want to. The trick is keeping them on the same page with the rest of the cast so you don't make two different movies.

Understandably, an actor might want to hide the fact they have an outside kibitzer. If you suspect that's what's happening and why you're getting weird work, don't ignore it. Politely flush it out into the open where you and the coach can work together, not at cross purposes.

Most coaches can be very helpful, though there are reliable reports of charlatans who work their mojo by physically abusing their clients. Hopefully coaches like this are an anomaly. God forbid you should have an actor doing a hell of a scene but wearing a black eye that appeared mysteriously.

Summary

1. No conflict = no drama. No drama = boring.

2. Intellectualizing the meaning of a scene is totally different from finding a way to play the scene. Intellectualizing is unplayable for the actor. Active verbs are playable.

3. Emotion comes out of the given circumstances combined with the action being played. It should never be imposed on the scene. It is what *happens* during the encounter that affects our state of mind.

4. Given Circumstances **+** Objective **+** Obstacle **+** Adjustment **=** Action & Reaction

5. Whatever the scene, we can always express it in a verb. A verb describes action and there is always a verb for our actions.

6. Acting is "Pinch" followed by "Ouch." Action followed by reaction.

7. Emotional scenes are like sunrises: fragile, ephemeral, and gone in an instant. Don't over-rehearse them. Do shoot close-ups first to capture them when they happen.

8. Sarcasm is deadly. An actor will shy away from you forever if you use it around him.

9. Make your actors and your crew have at least two solutions in mind before they come to you. If they are part of the problem, they can certainly be part of the solution.

10. Acting coaches can be helpful, but the director must work with them to make sure they are both flying to the same airport.

On the Day

Don't count on sleeping the night before the first day of shooting. Steven Spielberg said he feels anxious *every* shooting day, not just the first day. I myself never go to shoot without anxiety about that day's work. Director Arthur Penn was so nervous on the first day of shooting his first film, *The Left-Handed Gun*, that he let the star, Paul Newman (who was playing Billy the Kid), walk half a mile out of town until the assistant director suggested politely that Penn call "cut."

What we shoot today will be on film forever. In our minds this will be the only chance we have to shoot these scenes. There are re-shoots if you have the money, but no director approaches a scene thinking it can be re-shot if it doesn't come out right. (Yeah, yeah, yeah, I know, Woody Allen does it all the time.) Forget the budget and the schedule; for many directors it's a matter of pride. Get it right and get it good… not the first time, but the only time. This is stressful because each shot is a custom job. The director is not a worker on an assembly line who fits the same nut to the same bolt all day long. For him, every shot will be slightly different from the last one.

The passionate director will have it no other way. The audience will absolutely have it no other way. We go to the movies for many reasons. *None* of them is to see the same old thing we saw last week. I don't count your ten-year-old nephew Herman who has seen *Star Trek* 604 times. We want different stories, characters, plots and acting. *Seinfeld*, *Friends*, and *I Love*

Lucy may be very popular but wear out their welcome over time. We're not curing cancer; we just have to tell an entertaining, involving story.

What's the best way to set the stage for a successful shoot? Carb-loading at the catering truck upon arrival on set is the wrong way to spend your time. Make the rounds and talk to the cast who work that day. **Every one of them, stars and day players alike.**

Brad Silberling: "I always make a point of sticking my head in the makeup trailer in the morning and say hello and try to start a conversation about the day's work, and if there was testing to be done, it would start there."

You're not there to have deep discussions about the movie; you're there to warm up your team and to reassure them. Like the surgeon who drops in to see you before taking out your tonsils. The actors feel like they're about to choke anyway. Your being there says you will be there for them all day. If they have a big scene that day, check for a glazed panic in their eyes. The thousand-yard stare. Loosen them up now or they'll carry this monkey all day.

The day players need settling more than anyone. Settle them down early in the day. It's not that they don't know what they're doing; it's that they're working with all new people, they're being judged, they haven't worked in two months, they have a cold sore, they're overweight, and all of the above. You have to be their support, their guide, and their friend who will let nothing bad happen. It's not unusual to have to spend more time with a day player and shoot more takes than the star.

Coddling? It's anything but. What you've done in your dawn visit is start to create that comfortable environment that actors so desperately want.

Robert Forster: "So what do I hope a director gives me? A little bit of space. If the director has some confidence in me, okay, but I figure it's my job, in that first couple of days, to give the director, as close to the way it was written as can be before I ask for anything at all, just so the guy feels confident, whether I've worked with him before or whether he knows me or not. You get hired by people who don't really know you. It's my hope that I can deliver what the director needs of me in such a way that after a day or so he says to himself, 'This guy's okay. I don't have to worry about him anymore.'"

In a television series, the regular actors know their characters inside and out and feel very comfortable. They rule the roost, the director is just another "john." It's the guest cast that has to learn to feel comfortable. They are the ones that can blindside you with odd requests. If this is your first time on the show, the regulars are just waiting to see how much of an idiot you are before they trust you.

Michael Chiklis: "I find myself the most frustrated with guest directors on *The Shield*. When they don't understand what the show is about, they will come up with a direction or even a camera move that just doesn't serve the piece at all and doesn't show any kind of understanding of the characters. Five minutes on the set and you can tell if a director has the number one criteria that they need: confidence. One director will go into the set and rehearse with the actors. Another director will walk in and start setting up shots with the crew immediately. The cast hasn't even walked in yet. Already you know that the second guy is more of a technical director. He already has shots set up in his mind based on the set and what's on the page, and he's going to mold the cast to what he has in his mind."

What's the First Shot?

When the actors come on set, send the crew out for more caffeine and crois-sants. When it's quiet, warm the cast up. Just read through the scene and *don't let them act.*

Judge Reinhold: "The director has to make you feel like what you're doing is the most important thing in the world. The way he does that is to get everybody to shut up, out of respect for the filmmaking endeavor. You have to feel that it's really, really important. You need the director to create a safe haven where you can try anything. The actor should never have to do that for himself."

If you did your work back in rehearsal and talked through the where, when, why, and how of the scene there should be little disagreement. A good rehearsal period will have gotten everyone to the point where they focus on playing the objectives and emotions, not what the emotions and objectives are in the first place. **You don't want to be standing on the set at 7:00 in the morning deciding what the scene's about.** Alfred Hitchcock used to compare it to a conductor getting up in front of the orchestra and saying, "Ummm, what if we play an A flat?"

Steven Soderbergh: "It's rare that I've had an actor show up on a day of a scene with a big problem. Because usually I've given them opportunities beforehand to say whatever they want to say and raise whatever issue they want to raise. I don't recall anybody ever showing up on the day and saying, 'You know, I've thought about it and this just doesn't make sense,' or 'This scene is bullshit,' or 'I would never do that.' Because hopefully we would have discussed that before."

However, if you couldn't do the rehearsal work in advance for whatever reason, fasten your seat belt. Anything can happen. In a (non-existent) perfect world, actors wait obediently to be staged. In the (very existent) real world they have this nasty habit of being impertinent and asking tough questions. Questions you can't answer with a yes or no. Questions that shake the foundation of the story you are telling, not to mention your bowels.

Brad Silberling: "I'm sure that every director has his or her version of it. Your blood just turns cold, and you're like, 'Oh my God, here we go.' You literally feel your whole body stop. You can feel very swimmy in your head and the blood rushes, because you're trying to hang in there. 'Oh God, how are we going to pull out of this one?' It's like going into a road skid at 90 miles per hour. And the good news is, I still have that feeling. I'll have it sometimes not even about a moment with an actor, but suddenly something you were counting on in your day just went sour, and you have that feeling. At least you come to recognize it and not be as afraid of it. Okay, I've lived through this feeling before."

This is where you wish you'd worked this out before. On a long feature schedule, you only age a few weeks. On a TV schedule you look twenty years older. On some Martin Scorsese movies with Robert De Niro, the two of them have been known to retire to the trailer and not be seen again for two or three hours. Based on their track records they are entitled to have these extended discussions. The rest of us will get fired.

Brad Silberling: "I got Darren McGavin of *Night Stalker* fame to play this character of an old rich guy. He believed he was being cuckolded by his young wife and wanted to sue for divorce. We got in to rehearse the first morning, and he asked me a question about a choice that he might make. I gave him what I thought was a good answer. And he said, 'That is absolutely wrong. Have you ever experienced loss in your life?' And I said, 'As a matter of fact, I have.' And he said, 'Well, what was that?'

"I said, 'Unfortunately two years ago I lost a loved one. My wife-to-be was killed.' And he said, 'Oh, this is not the same thing. That's over in a moment. She's gone and she's done. This is a divorce that we're talking about.' The crew was like, oh, my God. Darren said, 'Clearly you have no idea about this character and clearly you weren't the one who hired me, so I don't know what I'm doing here.' It was classic. I said, 'Actually, Darren, I am the reason you're here, and to be completely honest, the producers didn't want you. But I did. I'm excited you're here, so let's figure it out.' It was wild. It was truly the old lion needing to just pounce. And it wasn't even that he was offering up a choice that got plowed over by a director. It was just this pure test."

Frank Langella: "Actors don't want to be made to feel problematic, however petty their concerns may seem at a given moment. Every department on a film set considers their contribution important — and every department is. Actors don't want to be made to feel difficult for caring about the things that are important to them in order to give a good performance. One of the best things a director can do is to instill in his crew that an actor must be treated with respect and dignity. If his concerns are legitimate they must be honored. Don't dismiss them as an actor's ego."

John Frankenheimer took over the directing of the remake of *The Island of Dr. Moreau* in 1995. Marlon Brando and Val Kilmer were the stars. On the first day of shooting, two hundred Filipino extras had been called at 4:30 in the morning to put on grotesque animal makeup. By 8 a.m. the jungle was a 100-degree sauna. The crew was preparing to shoot the entrance of Brando's character, Dr. Moreau. John Frankenheimer goes to Brando's trailer to say good morning. Brando's first question is "What are we shooting today?" Frankenheimer thinks to himself that reading the call sheet must be harder than he thought. "It's your character's entrance, Marlon." Brando replies. "Read it to me," says Brando. Frankenheimer diplomatically demurs. "Marlon, I'm not going to presume to read a scene to Marlon Brando." This little two-step goes on for a few moments. Brando finally picks up the pages. He scans them briefly and then declares, "This is crap." He must not have had time to read the script before taking this $10 million job. Frankenheimer says "Marlon, Shakespeare it's not, but we can work on it while they get the shot ready." "I don't think so," said Brando. "Crap is crap."

Frankenheimer takes Brando over to the window and shows him two hundred extras melting in the sun. "Marlon, these people have been here since 4:30 this morning and pretty soon all the makeup will be ruined." "So... what's your point?" Brando said. "Let me get this straight," says Frankenheimer, "We're making a picture called *The Island of Dr. Moreau*. And the man playing Dr. Moreau doesn't want to enter his own movie?" Brando did not respond. The extras were sent home. No work was done that day; $100,000 down the drain. Only after lots of saber rattling and ego stroking was the scene shot — as written. If John Frankenheimer — who could channel directors John Ford, Henry Hathaway, and Otto Preminger from the grave when he was shooting — can be stymied, what hope is there for a director who is not so tough?

Six-Hundred-Pound Gorillas

When Clint Eastwood directed Kevin Costner in *A Perfect World*, they were both among the ten most powerful movie stars in the world. The Hollywood grapevine had it that Costner, who played an escaped convict in prison garb, had to run through a farmer's back yard and steal some jeans off a clothes-line. Take 1. Eastwood calls "Action," Costner runs through, grabs the clothes. Eastwood calls "Cut, print, moving on. Next location!"

Costner is used to driving his own wagon train and doing lots of takes. "Wait," he says to Eastwood. "I want to do it again." Eastwood says, "Nah, it's fine, no need." Costner insists they go again and again. Eastwood demurred. This tense little pas de deux went on for a few minutes until finally Eastwood says, "Kevin, it's only laundry."

He turned to his crew and announced, "Wrong set, boys!" And he heads off down the hill to the next location. Costner is so mad that not only won't he come out of his trailer just to line up the next shot; he won't come out when Eastwood is ready to shoot.

Dirty Harry doesn't blink. He tells the assistant director that that his day has just been made and he will shoot the scene with Costner's double. He shoots it and moves on. Now Eliot Ness is really mad. He explodes from the trailer. "What the hell is going on?" he says, "You can't do this to me."

The Man with No Name gives him the patented *Fistful of Dollars* squint and growls, "You know, Kevin, I may be the only guy on the planet who *can* do that to you." This story is only from the grapevine, but things like it happen every day.

In *Nick of Time*, Johnny Depp, playing a mild-mannered father, shoots the bad guy, Christopher Walken, at the climax of the movie. At this time Congress was leaning on all the studios to back off on violence in movies. Studio Chairperson Sherry Lansing has assigned a new Paramount exec to make his bones on this movie and be sure the filmmakers behave. By phone, he instructs me that Depp is only to fire one shot when he shoots Walken. OK, fine. The exec says he has to take a call from somebody more important, and hangs up.

However, as we line up the scene, Johnny Depp says he would like to fire at Walken more than once. In fact, he wants to empty his pistol into Walken's face. When I tell him about Paramount's order, he gets that funny look on his face and starts digging his heels into the sidewalk. Sometimes an actor will relent rather than confront. Not Johnny. I was caught in the middle. I was damned if I let him and would sleep with the fishes if I didn't.

So our young exec has to get off his call from O.J. Simpson and hear what Depp wants to do. "Absolutely not!" he replies. "No way is he allowed to fire more than one shot. I'm not taking Jack Valenti's (head of the Motion Picture Association that deals with Congress) phone calls." I then suggested with malice aforethought, "Well, maybe you'd like to come down to the set and explain to Johnny Depp that he's in contempt of Congress." "No way," he replied. "That's your job. I've got to go, Winona Ryder is calling."

Just to make things fun, all this time it was getting dark. Johnny Depp had to leave for Paris the next day to start another movie. Meanwhile the production manager is starting to hyperventilate and the AD is reaching for the Valium. What's a director to do?

They say panic is the mother of desperate ideas. Pause, pause, bing! Right on cue I have a Desperate Idea: what if we go ahead and let Depp empty his gun into Walken, and we hide that take from the studio. So I go back to Depp and tell him something like "Great idea, Johnny babe, fire away!" Great sighs of relief all around. We do the takes, including one where the gun mysteriously only had one blank bullet loaded in it. (Gee whiz! Those dumb prop men!) That's the take we sent to Paramount. The takes where Depp empties the gun into Walken are quickly hidden under the cinematographer's stack of porn magazines.

Cut to a few weeks later: Sherry Lansing and our young exec — on his cellphone to Paul Reubens — are sitting behind me in the big Paramount Theatre, screening my director's cut. I can't concentrate on the movie, all my attention is focused on Sherry Lansing's reactions. By an hour and a half into the movie, she hasn't made any notes on her clipboard. A sign, a very excellent sign. We arrive at the part of the movie where Depp shoots Walken. He raises the gun and fires. One time and only one time. Young exec hangs up from Danny Bonaduce and smiles smugly. But suddenly the light on

Lansing's clipboard flashes on and she starts scribbling like crazy. Omigod, what is she writing! Panic! Stomach churn!

The lights come up at the end and we wait for the verdict. But Ms. Lansing has jumped up and left the theatre. We sit in suspense. After a few minutes she returns (bathroom break?). Standing statuesquely in the aisle she pronounces the movie... Terrific. She loves the performances, the story, the direction, and so on. Trumpets blare. Fireworks go off. The crowd roars! But, what about all that scribbling? "Sherry, what were you writing so furiously at the end?" I asked. She said, "Honey, you can't have Johnny shoot Chris Walken just one time. It's totally unsatisfying. We hate Walken's character now. We have to blow him away!"

Out of the corner of my eye I see Mr. Young Exec sliding lower and lower in his seat. His smug smile was morphing into a sage nod of agreement with Madame Chairperson.

I put on my best-troubled face. "Oh, gee. I thought we weren't supposed to let him fire more than once." I scratched my head and gave a dramatic pause for effect. "Well, it'll be tough but maybe Frank Morriss, our editor, can cobble something together and show it to you next week." Sherry Lansing nodded, thanked us all and went on with her day. Frank Morriss and I went back to the cutting room, where he spent all of two minutes cutting in our secret take. Then we went out for a three-martini lunch. Watch the DVD and see Depp blast Walken to pieces.

Mark Rydell: "On the first day of shooting on *The Rose*, which was unusually tense because of the mixture of New York and L.A., I started to walk up to Bette Midler to talk to her. Her manager, Aaron Russo, who is a big linebacker sort, gets in my way and says something like, 'What are you doing?' I told him I'm going to talk to Bette. He said that I had to talk to him first and then he would talk to her. I said, 'I beg your pardon?' Aaron was a producer on the movie because of Bette. He repeated that I wasn't to talk to Bette, that he was to talk to her.

"A security cop was nearby. I called him over and I called Bette over and said to her, 'Look, you have ten seconds to change your allegiance from your manager to me, because all he can do is help you get a better trailer. I can help you to be good in this picture. What do you want to do?'

"Bette stood there for a second, and then she looked me in the eye and nodded yes. I said to the cop, take him out. I don't want to see his face again. Aaron was escorted off the set and Bette and I were standing there alone. At that moment she became 'the Rose.' It was a very important moment to the whole picture."

Forget Them, What About Me?

So meanwhile back at your set where the actor is giving you angina, you've fought off the urge to throw up. You proceed calmly as though nothing unusual is happening. Never scream. Never yell. If you scream, about the schedule, about "who's the director here," or try to bully the actor in any way, you've given them even more control. He's got you by the shorts. Richard Donner relates an explosive incident with Gregory Peck on *The Omen.*

Richard Donner: "There's a scene where Gregory Peck finds out his wife is dead. He and I had discussed it many times. The prop man came to me one morning and said, 'You know, Mr. Peck has asked for all break-aways in the set.' I said, 'What do you mean?' He said, 'He wants mirrors and the glassware all duplicated in break-aways.' So I went to Greg and he said, 'I want the rage to come out in me when I hear this.' I said, 'You know, I see it differently. I'd like to see you after that rage. I'd like to find you in bed. You're not at peace with yourself and now the reality of it is coming to you. When David Warner comes in the door, you just tell him without even looking at him what happened — that she's dead and what you have to do.'

"Greg said, 'No, no way, that's wrong.' We got in this terrible argument. I said, 'Well look, if you want me to shoot it your way, I'll shoot it your way, but we're also going to shoot it my way,' and he said, 'No, we're not going to do it two ways. It's one way — it's my way.' So I said, 'No, it's going to be my way, Greg. I love you, but I'm the director and this is what I want. Two ways I'll give you, but if it's only one way, it's my way.' And he stormed out.

"I got a call from him later that night and he said, 'Okay, you're the director. It's totally wrong, but I'll do it.' So I took the crew into the bedroom set that night and I put a stand-in on the bed. The camera was on a high crane and set to move in slowly on Peck during his speech until it's on a big profile of him lying on the bed. The focus and speed of the move was critical to making the scene work. I said to the crew, 'Listen, guys. I want you to practice this. If you have to stay on overtime tonight, I don't care. Practice this and practice this and practice this until it's perfect. I don't want to have to go through it again.'

"The next morning Peck comes onto the set. He said, 'What do you want?' I said, 'Here's what I'd like.' In front of everybody he said, 'You are so wrong.' Then he lay down on the bed. We rolled and the camera slowly moved in. It was a long speech and by the time it was over, I was crying.

"I looked at everybody and they went — 'Perfect' — and I said, 'Cut.' I said, 'Thank you, Greg.' He said, 'Okay, well let's do it one more time.' I said, 'No, it's perfect.' He said, 'I'd like to do another.' I said, 'No, you can't do it better.'

"The next day he came into dailies and he sat down with his wife Veronique and we ran the take. And at the end he stood up and he said, 'I told you, Mr. Donner, that you were wrong. Well, I was wrong. I couldn't have done it better, and I appreciate it so much.' Later he apologized to me in front of the whole crew."

In *Whose Life Is It Anyway?*, John Cassavetes stopped us cold one day. He said the scene we were doing didn't work, it was terrible, we couldn't do it, etc., etc. As I dug deeper, one particular word popped up as the culprit. He had a line to Christine Lahti: "I have to teach a bunch of retards on the Hospital Board of Directors about inflation." John worked with developmentally disabled children 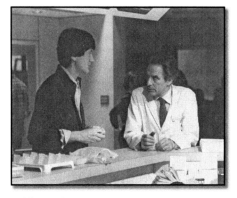 and felt very sensitive about using the word "retard."

Fortunately, the cameraman, Mario Tosi, had a big lighting job. I had learned awhile ago to make actors come up with their own new dialogue if they didn't like what they were given. So Cassavetes paced around to think. And we waited and we waited. (Any suggestions from me were deemed terrible and the writer wasn't available to help.) After forty-five minutes he finally comes up with a new phrase he likes to characterize the Board of Directors... (drum roll)... "Tight-ass tick-tocks." Say what? I had no idea what this meant, but after spending an hour on it, I would have let him say the Pledge of Allegiance.

We start to shoot and when Cassavetes got to his new line, "Tight-ass tick-tocks" he... went up, blanked out, couldn't remember his own line. We cut. We shot again, and he went up again... and again and again... It took *twenty-three takes* before we got a usable print.

Ask your pain-in-the-ass *du jour* to explain his ideas to you. Hear him out. Make sure you are really hearing him. Repeat back to him his concerns to let him know that you are taking his worries seriously. Try to determine if he is worried about the scene itself or some other hidden issue as we saw with Darren McGavin. You may think the actor is throwing a fit about the whole scene but when you pull it apart you may find he's talking about something minor. Minor to you maybe, but so major to this actor that he's made a psychodrama out of it. Just talking the scene through can calm his fears. Very often what he says is the problem is not the problem at all. It's just the problem he'll admit to. The real problem will out soon enough. Find out what his *real* concern is so you can deal with that.

Brad Silberling: "When making *City of Angels* we have several scenes where Nick Cage is sitting on a high girder of a building under construction, feet dangling into space. The day before we shoot Nick casually says, 'I don't know if I mentioned, but I'm basically terrified of heights.' And I think he's kidding, and he says, 'No. I'm like oh-my-God scared.' And I said, 'I've got to get you up to the roof of this building to show you what we've built. If you can't do it I'm going to have to go back to the studio and ask for two or three million more dollars to do it in the computer.'

"I take him up on the roof of a building on Wilshire they say was built by Chinese mafia. I get him up one of the largest ladders made. We get it close to the edge so he can see all of L.A. Nick's like white. I say, 'What do you think?' And he said, 'Well, I'm really scared. I may not be able to speak.' I said, 'Well, It's okay, they love you at the studio, and we'll find a different way to do it.' He stopped me and said, 'No, I can't tell them that I can't get up twenty feet. I'm supposed to do Superman for them next.'

"I said, 'Okay, in exchange for this, you can tell me to do anything you want, short of running down Sunset Boulevard naked.' He thought for a moment and came up with the scariest thing he could think of. He said, 'I want you sitting up on the girder for fifteen minutes.' I said, 'Cool.' I took the producer up with me, who was on his cell phone the whole time. Nick and the crew loved it. I gave him the bullhorn and he's yelling up at me. But he was very sweet and he appreciated that. And good to his word when we shot he got right up there.'"

It's About Respect

Among other things, *Saturday Night Fever* started the careers of many young actors brand new to the Screen Actors Guild. John Travolta was not a major star at the time. Adults only knew him as the big goofy teenager on TV's *Welcome Back Kotter.* However, when I watched Travolta dance, it was a no-brainer to see that he was a major undiscovered star. Barry Diller and Michael Eisner, then the Chairman and President respectively of Paramount Studios, thought my enthusiastic predictions of Travolta's future career were just hyperbole. Only after the movie was released and they saw the incredible box office figures pouring in week after week did the reality of his stardom sink in.

He was not the only discovery of the movie. Fran Drescher became the star of TV's *The Nanny*; Donna Pescow became the star of the sitcom *Angie.* The cast was filled with talented, high-spirited young actors, excited to be in a movie. When they realized they could ad-lib anything that sprang to mind, including profanity, scatology, racism, and sexism, they were like winos set loose in a liquor store. As the director I had Frankensteined this bunch of crazies. It was inevitable I would have to rein them in.

"Where's my close-up?" said Paul Pape, who played Double J. He stopped the rehearsal cold. I was in the middle of staging a scene that had the camera placed behind Paul over his shoulder. He didn't understand that I would have to get his close-up eventually. But he needed to be talked to. I took him *off to one side* to Roto-Rooter his nether regions… tactfully. **Always have actor conversations about anything to do with the actor personally, in private.** There is nothing to be gained and a lot to be lost by having public confrontations. Sometimes even the most seemingly harmless comments can humiliate an actor. Humiliation always breeds resentment and bad blood that can almost never be healed. If I've lost my temper in front of the crew, or cast I have always regretted it. It has either cost me a job, a friendship or loss of respect from cast and crew.

So I take Paul to one side and I say, "You're lucky I'm a low-key person. Lots of directors would jam your jewels in the microwave. No director appreciates being told how to do their job. All you have to do is ask nicely,

'Is there going to be a close-up?' Even a cucumber knows the scene won't work without a close-up of you." Paul apologized. We went back to work. I thought that was the end of it.

Where's My Close-Up: The Sequel. Six weeks later, I staged a scene in a hospital room where the gang was visiting Gus, played by Bruce Ornstein. In the story he had been beaten up by a rival gang. We are lining up the shot by his bedside and I hear that dreaded phrase again: "Hey, where's my close-up?" from… guess who? Sarcasm, that dreaded sarcasm, seized my brain and I blurted: "Gee, Paul, you're right, I guess we don't need you in the scene after all. You can go home. I'll just give your lines to the other guys."

The whole set stopped cold to see what would happen. Paul, who was hot-tempered even when calm, looked like he was ready to hurt someone… me. He wrestled with this for a few seconds and then decided being in the scene was cooler than hitting me. "Sorry," he said. I started the rehearsal again and shot it the way I always intended… with a close-up of him.

A more mature me would have taken Paul aside and worked this out with him privately. The tunnel vision tension of a tight shooting schedule can blind one to bulldoze over anything that gets in the way. **That still doesn't excuse my sarcasm, which was humiliating to him.** All I had to do was take him aside and say something like, "We spoke about this before. Obviously, the scene won't work without a close-up of you. When you learn how scenes are shot you'll know not to ask dumb questions in front of the crew. You're a good actor and you're doing a very good job in this movie. If you want to become a professional, come to me privately and ask those questions."

There is a great temptation to be sarcastic and make fun of the actor. Do not do this. **Banish sarcasm no matter what.** No matter how clever you think you are, avoid it like the IRS. **The consequences are not worth the pleasure of the moment.** The minute the actor thinks he is being made fun of he'll hate you for it.

Where's My Close-Up: The Postscript. Nearly twenty-five years later Paul and I talked about this incident. He has a successful career as both actor and voice-over performer. Remembering the incident as clearly as I did, he was hurt and puzzled at the time by my sarcasm. Filled with the passion of a hot-blooded young actor he had to restrain himself. He kindly reminded me we were in the last two days of shooting the film and that I was visibly exhausted. He also knew where he had overstepped his bounds. Of course my exhaustion is no excuse for anything, even though that's a time when one's self-control and good sense are at their weakest.

David Ward: "I learned watching Robert Redford direct on *The Milagro Beanfield War* you never want to say something to an actor that might embarrass them in some way in front of the other actors or the crew. Bob is very much 'an actor's director' in the sense that he is extremely patient and understanding. I've never seen him raise his voice to an actor. He is always very concerned to keep the actors in a certain comfort zone where they feel appreciated and understood. One of the first things you have to realize, as a director, is the extent to which actors feel vulnerable and at risk. They want to believe that you know what's good... for them, specifically. And if they don't get that feeling, they won't listen to you. Bob was difficult to observe in his directing because, if he had something to say to the actor, he would always take the actor off by himself. He would never talk to an actor in front of the crew."

It's very important to make personal contact with every actor after every take. This may only mean that the director touches their arm reassuringly; it may mean praise or a quick suggestion; it may mean that the director takes the actor aside and gives them a new task for the next take. Surprisingly, it doesn't take very much time even on episodic shows with brutal schedules of ten pages a day. It keeps the actor's morale up and assures them that you're watching.

Summary

1. Visit with every member of the cast in the morning. Talk briefly about the day's work. The day players are the most nervous and need your support.

2. Get the first rehearsal in private on the set. Send the crew out for carbs and coffee.

3. Work problems out in advance, if possible.

4. When problems arise — and they will — never get into a shouting match with the actor. You will lose, if not today, then tomorrow. Stay calm and reason your way through the problem.

5. Avoid sarcasm. It will cost you dearly in the end, pun intended.

6. Talk to every actor after every take, even if it is only to give them a reassuring nod or pat on the shoulder.

Actors Are Not Apples

Nobody likes to talk about it, but the truth is that many, too many, actors **come to the set having sort-of learned their lines but little else.** They haven't thought out what their character is trying to do or any character business that could give the scene more life. And it's not necessarily their fault. Writers work for months on the script, directors have intense preparation time, and actors get very little, if any. Many are cast only a couple of days before the shoot. I have had lots of actors come on set at 7 a.m. having received the script at 10 p.m. the night before. We expect them to be like Apple computers: plug-and-play, performing perfectly right out of the box. They need time to catch up to the writer and the director.

Any good teacher knows that letting the student discover things on their own and at their own pace is the best way to learn. **Let the actors have the freedom to discover the staging of a scene with very little input from you.** Not only is it less work for you, the actors will make the blocking their own. When the actors discover it themselves they grasp the dramatic logic of the scene. Almost invariably, the staging will not only look like what you planned, it probably will have unexpected and exciting moments that you did not think of.

Jenna Elfman: "When we rehearsed *EdTV*, we rehearsed on an empty sound stage that had the dimensions of the set taped down on the floor. Ron Howard taped out the entire thing and told us where the doors were. We really moved through this maze of tape as if it were a set, so I felt 'I know where I'm going... can we go here and over there?' We worked that out, and he very much put the acting first and then worked the cameras around what the cast was doing. However, I find so many times on other films, it's cameras first and acting second."

The very safest way to begin is to gather the cast in a small group and just stand there on the set and say the words to each other. They need to warm up their brains, hear what the other actors have to say and gently ease into the creative process. In the previous chapter, when we discussed table readings, we emphasized having the cast just talk and listen to each other at first. Even if you've had the luxury of a previous rehearsal it's still a good idea to start every single scene rehearsal this way.

Having warmed up the dialogue, you want to get the scene on its feet. Give them only vague instructions to get them started: "Christine, what if you come in from that door?" and "Bill, how about if you sit at your desk paying bills? Move wherever you feel like going on the set. Let's just play around and see what the scene wants to do. If you don't like what you are doing, try something else." Now step back and let them have at it by themselves. The first time will be a mess! Like a bunch of cats turned loose in a new place, the actors will walk all over the place, around the set, out to the parking lot. Check out the crew as they start to panic over how to light this mess.

Shooting a remake of the French classic *Diabolique*, I was fortunate to work with Sam Waterston, Tuesday Weld, and Joan Hackett. We were staging a scene in Joan Hackett's bedroom set. Tuesday Weld comes in the door to comfort a paranoid Joan Hackett who thinks that everyone is out to get her. She sees Tuesday Weld as an enemy and tries to protect herself. I knew how the scene should stage but I had no intention of sharing it with the actors unless absolutely needed.

"Where do you want us to go?" said Joan Hackett to me. "Wherever you want," I told her. The next thing I know, Joan Hackett is chasing Tuesday Weld around the room wielding a poker. This was *not* in the script. It was very dramatic. It was also way over the top.

Aaron Rosenberg, the producer, turns white. He comes quickly over to me. "What's this?" he wants to know. "What are you doing?" "Just watch," I said. When the women breathlessly finished, I said nothing. Except "Try it again." This time the two of them didn't move around as much though Joan was still waving that poker around dangerously. Again I said nothing and had them do it a third time. By the fourth time through, Joan had abandoned the poker without a word from me and the two actresses had developed an electric version of the scene that looked a lot like the staging hidden in my pocket — with one big difference. They came up with it, so they owned it. Now they would fight to the death to protect their staging because they understood why it worked.

If you think you are saving time just giving actors the blocking yourself, right away you'll find that it takes just as long, if not longer. They may even resent being restricted and "put in jail" as Anthony Quinn once phrased it angrily to a hapless TV director noted for his overly precise staging. Quinn was a highly instinctive actor who wanted to discover the scene himself in a way that worked for his character. And he was not wrong. Why would we want to bring greatly talented actors to our set and then not allow them to contribute to what we are doing?

Oliver Stone: "But sometimes in shooting *Alexander* I found that she [Angelina Jolie] would pre-choreograph it in her head before she ever did it. You know, she would see the scene a certain way, because we didn't have all of the sets to rehearse on. So, what do you do? You're not going to fight and say, 'That's not the way it was set up or the way I want to light it.' But you say, 'Okay, show me,' and then she shows you her way. Fine, I see it. 'Okay, now how about this? This is an alternative way.' And then you let her work her way into exploring alternatives. You lead everybody as much as you can, if you can, if you're ahead of them. Sometimes the actor is ahead of you and knows better what he can do or say. 'I don't need that line. I can show it.'"

Why does this technique work? First of all, every scene has a dramatic logic that will not be ignored. **The writer wrote the scene for a specific reason. That reason contains the dramatic logic of the scene.** If we ignore the dramatic logic, the scene won't work! As the actors explore the staging, they will discover it for themselves.

Richard Dreyfuss: "I want to be able to feel with a director that I'm a creative partner in this endeavor. Anything that happens that makes me feel otherwise I am going to resent."

Another reason that it works is that when you pick a location, **the location will limit your choices.** There are only so many places the actor can go.

And the beauty part is that this technique of letting actors discover the scene for themselves takes no longer than any other method for staging dialogue scenes. And how long is that? Usually it takes fifteen minutes to half an hour and often even less. If it's a long dialogue scene or complicated action it will take longer. But that is the same whether the director hands out the staging or lets the actors discover it on their own. The point is this method is not a short cut; it is a more creative way to work because it involves the creative input of the actors as well as the director.

If we don't listen to actors' ideas we might as well use computer-generated characters that do what we tell them to do. They will be about that interesting too.

Get a Stuntman

Action scenes, special effects scenes, or cleverly lined-up shots require precise staging. Shots where the actor cannot deviate from a predetermined plan. Now you *will* have to "put them in creative jail." But take time, *before you stage the scene*, to explain to the actors why they are being limited. Actors will respect directors for doing that, respond to the challenge, and even come to enjoy it.

Many times the actor will want to do a stunt themselves. *Don't allow this*, unless the actor is named Jackie Chan. Even though a stunt seems really simple, actors can and do get hurt, often. Not just tragic examples, like Brandon Lee who was killed by a *blank pistol* on the set of *The Crow*, or Jon Erik Hexum, who shot himself on a set, playing Russian Roulette with a *blank pistol*. Your accident might only be a twisted ankle but it can be enough to turn the whole shoot into a catastrophe. We often read in the entertainment rags how this star or that star did all their own stunts. There are two, and only two, explanations for this: they are lying or they are idiots.

Rehearsal of action scenes should only be done with the stunt coordinator present. He is as concerned with safety as he is concerned with the successful execution of the action scene. If there are specific physical things the actor needs to learn, such as kung fu or sword fighting or driving an unfamiliar vehicle, those things have to be rehearsed before shooting. **And never, never, never believe what an actor says he can do.** Every actor *says* they can ride a horse, play baseball, shoot a gun, and dance like Baryshnikov. Bullshit. They lie to get the job. They lie out of pride or embarrassment.

Goldie Hawn is a fantastic driver. She handles her Porsche like a pro. In *Bird on a Wire* she had to drive through a city street and throw her car into a 360-degree spin. Unbeknownst to me she spent the weekend in a huge empty parking lot learning how to do this. On Monday morning, she proudly told me she wanted to drive the car herself for the stunt. My stomach did a flip-flop as I realized I would have to tell her no.

We were not shooting in a big parking lot. We were on a narrow city street with curbs, lampposts, buildings, buses, and other cars. If something happened with Goldie driving and she was injured… not only would the production be shut down but also the entire crew would be out of work. A really bad idea overall. So we did the shot using a British-made right-hand-drive convertible. She could sit in the passenger seat and pretend to drive while Mic Rogers, the stunt coordinator, did the driving from the right-hand side.

In *Stakeout*, Richard Dreyfuss and Emilio Estevez, playing detectives, startle each other in a dark alley. Dreyfuss' character clocks Estevez with a right cross. The right way to do this would be to use stunt doubles. But noooo: the actors wanted to do it themselves. Because both actors were inexperienced at stunts and perfectionists at the same time they wound up punching each other ten times before they were satisfied. The next day Estevez couldn't move his head because he'd strained his neck muscles, which had totally locked up. We couldn't shoot with him the next day. Whose fault was it? Mine.

Two days later we start an action scene where Dreyfuss has to jump into a backyard and meet a mean German Shepherd who chases him.

All Dreyfuss has to do is jump off a little platform one foot high. That's right, twelve inches. We roll, "Action" is called, and Richard jumps onto the grass… and twists his ankle. He is taken to the hospital and the company has to shut down for the day. Whose fault was it? Mine, of course.

Who Made You God of Good Ideas?

Many times as a beginning director, actors would sidle up to me with suggestions. Being insecure I reflexively said "No, that won't work." Only after they walked away dispirited would I realize they had a very good idea. This was a real dilemma. My pride said ignore their idea but my director's sense said they were onto something.

David Levinson: "Don't be a schmuck. If it's a good idea, use it. Who cares about your pride, anyway?"

I'd then have to tell the crew, "Bennett, our writer, had a good idea, why don't we... etc." The film profited and importantly, in the future, people were more likely to share their ideas with me. You always have the option to reject an idea. But if you do you want to encourage that person to keep coming back to you with other ideas. By me, **good ideas always win over pride.**

Mel Gibson: "Even if an actor comes up with ideas that you don't think are the right way to go, always, always say, 'Try it.' Even if you're up against the clock. It'll become apparent quickly if it's not working. Unfortunately, there are a lot of egos involved. Once people's egos get involved, it becomes very difficult. It's hard to leave your ego at the door. It's like, 'What are you doing? This person is trying to help you. Accept the help. He's only going to make you look better.' There are directors who are really cranky and miserable, and people help them anyway. You're thinking, 'Why? How do they get away with that?'"

Martin Scorsese is the poster child for director openness. Since he is obviously such a great actor's director we can crib from him. In *Casino* he cast the great character actor L.Q. Jones from *The Wild Bunch*. L.Q. came to rehearsal the day of shooting with several unusual ideas.

L.Q. Jones: "I couldn't believe how open Marty was. If I'd tried that with Sam Peckinpah I'd of eaten a fist sandwich."

"Let's try it, sounds great" seems to be Scorsese's response to almost any actor suggestion. The actor realizes his ideas are welcome. **An actor will always be wary around a director until he learns what to expect from him.** The interchange between director and actor can get richer and richer. The scenes in *Casino* with L.Q. and De Niro are terrific: real, fresh, and to the point. If the director isn't open to others' ideas then he is stuck with what he brings to the party by himself. Unless you are Scorsese or Spielberg or Michael Mann at the very apex of your talent you can probably use some help. One of many reasons for these directors' success is their ability to be wide open to other people's ideas all day, every day.

Kurtwood Smith: "If a director is always saying 'No, no, no, no, it's got to be this way,' then pretty soon you just sort of give up and wait for him to tell you what to do. Or you fight him, and then all that does is create a lot of tension."

Gary Busey is a real free spirit; well, wild man is closer to the mark. Gary is a unique talent living on the planet of improvisation in a universe far, far away. Scenes with him will always be unusual, quirky, and interesting; and he is loved for his eccentricities. If we want fresh characters and fresh points of view we will always seek out actors who don't necessarily march to the production department's drummer. Gary Busey talked about what an actor can improvise when he's in tune with his character. Specifically, how he came to wear a dress in several scenes in *Under Siege*.

Gary Busey: "Up to that point in *Under Siege* we didn't have Navy cooperation. They thought we made the Navy look bad. Polliwog Day is the day when a Navy ship is on a combat mission and they cross the equator. One whole day is spent making first-year sailors go through a lot of hardship. Like sticking your head in loose Jell-O and sending Morse code about how short your dick is.

"There's an enlisted man that will come out and be Queen of the Wogs. I said, 'This is great.' I went back to Andy Davis, the director, and said, 'Andy, I'm going to kill the Captain in drag.' He said, 'What? What?' Steven Segal said, 'Whose idea was this?' They were expecting Erika Eleniak, the 1989 Miss July to emerge in a thong... and out came me. Tommy Lee announces, 'It's Commander Krill, former Queen of the Wogs,' I had a 44D stuffed bra, and a little short blue-and-white striped dress, with four brass buttons and a Tina Turner wig on. I looked at Tommy Lee Jones, and said, 'Do I look like I need psychological evaluation?' And Tommy Lee went, 'Not at all.' Warner Brothers got on the phone and said, 'Gary, we don't want to do it this way. We don't want to get into some psychological thing where you dress as a woman and go in drag. It won't work.' I said, 'I'll make a deal with you. I'll do both genders. I'll do Commander Krill like you want him and I'll do him in drag. Warner Brothers told Andy Davis it was OK, but only if the movie stayed on schedule. We did the drag scene before lunch, and did the straight version in the afternoon. Stayed on schedule.

"The Navy said, 'We now accept your movie, because we know the executive officer is insane. So it's not a black mark on the Navy.'"

Don't get all excited and think because you've found an eccentric actor that he is necessarily talented. Conversely, a compliant actor is not necessarily dull. Off the set Chris Walken is quieter than a flea peeing on a blotter. Yet when he lets the genie out of the bottle and steps on the set his performance is riveting.

Of course, we can never forget that an actor is only going to reach for a deeply buried emotion if he trusts the director — even an actor as experienced as Martin Sheen.

Martin Sheen: "If you trust the director, you say, 'Well, I'm going to go into this darkness for a little bit.' And you'll only do it with a director that has confidence and that will protect you, because acting is such a private thing. You're revealing something from deep inside you. It may not be your wife or child that just died, but somebody or something has died in me that I'm going to have to get in touch with. That's what we do. We have this store of emotions that we go to and it's personal and very special. If it's personal you can always tell. It's not some faint Xerox copy of some other actor's performance."

Summary

1. Let the actors have the freedom to discover the staging of a scene with very little input from you.

2. All scenes contain a dramatic logic that will not be ignored. If staging doesn't work, look to the scene for the solution.

3. The location chosen for a scene will also dictate staging.

4. Never permit actors to do their own stunts.

5. If you are not open to ideas from others, you are stuck with what you brought to the party yourself. When the film is finished what counts is how well it works, not who thought of something.

6. Good ideas always win over pride. If you think you were wrong about something, admit it. Everyone knows you're not perfect anyway.

What Am I Doing?

The opposite of people coming at you with ideas are the dependent ones who don't have any. At least that is what they say. **They have plenty of ideas but are afraid to voice them.** They may even be afraid to think them. That's the last thing you need on a set. Fear is the enemy of creativity. Everybody has to be thinking. Not just about their part but alert to what's going on all around. So the person who comes to you wanting to be told what to do has to be retrained to think for herself or she is dead weight. And guess who has to drag them around?

If you sense hesitation or concern on the part of an actor, don't wait, go directly to them and talk about it. Never kid yourself that they are in their trailer working on the scene. If they need help understanding the scene, or mastering a tricky bit of dialogue, or handling a devilish prop, now is the time. When the crew is ready, the cast should be ready too.

There are plenty of times you have to engage the actor who needs to talk about the scene. **However, make them do the work.** If they get the idea you'll do their thinking for them, you've dropped another monkey on your back. Draw them out with questions. Get them to articulate what they think is happening in the scene and particularly with their character. It's perfectly possible that they don't understand the scene. **The key question: What does your character** *want to do* **(to the other person), or what do you** *want to get* **(from them)?** Very likely you will hear answers that are intellectual or unspecific and therefore un-actable. Don't accept this. Press for a verb, an active verb. If the actor doesn't give you one, keep asking questions to lead him that way.

Look at the opening of *Saving Private Ryan*. We see soldiers running onto the beach at Normandy. We follow them as they dive for cover and attempt to return fire. We can look at this on two levels: intellectually, we can see the horror of war, the toll it takes on young men we send to fight, man's inhumanity to man blah, blah, blah. These are *totally unactable directions*. Specifically, we follow an individual soldier who is doing his job: advancing on the enemy and trying to save his own life at the same time. This scared soldier knows that to do his job he must aggressively protect his life and the life of his buddies. The soldier is not thinking on some larger philosophical level. He's not thinking about the absurdity of war, of man's inhumanity to man. This poor GI is diving into the sand to avoid getting killed. It's that simple. **It's not the actor's job to play the larger themes. It's his job to do the actions... that create the themes.**

Sydney Pollack: "The difficult work for the director is to try to be the Sheriff of Specificity. Scenes get general and vague. You want to say to the actors, 'Look, suppose this was in Japanese. Would I understand what this scene is about?' And if you don't get it there's something wrong, almost always."

To repeat what was said earlier: **It's only possible to act one thing at a time and that thing must be a very specific active verb.** All those grand philosophical and cosmic ideas that actors and directors come up with are a total waste of time. They may make up part of the back-story of the character or part of his psychological makeup. But they cannot be acted upon at the moment in the scene. Those ideas are part of the Given Circumstances or what the character brings to that moment in the scene from his past history. **Use William Ball's "crowbar" technique. "What does the character want or hope to get in this moment?"** Ask "what if" questions.

William Ball: "Some directors desperate to cover for lack of preparation manage to get through the entire rehearsal period on these two sentences alone. They use them as a crowbar. In fact there are some directors who, unable to be bothered with refinements, have built an entire career on these two sentences: 'What are you trying to GET from him? What are you trying to MAKE him give you?'"[1]

Any right answer will contain at least three things:
1. A verb. "I am trying to CONVINCE."
2. A receiver: "I am trying to convince HIM."
3. A desired response "I am trying to convince him TO GO WITH ME."

---

[1] *A Sense of Direction*, page 91

The hardest thing about getting good answers from actors is keeping them to the *facts* of the situation. They always want to ladle explanations and states of mind onto the scene. Don't allow it. Keep coming back to the simplest facts.

Result Directing

A famous director of movies in the 1940s and '50s, Mervyn LeRoy (*Mr. Roberts*, *Quo Vadis*), was said to have one direction and one direction only. Before the camera rolled he would step up to the actors like a referee in a boxing match and say: "Now kids, give me a good scene... with lots of feeling." A former dean of the Yale Drama School was reputed to say to an actor, "This time do it... funnier... and better." Somebody joked that the dean once said: "I'm not giving you a line reading... just imitate me." That's result directing, the lazy way of the unprepared director, the director who hasn't done his homework. What is wrong with it? What is right with it? It is so vague it can't even qualify as general.

These are some favorite useless result directions:
Have fun with it.
Do it better.
Be funnier.
More energy!
Do something offbeat.
Be sad.
Do it faster.
Do it with attitude.
You have to cry here.
You're the good guy.
You're a mean guy who hates everybody.
You're a bitch.
You're a killer.
You're in the nude.

John Frankenheimer: "The terrible trap that so many directors fall into, is that they continually talk to actors in result terms. Like I want it faster or I want it louder. I want it this. Sometimes there are moments when probably you're going to have to say that, but most of the time if you want to help an actor, that's not what you want to say. You don't want to say, 'Better.' You want to be able to tell the actor a reason why he or she has to be quicker in this scene, why there has to be more urgency."

A television series with George Kennedy called *Sarge*, the third TV episode I directed, guest-starred Vic Morrow, a tough, talented actor who was sense-lessly killed in a tragic *Twilight Zone* filming accident. He was intense, exciting, with danger simmering underneath. But at the same time he was very low key. The camera had to be right in his face to see the strong, truthful work he was doing. All Vic's characters took their time. If Vic ever played a character that was supposed to be fast-talking, he wasn't fast after Vic got hold of him. But you never took your eyes off him.

So I'm young and stupid. On the first day, I watch the rehearsal and see a scene that just looks slow to me. I sidle over to Vic Morrow, who was twenty years older and say to him with stupid confidence: "Vic, let's pick up the pace." His eyes flash with anger and he gives me the look of death. I can still feel it in my chest. "Don't ever tell me faster!" he says. This phrase made such an impression on me that for awhile it was going to be the title of this book.

Moral: Yes, you can go to the actors and ask them to give you more pace, more energy, more tears. But there is a good way and a bad way to do it.

Pace or speed is one of the last things you add to a scene. Not in the rehearsal. It's destructive to do it too early. Pace is easy, energy is easy. Wait till they know the damn scene first. If we get impatient and ask actors to speed up long before they have control of the scene, all we'll get is people who talk faster… and louder. It will have no nuance, no body. In the brief time they have to rehearse, they are still discovering and experimenting. Wait a couple of takes and see what develops by itself. You'll get it all, the nuances and the pace and energy. Actors are not machines. It takes time… even when there is no time.

You can get much better results giving actors specific reasons *why* they speak faster, *Why* they are more energetic. Example: Two men stop on the street. One asks the other for directions. Yawn. Boring expositional scene, right? The actor giving directions takes forever to get the dialogue out. You're in a hurry so you want to blurt out "Faster." Don't say that. Give him something he can act. Tell him he is late for his train home. If he misses this one he'll have to wait two hours for the next one. Tell him it's about to rain and he's wearing a new suit. That he can play. Tell him he has to go to the bathroom right away. Tell him he has just shoplifted and is trying to get away without getting caught. Any of these and a thousand more are much more interesting than "faster."

I'm directing Candice Bergen and a young actor named Bug Hall in a suspense movie for CBS, *Footsteps*. In the middle of the night she has caught him snooping in her house and he is trying to talk her into letting him go. Fairly simple, right? Clean obvious objective. No mystery here. So then, why did each take start with great energy and bog down right away? Ken Raskoff and David Madden, the producers, kept whispering to me, "Make him go faster." I ignored them for a couple of takes in order to give the actor time to feel on solid ground. But it got no better. Indeed, it got deadly.

I took Bug Hall aside and said he should act "as-if" he could hear a cop car coming. If he's caught, he's going to jail. Find an escape route. And on each new take he has to think of a different way out. As I'm writing this I realize I should have made him tell me his escape route after each take to keep the pressure on him to think of something new each time.

During the next take I talked out loud. "There's a siren! Cops are coming up the drive. They're coming into the house. Etc., etc." Now Bug began to go faster. But not just faster, faster with a difference: now it was organic. Now we could see his panic. Now the scene began to click. Not just because he was talking faster, but also because we could see other things going on in his head. Big difference.

Candice Bergen's character had a lot more to work with now. She does not have to stand there tapping her foot while he plods through his lines. She can see he's up to something. She has to think what to do if he tries some trick.

Is this a lot of trouble for just one scene? Absolutely not. Scenes take a lot of work to keep them interesting. All audiences have seen hours and hours of movies and TV shows. They are way ahead of us. We have to outsmart them or lose them.

In the same movie Candice Bergen, playing a famous novelist, is giving a talk to her fans. While waiting to go on, a very shy assistant comes in to tell her the audience is ready. Candice calms her, saying: "Don't worry, it's just an audience, not a posse."

Our young actress only has one line, "Miss Lowendahl, they're ready," to convey her nervousness. But she is too nervous to say her own name. She has gotten so stiff she comes off like an automaton.

I could have run over and given her a result direction: "Remember, you're very nervous here." Wrong. Instead I took her aside: "You're kind of nervous now, aren't you?" She nodded. I said, "That's OK. It works for the character." She looked puzzled. "Since your character is scared of Candice, don't try to hide your own nervousness. Use it." This was just a fancier result direction and she needed to be given an adjustment that was more specific, more actable, to help her act the scene better.

The specific idea was: What if she constantly garbles the name of Candice's character, "Ms. Lowendahl"? She could screw up the name every time. Ms. Lowenthal, Ms. Lowenberg, Ms. Lowenstein, etc. The actress brightened, "Got it, I know what to do." I deliberately didn't ask her what the "what to do" was. Acting ideas, like jokes, are ruined if you try to explain them. The camera rolled, she entered, stumbles over the name. Then she stuttered and blushed while finishing her line. Now Candice's reply makes perfect sense and we have a scene with a little bit of character in it. **Specific directions work. General directions give general results.**

Tricky, Tricky

Elia Kazan was famous for the tricks he used to keep his actors off balance. He would set up lose-lose situations for the characters. His favorite trick was to give two actors in a scene contradictory jobs. In William Inge's play *Dark at the Top of the Stairs*, a young girl comes into her boyfriend's house for a study date. The mother doesn't like this girl and makes no secret about it. No wimp, the girl responds in kind. Kazan could have just let the women say their dialogue and play general don't-like-each-other attitudes. Stage directions say the mother *has* to take the girl's coat when she arrives. Instead Kazan secretly told the girl *not* to let the mother have her coat — no matter what. Now the two of them struggle over the coat, and each actress thinks the other is trying to screw them. Kazan had devilishly set in motion a real-life hate relationship between the two actresses, which of course affected their scenes together. The result was great for the play and terrible for the two women who may never have spoken again after that.

Elia Kazan: "When I did the play [*Streetcar Named Desire*] with Jessica Tandy, I did a lot to break her out of her schooled RADA, Royal Academy of the Dramatic Arts, habits. I once tied her up and had them threaten and make fun of her. I did all kinds of wild things in those days with actors in order to make them feel helpless or whatever the hell I wanted to make them feel."[2]

A lot of people say this kind of directing is dirty pool. Actors should be respected enough to do the job without trickery. I myself am a terrible liar

[2] *Kazan*, page 81

and can't even trick my dogs. But at the same time I know that unexpected events can bring terrific unexpected results.

If the director can cleverly set up these situations, the actors don't necessarily resent being manipulated.

Jodie Foster: "Dick Donner does this amazing thing: While you're doing a take, he yells at you things to do. In comedy it's funny, because it makes the comedy very chaotic."[3]

Richard Donner: "God love Jodie Foster. I mean, I've been the luckiest guy alive with getting actors. Jodie's a person you can do that with. Because if you get an idea and you wait until the end of the take to say it and do it again, it's lost. But if you can just say 'the telephone,' and you don't have to say another thing. 'The wallet.' You never say anything more. Bang, all of a sudden Mel Gibson has lost his wallet. And Mel figured it out without a cut. Jody's so quick she does the same thing. I love her."

In *Saturday Night Fever,* Travolta is sitting at the disco bar with Donna Pescow watching a stripper denude. Pescow's character wants to date Travolta's in the worst way. He could care less. During the rehearsals I had him light a cigarette and then light hers also. On the take, however, I told him not to light her cigarette, just ignore her and blow out the match just as she reached to get a light. Donna Pescow is a terrifically intuitive actress who always responds freshly in the moment. The look on her face was wonderful. In one second it told all we needed to know about her vulnerability and about this going-nowhere relationship. Was this a dirty trick? No, it's all part of the playing around that makes for good acting.

They used to tell Judy Garland her parakeet had died to get her to cry. *That* was a dirty trick. Come to think of it, she did a lot of movies where she cried. She must have had a lot of parakeets.

Mark Rydell: "In *The Cowboys*, I wanted to create an environment that made Duke [John Wayne] uncomfortable... He wanted all of his regular crew guys, and I wouldn't hire any of them. I hired a bunch of left-wing hippies who made him uncomfortable. The woman playing his wife, Sarah Cunningham, was a blacklisted communist. I wanted him to feel unstable. Actor's Studio people surrounded him, and he knew that I was a director of the Actor's Studio. It just did the right

---

[3] *Actors Turned Directors,* page 58

thing. He was challenged, and he was the first guy on the set and the last guy to leave. He worked like a dog. He was a hard worker. If people challenged him, he rose to the challenge. If I had let him do what he had wanted, which was what he always had done with those old cronies of his, it would have been just like his other movies instead of the very fresh performance that he gave."

Many memorable film moments come from the insights of the moment. Martin Sheen's accidentally cutting his hand badly in the opening of *Apocalypse Now* unleashed a torrent of emotion and feelings that made the scene frightening and shocking. Another scene that was restored for the re-release of the film was a clever use of acting in the moment.

Martin Sheen: "Kurtz [Brando] had me put in this little prison. And he comes around to proselytize me and to brag about his achievements. Marlon sits on a mud step and starts reading his war reviews from *Time* magazine. Francis [Ford Coppola] put all of these children who spoke no English... Now mind you, they didn't speak Vietnamese either, and he told the children through the interpreter, 'Just distract Mr. Brando. Do anything to him that you like.' So they would come up and they'd feel his head, which was bald. Then they'd laugh and poke him in the eye. Marlon is going like this, [waving his hands] like they're fleas. But they were just all children. And Marlon starts... speaking Vietnamese! Not really. He's just doing crazy double-talk like Sid Caesar and Carl Reiner used to do. I mean, he created that whole scene just by being available to it."

If you are working with a really sensitive and talented actor they will respond in the moment to what is put before them. If they are untalented you may get nothing more than a puzzled look. Remember Sanford Meisner's "Pinch-Ouch" rule. One character does something to another character (pinches them) and the other character reacts (ouch!).

If you are not getting "Pinch-Ouch" responses from your actors, when the acting is all stiff and wooden, something is very wrong with the scene. The scene itself may be poorly written, or more likely the actors aren't living moment to moment in the scene.

Jeremy Kagan: "You can motivate a performance. I will use an active, intentional verb: something that they want at this moment in this scene. I sometimes will give a personal reference, 'You know what you were telling me about when your dad threw you out of the house? This is the same moment here.' Sometimes I will give them a goal like, you've got to say this before you leave the room.' Or, 'You know what I want you to do? You see that beautiful girl over there? Think about her while you're doing this scene.' The actor might say 'But I'm supposed to be firing him.' I'll say, 'I know, but that's what I want you to have on your mind." And these are purely the bag of tricks or tools to help if the actor is suddenly frozen."

Skip the Bullshit, What Do You Want?

James Woods is a guy who takes directness into lunar orbit; he makes you laugh at the same time that he's slicing you up like salami. I learned early on that if I gave him a really good correct "actable" direction like "do this as if you have to leave to catch a train," he would look at me; head cocked, and say out of the side of his mouth, "Oh, you mean go faster." Woods is the kind of actor who says in effect, just give me the result and I'll get there on my own.

James Woods: "Actors always say, 'Well, I feel this character's back-story is such and such.' You know, if you want a back-story, pass out a pamphlet to the audience. I want to see what's happening right now.

"Here's the key to what I feel about acting and how I feel about directing. I took one acting class for one session my entire life. I went into one of these acting schools in New York. I'd already done thirty-six plays in college and summer stock and stuff. I had a lot of experience, and I just always flew by the seat of my pants. I did the 'to be' soliloquy from *Hamlet*. Then the teacher opened it up to the class, who were a bunch of people who'd never been on stage in their lives. And the first thing anybody said was, 'You know, I watched you, but I couldn't tell what Hamlet had had for breakfast from the way you did the soliloquy.' And I said, 'You know what, I think he's fasting right now. And so am I.' I left the class and that was it for acting classes for me."

A good response to an actor who is Method-resistant could be, "Yes, but also what would happen if you played it 'as-if...' (giving an 'as-if' direction)?" Because even if the actor knows the result you want is (faster, louder, funnier, better), any actable input you give him can spark his imagination to create new behavior that goes beyond the "result" response of (louder, funnier, better). No actor is able to resist putting a fresh twist on a scene. Very often the funniest lines in movies come not from the script but from an actor who ad-libbed the line on the spot. Mel Gibson can always be counted upon to keep a scene fresh.

Richard Donner: "You take a guy like Mel Gibson and you say, 'Hey Mel, what about the phone?' 'Leave me alone,' he says. 'I got it.' And he'll turn that phone into the most incredible piece of business you've ever heard in your life."

Richard Pryor, Will Smith, almost any comedian can find unusual twists in a situation. Classically trained English actors are the biggest devils in this area. Any excuse to horse around in a scene and they are off to the races. They are in such control of their technique that they get bored doing the same thing time after time.

My favorite story of sensitive "good direction" misunderstood is from a production of *The Cherry Orchard* at the Williamstown Theatre Festival. Nikos Psacharopolous, the director, had hired an eighty-year-old actor to play Firs, the aged butler. In the rehearsals the actor was doing odd, very stylized movements and spoke with a very crackly voice unlike his own natural voice. Nikos kept trying and failing to bring him around to more natural behavior. No matter what Nikos told him, the old actor moved even more strangely and talked even slower.

One day, desperate to get Firs to be more natural, Nikos — a master director — tried once again to get through to him using all the good active actable verbs. Suddenly the eighty-year-old actor brightened and said: "Oh, you mean you don't want me to play the age?"

Jeremy Kagan: "I found this ten-year-old kid, wonderful and very smart and energetic. I want him to cry, and I can't motivate him. And his mom has told me, 'He doesn't cry. He's not a crier.' It's just not happening. He's pretending to cry, but I want him to go one more level. And finally he looks at me and says 'Oh, you want me to blubber.' 'Yeah.' And bam, in seconds, he does it and it's a delicious moment. I would never use the word blubber, but he's seen other people blubber, and he's an actor."

There are lots of actors who agree with Laurence Olivier's line to Dustin Hoffman during the shooting of *Marathon Man*. Hoffman's character has been running away from bad guys for two days without sleep. When Hoffman shows up to shoot the scene looking awful, a compassionate Olivier asks what happened and Hoffman explains that he actually stayed up all night to achieve his haggard look. Olivier responded, "Dear boy, why don't you just try acting?" These actors look upon this "as-if" business with suspicion and disrespect.

Craig Modderno asked Harrison Ford in a 2006 interview in *Hollywood Life* magazine, "What don't you want to hear from a director?" With characteristic dry humor, Ford replied (*lowers voice dramatically*), "Think back to when you were a child. Did you ever have feelings about your parents having another child?" Then he added, "I don't want to talk about acting at this point in a movie. I want to talk about the story, how we can best serve the audience."

You may not know the actor feels that way about acting until you step right into a steaming bit of cow plop. I tried a couple of "as-if"s on Michael J. Fox in *The Hard Way* and got frostbite of the balls. Michael, normally a very lovely guy, looked at me coldly and said in effect, "I don't want to hear that psychological crap." Only afterwards did I find out that Brian de Palma and Paul Schrader, who both had directed Michael, were also sent to the ER for gonad hypothermia. No need to tell me twice. I stayed away from directing him that way. Too touchy-feely for Michael. And that's OK. It's the way he works.

Both Michael J. Fox and James Woods are talented, intuitive, and smart people. They understand the scene without being told and their emotions lie right where they should be... on the surface. Instantly accessible. James Woods is one big raw emotion running at full blast all day long. Woods would sooner date a chimpanzee with chlamydia than he would go off in a corner to do "sense memories."

James Woods: "The story's always about one thing. Character A wants something from Character B that Character B doesn't want to give up, and Character A has to find a way to get it. It's all about this: First Act, get the guy up the tree. Second Act, throw shit at him. Third Act, try to get him back down without hurting him. And every scene has that structure too. What's this scene about? It's pretty simple. What does it say it's about? 'Well, I walk in...' It's easier than you think it is."

With actors like this we have to rely on the very basics of acting: objectives. **Get clear with them what their character *wants* and is *doing* in the scene and turn them loose.** There is nothing touchy-feely about a direction like "You want to bombard the police captain with the facts of the case." It's straightforward. A strong actable sequence of 1) verb; 2) receiver; and 3) consequence will be plenty for this kind of actor.

The other kind of actor that despises "The Method" may be British or from another country that trains actors differently than in the U.S. British actors often come at the character from the outside rather than the inside. They may start to build a character with a prop or piece of wardrobe. Olivier loved to use false noses, Gielgud used wigs. Yul Brynner discovered his character in *The King and I* when he tried on his wardrobe for the first time. He stared in the mirror for a few seconds, then suddenly slammed his fists on his hips. A King was born.

With non-Method actors you depend on the actor having instant intuitive access to his emotions. Here is where careful casting pays off. Know the actor before he shows up on the set. Do your homework. Get the 411 from directors who have worked with that actor. With the instant accessibility of videos today there's no excuse not to know an actor's work.

Even a Method-trained actor who is a pro knows how to cut through the bullshit and get to the point. Even if the point is something they despise.

Ed Asner: "I went down to see the director and the line producer the next day. They kept talking about the scenes. I didn't know what in the hell they wanted. So, they were talking and talking and talking. Then I said 'Oh! You want me to play it like a villain!' I don't know if I said that, but that was the implication. They nodded 'Yes.' My friend Bob walked me out to the gate and said, 'I don't know. You've got to do what you've got to do. Sometimes you've got to be in the whore business. It's up to you if you want to do the job or not.' I said 'No! I don't consider it being a whore. If that's all they see in the character, they're getting what they want. No problem!' They wanted all the subtlety removed."

When dealing with beginning actors it would be a mistake to try to throw actor jargon at them.

Betty Thomas: "I just think everyone is a smart human being. That's my original assumption when I walk on the set — you're a smart human being and you understand English. If those two things are true, I know I can talk to you and say, 'Here's what I'm trying to do.' If you're not an actor, I say it very clearly. 'Here's what I'm looking for and trying to get to. Is there a way you think you could do that and still feel like it's natural to you?' So I don't try to bullshit anybody and talk about different acting terms with people who are new to acting. I just try to be as clear as I can. My favorite is, 'Try to act more human. That would be the best thing you could do. More human.' I find people forget that they're just playing a human being."

Off the Wall

If actors have a lot of stage experience they may bring along habits learned on stage that are tough to break. Ignorantly, some call them "over the top," "hams," "showoffs," and worse. They are not bad actors, they just have bad habits that don't work on film. Watching them nuke a scene can be scarier than watching a hockey player stiff a Viagra commercial. Hamlet's advice to the players was meant for theatre actors but applies even more to the film actor. **"Nor do not saw the air too much with your hands... but suit the action to the word and the word to the action."**

In 1978 the hottest ticket on Broadway was *Dracula* played by Frank Langella. Langella, one of the boldest and physically daring actors of our time, delighted audiences with his chilling portrayal of Dracula in a clever tongue-in-cheek production. In the climactic confrontation between Dracula and Professor Von Helsing, the Vampire Hunter, Van Helsing thrusts a bunch of garlic in Dracula's face. Langella is repelled so forcefully that he seemed thrown against the flimsy walls of the stage set, specifically strengthened for that purpose. Langella is one of the few actors of our time that has the physical courage to do something like that on stage. The legendary Laurence Olivier, who played opposite Langella in *Dracula*, was also an amazing physical actor in his prime. Olivier, in the final act of *Coriolanus* at the Old Vic, would hurl his body backwards off a platform twenty-five feet above the stage, to be caught at the last nanosecond by his ankles.

Dracula was shot in Cornwall, at King Arthur's birthplace in Tintagel. Peter Murton, the production designer, transformed a weird Victorian building to look like the insane asylum described in Bram Stoker's novel.

On the day we shot this confrontation between Langella and Olivier, Frank wanted to repeat the staging as he had done it on Broadway, complete with being thrown against the walls. These walls for the movie were made of stone, no reinforcing needed. I wasn't so concerned that he would hurt his shoulder as I was that his movements and acting might be way too big for film. On a theatre stage... spectacular. On a film set... over the top? Taking Frank aside, I told him, "The movie screen can't contain the size of what you're doing. It's so much bigger than normal human behavior that it could easily look ridiculous." Frank was unperturbed. With the confidence of eight months success on Broadway he smiled. "John, we need to see the power of Dracula."

I shifted to Plan B. I made him an offer he couldn't refuse. "You know this character better than anyone. I have to respect what you're saying. Let's shoot it your way. Come to dailies tomorrow and watch it with me. If you like it I'll shut up. If you don't like it we can re-take it." If ever something could backfire big-time, this was it. If I was wrong or he was stubborn, I would have abdicated my rights as director.

The scene was shot Langella's way. In my mind Laurence Olivier, frail and sick with cancer, upstaged Langella by simply standing still and watching him be thrown against the walls.

When the film came back from London Technicolor, everyone gathered in the makeshift projection room in our hotel in Tintagel. Langella sat behind me. The first take unspooled on the screen and the room got quieter and quieter. After three takes I could hear rustling and muttering behind me. Suddenly, in his sonorous bass-baritone Langella said, "Oh... dear. God!" At that moment he realized he needed a new approach to the scene.

Eight weeks later we re-shot the scene at Shepperton Studios. Forcing himself to contain his character's rage, the most powerful things about the scene became the extreme close-ups of Frank's eyes, which literally vibrated with hatred as he confronted Van Helsing. It is one of the best scenes in the movie. Less is more when it comes to screen acting.

Frank Langella, having years of film experience behind him, would have adjusted more quickly to a film acting level except that he had been doing this scene for over 250 performances on Broadway. If he had done less on film he would have felt he was not doing his job. All his alarm bells would go off saying "Wrong, wrong! Not enough!" After he had time to adjust to film from stage he performed the scene spectacularly.

If you really want to see what over-the-top acting looks like, tune into the Tony Awards when excerpts are shown from the nominated shows. There is always a feeling of gross unreality to these scenes when seen on TV no matter how good the acting was in the theatre. The voices are too loud, the gestures are too large, and the facial expressions as big as Mount Rushmore. The actors have been playing the scenes on stage for an audience in a big theatre, not the camera. So it's horribly unfair to show the world their work in this form.

It is one reason why many filmed versions of plays and musicals almost always fare better when they use different actors and directors from the Broadway version. The original creative team is so wedded to how they did it on stage they can't see how excessive it looks on film. Laurence Olivier's film of *Othello* is an example of the most brilliant actor of his generation repeating his magnificent theatrical performance on film and appearing false and over-done. The 2006 film of *The Producers* is directed with the same intensity as the stage version and seems over the top.

Rx for Stage Actors

Craig Modderno: "Can you give some technique tips to actors who work both in television and in films?"

James Woods: "Yeah, don't change a f— thing."

CM: "Really? That simple?"

JW: "Yeah. There's absolutely no difference between television and films and stage, except maybe the volume level on stage. But acting is acting. It's all about truth. Would this character do this at this moment?"

CM: "You don't tone it down for TV as opposed to bringing it up for film?"

JW: "No. I don't. Why would I?"

CM: "Because TV is a medium of close-ups, and you have to be larger than life on a big screen."

JW: "What, did they say that at some film school or something?"

The solution to this horrendous problem of "ACTING!" is fairly easy. There are only one or two simple principles. On a theatrical stage an actor has to communicate his feelings to an audience who may be sitting one or two hundred feet away. Therefore, not only does his voice have to carry a great distance, his gestures and facial expressions must be enlarged as well. The director, the audience, and her mother always urge him to "Sing out, Louise!"

John Travolta appeared on Broadway in *Grease* in a supporting role before he did *Welcome Back Kotter*. He told me he was constantly being told to "Speak up, talk louder, nobody can hear you." And the director was not wrong. If nobody can hear you or read the expressions on your face, you've failed in your job of communicating the play.

So actors get into the habit of enlarging everything, making it bigger. "It's got to read in the back of the house."

Woody Allen: "Good acting on stage is determined by who shouts the loudest."

For film this is the last thing the actor needs to do. **The camera and the microphones do all the work of projecting.**

At a Film Technique Workshop for actors at the Yale School of Drama, I teach them the difference between stage and film. Few of them have worked in film and are anxious about making the transition. On the first day of the Workshop the actors bring in scenes from Shakespeare or Chekhov. No modern plays allowed. Too easy. Since they are already skilled actors they have to act difficult scenes. Scenes that require size and style on stage.

In front of digital cameras they perform the scenes the way they play them on stage. Afterwards I tell them three things:

1) The eye of the audience is not a hundred feet away from you, it is only three feet away. The camera captures your smallest expressions. No need to project your gestures, body language, and facial expressions anymore than if you were talking to somebody standing next to you.

2) The ear of the audience is as close as the mike pinned to your chest. You never have to project your voice any louder than you would in a normal situation.

To drive these points home, I have them stand very close to each other, a foot apart, and do the scenes at a stage volume and size. Two people standing a foot apart and shouting at each other "O Romeo, Romeo, wherefore art thou?" is very funny. Within three or four lines of dialogue the actors break out laughing at the absurdity of it.

3) Listening on film is as important as speaking. There is no camera on a theater stage to cut back and forth between two actors in a scene. Even though one actor has to listen to the other on stage, it doesn't have as much impact as what is seen on film. One of the reasons there is so much less dialogue in film is that the character who is listening conveys much of what has to be said verbally on stage.

Oliver Stone: "The great stars were always great listeners. You know, if you watch Gary Cooper or watch Michael Caine, and it's the way they listen. You're watching them. You're not watching the person that's talking. It's the way they listen. So an actor who says, 'I've got three lines in the movie,' is really not looking at this correctly."

As simple as that. Once experienced actors understand the idea of scale, they adjust quickly. At first they may be uncomfortable because they have always worked on such a bigger canvas that they feel they are not doing their job.

Now I have the class repeat their scenes on camera, using these new techniques, and then show them the result on the TV monitor. First they see their "stage" version. Inevitably they comment how *big* their acting is, how false it seems. Then they are shown their "film" version. They are flabbergasted by how much better it works.

In one session two men performed the big confrontation scene from *Macbeth* between Malcolm and MacDuff. In this scene the two men are enemies but come to realize they have a bigger common enemy in Macbeth. On stage the scene is huge. The men are angry and verbally jousting. They move around the entire stage and their loud voices echo from the back rafters.

I gave them radical new adjustments to the way they were playing the scene. They were to imagine they were seated at a table in the Four Seasons restaurant in New York, where the phrase "power lunches" was coined. One actor was to imagine he was now the chairman of MCA Music and the other the chairman of Sony Records. They hate each other, but have a common enemy in Napster. They were told to play this scene like the ruthless CEOs that they are. However, in the Four Seasons they have to temper their behavior. Anyone who overheard them wouldn't know they were fighting tooth and nail.

The two actors looked at me like I was crazy. I had the rest of the class sitting across the classroom, fifty feet away, to watch the scene. The scene began with the actors talking quietly and went on for a couple of minutes. Then I stopped them and asked the class what they thought so far. The class was unanimous in saying I had just ruined a perfectly good scene. They couldn't hear the actors; they couldn't see any expression on their face. My Grade: F-.

Now I had the class move very close to the actors. Three feet away. The scene began again. After about thirty seconds the class began to smile, the kind of growing smile when something pleases you. They were now seeing it and hearing it the way a camera would. They could see now that it was possible to shrink giant thoughts and epic gestures to a human scale without losing power. In fact, from a film point of view, the scene gained great power.

After that the class realized the subtlety of film acting was not to be feared but to be welcomed. The actor is able to be very truthful without having to worry about "projecting" it.

David Ward: "I learned a lot watching George Roy Hill during the making of *The Sting* dealing with two stars, Paul Newman and Robert Redford. He had worked brilliantly with these two guys before on *Butch Cassidy and the Sundance Kid*. I went to a rehearsal that involved Newman and Robert Shaw. I felt like Shaw was blowing Newman away. Newman wasn't coming across. Shaw seemed so big and powerful and was stealing the scene. I went to George and I said, 'George, don't you think Paul needs to increase his intensity a little bit?' And he said, 'David, wait until he gets in front of the camera. Paul is a movie actor. When he gets in front of a camera, he knows how to play to the camera. He knows where the camera is. He knows how much to do. And believe me, it will come across.' George was right."

Film Actors Can't Throw Stones

In preparation for the film version of *Whose Life is it Anyway?* I took Richard Dreyfuss to the Williamstown Theatre Festival in Massachusetts where we produced the play as a kind of rehearsal for the movie. Dreyfuss, who had won an Academy Award for *The Goodbye Girl*, had a hard time adjusting to the stage for the opposite reason: He played it at a film level. Too small… for stage.

When the curtain went up on opening night an eager and attentive audience strained to hear and see him. What he was doing on stage was wonderful. The audience just couldn't hear it. Or see it. Though he was center stage the whole play, he might as well have been the wallpaper on the set. Sitting in the back row of the theatre I started to feel ill. Really-bad-reviews flashed before me. Dread danced on my skull. I wanted to to yell "Bigger, Louder. Help!"

At the intermission I ran back-stage. Dreyfuss looked at me, "Going OK, don't you think?" he asked. With all the tact of a two-year old I blurted, "No, you need to play a lot bigger. Right now, microbes are bigger than you." He gave me one of those "I don't know whether to clock you or to kiss you" looks. Long pause. Then he said "OK. I can do it. Watch this." I gave him a hug and assured him he was really good, it was just a matter of scaling it up. **He had been playing it as though he were in a movie. He had to re-gear his instincts.** The second act, Dreyfuss brought the play to life. Spectacularly. The show was a big hit with audience and critics. Nikos Psacharopolous, the theatre's artistic director, extended its run to the end of the summer. "134% Capacity!" he chortled. "The biggest hit in Williamstown since Dicky Cavett did *Charley's Aunt* in a dress! "

Summary

1. If you sense hesitation or concern on the part of an actor, don't wait, go directly to them and talk about it.

2. Make the actor do the hard work of figuring out a problem.

3. If they are stuck get them to answer the following: What does your character *want to do* (to the other person), or what do you *want to get* (from them)?

4. "Pinch-Ouch" is the basis of drama. Act, react.

5. Avoid unactable directions. "Go Faster" is a mechanical direction. "Act 'as-if' you have a plane to catch" is an actable direction.

6. Tricking actors during a scene to get a reaction is OK, just let them know about it afterwards.

7. Working with non-Method trained actors, you depend on them having instant intuitive access to their emotions. Encourage them to be "more human," more "real."

8. Actors who have worked mostly on stage tend to do everything too big. Teach them to let the camera and the microphones do the projecting. The reverse works for film actors going on stage.

Chapter 12

911 Directing

The rehearsal is underway. You and the actors agree on the approach to the scene. The staging is good. The camera setup is unique and the cinematographer has an innovative way to light the scene. But the scene isn't working. For now forget about the writing, set design, cinematography. What's going on here that doesn't work as far as the actors are concerned?

Obvious Possibilities
They are too tense or frightened.
They don't know their lines.
They don't understand the scene.
They understand it but just indicate it.
They don't know what the real emotion called for is like.
They are afraid of the emotion.
They don't want to play it as written.
They don't want to play it at all.
They're no good.
They're really crazed.

The Dog Ate My Dialogue

The entire planet, except for the bozo that doesn't know his lines, will agree that this is unforgivable. Worse than an NBA pro missing free throws. I'm not talking about forgetting lines. Everybody forgets lines. I'm talking about not having learned them in the first place. I'm talking about coming to work unprepared. It's lazy, disrespectful, and inexcusable.

In the very first rehearsal I say to the actors that I only expect three things of them: 1) Be on time; 2) Know your lines; 3) Know your character's history and objectives. We should no more have to tell them this, than we should have to tell them not to eat razors. But… well, you know.

Oliver Stone: "You cannot have an actor coming onto the set to play a character who has to keep a large part of his energy for remembering lines. It's a waste of his energy. He has to have those lines inside himself, and he should be looking for attitude on the set for how to deliver them. In *Wall Street* I had an actor who was blowing lines right and left. And he had a ton of dialogue. I called into question his commitment to the role on the fourth or fifth day, because I was nervous, and I never saw a guy change so fast. He may not understand, but he really concentrated, in a way. He re-concentrated himself."

Before you act out and stuff the lazy actor's head where it belongs, first get the scene in shape to be shot. For the moment just give them that *look* your mother used to give you. Complete the rehearsal with Lazybones carrying his script. Then the rest of the cast can rehearse without waiting for him to catch up. Also, it's a lot easier for anyone to learn the dialogue when they can relate to other actors, the scenery and furniture. They can associate lines of dialogue with a particular part of the set. Mnemonics 101.

Once the crew has the set, get someone else to take the actor aside and run lines with him. Don't *you* do it! If you do, you give them the power to control your attention.

After you have completed the scene, *then* you can drill him a new bodily orifice. Why wait to do this fun part? Because they will always get defensive and uptight, which will blow back onto your scene. There will be no end of lame excuses. If it's a big star and you are not a confrontational person this may be tough, but you have to do it. It's really not as terrifying as it may sound. It can be done without screaming and shouting. It can be done politely and in a way that preserves some of the errant actor's dignity. He knows he's wrong and he's been busted. It's disrespectful to the director and the other actors. It's expensive in terms of time, film wasted, morale. It's unprofessional.

Do not wimp out on this. Once they know they can flake out with impunity, they'll do it daily. Even if it means you get the actor angry, you have to do it.

If it means you get fired, well you just get fired, you don't get killed. It's happened to everyone. It's better than becoming some actor's bitch.

Steven Soderbergh: "What we do is a real luxury, and if you're being well treated and with respect but you still can't bring yourself to be a professional, then I won't hesitate to let you know how unhappy I am. That doesn't play — unprofessional behavior. That could mean not knowing your lines or being late or being inconsiderate of another actor to further whatever agenda you've got. Any of that stuff, I don't see any reason for it. It's not fair."

Older actors do have a legitimate reason for not being able to remember dialogue. If you have an actor who is genuinely having trouble remembering dialogue, the only answer is patience, print, and pick-up. I have had to do scenes where we could only shoot one sentence at a time with an older actor because that is all he could remember. We would cut and print what we had, and pick-up a new take at the next sentence. No matter how frustrating this is for the director and the shooting company, it is just as frustrating and upsetting for the actor. They know they can't remember dialogue like they used to and it drives them nuts. The late Dorothy Malone and Lloyd Nolan were both wonderful actors with great charm and talent. Working with them toward the end of their careers, we had to print and pick-up constantly because they were having trouble remembering lines. The producers were worried the performances wouldn't cut together. To their surprise both actors wound up stealing the scenes they were in. Their inherent talent and charm blasted through all the difficulties. And the producers of course took all the credit.

This Scene Is Stupid

An actor's idea of what the scene is about may be unfocused, unspecific, or flat wrong. Remember to always begin by asking them what their character is doing. Almost invariably they can't verbalize their objective clearly. Their explanation will frequently be general, unspecific, and intellectual. **They need to have something they can act, they can do.** Find active verbs that describe their objectives.

Mel Gibson: "It's really important to just go up and keep talking, and trying to find an access point that they get. Sometimes they don't get it. Sometimes all it takes is you start talking about it, and they say, 'Oh, I know what you mean.' Then they'll take off and do it. It's amazing. Eight times out of ten you don't even have to try though. Most of them will come with their own thing. They may just not understand the way the shots are working, and what they need to do for the maximum punctuation and affect, but I love to include them in that. I say, 'Look, this is what's happening here.' Give them a blueprint for what I'm doing in particular for the effect of what I want so I can see if they can help me with that."

Perhaps they don't understand a line of dialogue and it throws them off. Ask them what they think the line means. Remember to ask them before you tell them. Make the actor actively work to figure something out, not just passively wait for you to tell them the answer. Good directing is Socratic. It's a series of questions from the director that helps actors discover the answers for themselves.

Sydney Pollack: "An actor will say something, and then I will say, 'What does that mean to you?' And they say, 'What do you mean?' I say, 'You just said, "I'm never going to speak to you again." What does that mean to you? Are you sorry you say it? Are you thrilled? Have you wanted to say it for two years? I can't tell from your acting what it means to you. I hear the words, but I don't understand what it means. Because the only thing that I understand is behavior.' Nobody understands words; otherwise, there wouldn't be all these misunderstandings."

If you can't break a scene down into objectives that can be described by strong actable verbs, the scene is very likely no good. It has no place in the movie. You can shoot it anyway but it will be a blight on the final cut.

When a scene is broken down into its elements and strong actable verbs are used, the actor who was confused about the scene will know what to play.

Oliver Stone: "Let's say it doesn't work at all on the set. It's the worst-case scenario. You rehearsed it and it worked and you come to the set and it doesn't work. 'Okay, what are we trying to do here?' Go back to basics. What's the objective? Who did what when? Why are you doing this? Then an improv is probably necessarily, just for the actor to get in touch — without remembering lines — with what he's really doing. That's what the improv is for – not to find something new, but to remember your feelings and to remember what you're doing in the scene. What are the words? Words are nothing unless you have an attitude, a feeling or an action. If the actor is pushing, the director can't just say 'don't push' ...the reason they're pushing, in my opinion, is that they don't have a choice there. They're exerting this energy to try and fill the void of a choice. So it's the director's job to inform that choice for that actor, and give him something to play so he doesn't feel the need to push."

Can't Play It Truthfully

This is rudely called "hamminess" or "faking emotion" or "indicating." The actor can't truthfully reach the emotion called for so he pretends to do it. In other words he is just lying. What is worse, he is so bad that everyone can tell.

But isn't all acting lying? Yes, in one sense it is. In acting there are good liars and there are bad liars, Indicators are bad liars. Indicating rings phony to our finely tuned instincts for judging human behavior. The actor doesn't seem to feel the emotion; he's just imitating it badly. Another word for this is "ham" acting.

Elia Kazan: "That's what hamminess is, pretending there is more in something than there really is. There's no harm in saying, 'This isn't very deep. It has other virtues.'"[1]

Do we care if actors are *really experiencing* the emotion? English actors, for example, in general approach emotions externally, whereas American actors in general come at them internally. Are English actors fake and American actors real? Who cares? If it works it works. "If" is the key word. I have seen actors on stage in the West End of London who have moved me deeply. They do it exactly the same every night without variation. They are just doing it technically. However, if the audience buys into it, isn't it just as valid as the actor who gets there using internal technique like the method? We are not doing psychotherapy, we are acting.

As in the Lawrence Olivier/Dustin Hoffman exchange on the *Marathon Man* set mentioned earlier, it doesn't mean that one actor is right and the other wrong. It means that actors have different methods of doing their job. Whatever works is just fine. Acting is not an art of absolutes. The goal is to communicate truthfully, not have a personal psychodrama.

Sydney Pollack: "If a director cannot tell the difference between a fake bit of behavior and a true bit of behavior, they have no business directing. It's not something that can be learned. You have to know the difference between truth and fiction... That's all you have as a director, the ability to recognize reality in behavior."

Correcting indicating is a very tall order. The fault goes all the way back to casting the actor in the first place. That does you no good when you are standing on the set and have a "ham" on your hands. Now is a terrible time to begin teaching honesty in acting. But of course you have to try. The meter is running.

---

[1] *Kazan*, page 69

You have to take the actor aside and say, "I'm having trouble believing your work. It seems forced and not real. Let's get clear about the scene's objectives first. Then let's improvise the scene so we can get you in touch with the reality of the situation." Be careful with your actor. Taking them aside to talk to them is critical. This is one of the most embarrassing things to say to an actor and you have to be very respectful of their dignity. Otherwise they may get intimidated and shut down creatively.

When improvising the scene, don't allow the actors to use the written dialogue or they'll never make any progress toward honesty. They have to make up the scene in their own words.

What is the Real Emotion?

The first actor I was lucky enough to direct was Hal Holbrook, the brilliant interpreter of Mark Twain. His attention to detail, his incredible comic timing, and his ability to layer three-four characters at a time on top of one another is extraordinary. For example, at one point in his classic one-man show *Mark Twain Tonight*, Holbrook simultaneously plays: 1) Mark Twain as a seventy-year-old man; 2) Mark Twain playing Huck Finn, a sixteen-year-old boy; 3) Huck Finn playing Jim, a twenty-five-year-old escaped slave; and 4) Jim playing his forty-year-old slave owner. Each character is distinct and built on the one that came before it.

On the set of *The Senator*, the Emmy-winning series for which he won Best Actor, Holbrook was reading a script for another movie he had been offered. Not as the hero however, but as a murderer. Holbrook said he was wrestling with whether to do it or not. He didn't think he could play a murderer because he didn't understand the kind of emotions that would lead a person to murder someone else.

In his seminal book, *An Actor Prepares*, Stanislavsky says that there will be many situations where actors won't actually have lived the emotion called for in the scene. If our character is a heroin addict, do we have to shoot up to know what it feels like? His answer is no. We don't need to take heroin to experience craving. We don't have to become the Sultan of Brunei in order to feel what power is like. We don't have to murder someone to know that feeling. What we can do is to find something that we have actually experienced that is analogous to the situation in the script. We search in our memory for something that is as close as possible to what is in the script.

A fairly peaceful person, for example, could think of times that they were so angry they could kill without regret. For example, a fly is buzzing in the bedroom at night. It makes us nuts. We get a newspaper, and have at the fly. When the deed is done we go back to sleep without a second thought. The only guilt we feel is having made a stain on the wall. If that fly had been a person we would be a true sociopath. This is another use of the "as-if" technique, combined with emotional memories from our past.

After I told Holbrook this concept he immediately saw how he could use the "as-if" approach to understand the urge to kill. And he made that a part of the character that he would eventually play (Mathew Sand in *Travis Logan, D.A.*).

Once actors have found an appropriate "as if," they have an idea what that emotion feels like. You as the director are the judge of its truthfulness. All this being said, it's a bad idea to concentrate on the emotion itself when acting the scene. This "as-if" technique is only good for an insight into what the emotion is like. The actor has to do this before shooting, not when shooting. When performing the scene, the actor has to forget the preparation and just play the action, the behavior. The emotion will come by itself.

Actors who are used to doing this kind of "as-if" work find it such a useful tool that they will store away feelings that are happening to them in their current daily life. Lou Antonio, a wonderful actor/director who acted for Kazan in *America, America*, said that he could be arguing with his wife and feeling frustration and rage. Then some objective calm part of him would say. "This is really cool, I have to remember how this feels. I can use it in a scene some time."

Sydney Pollack: "You're always working in metaphors anyway. These are always 'as-ifs.' That, by the way, is the other tool I use with actors all the time. It's 'as-if,' and try to find a parallel situation, which clarifies. It's 'as-if' your whole body was burning and you couldn't touch it and you're trying to find one spot on your body that doesn't hurt. Now play the scene. Because you lead a person to behavior that way. And then what happens is, whether it's right or wrong, they will almost always find the text a hundred times easier."

This technique is so easy and so useful that we as directors get caught up in it and start thinking of our own "as-ifs" and wanting to impose them on the actor. This is a waste of time. Always have the actor come up with his own "as-if."

John Frankenheimer: "The other mistake that you can make as a director is to try and impose your own sense memory on an actor. Everybody's sense memory is different. What might make me cry would be totally different than what might make Angela Lansbury cry. She's not going to react to me telling her this tragic story of whatever happened to me in my life that I can recall. It means nothing. And you never say that you want them to cry. What you want to be able to do is to have them tap into something of their own that will achieve the result."

Fear of Failure

I'm standing on the Santa Monica pier with Carrie Snodgrass and Michael Brandon. Snodgrass had been nominated for an Academy Award for *Diary of a Mad Housewife*. She had just won two Golden Globes for the same film. This film, *The Impatient Heart*, was my first TV movie and I was greener than green. We are rehearsing a scene where Michael Brandon's character, Frank, tells Carrie Snodgrass' character, Gracie, he is quitting the fish store where he works. He tells her he's going off around the world... by himself. Gracie was hoping Frank would take her with him and can barely cover her disappointment. In rehearsal on the set, both actors hit a roadblock and were fighting the emotional core of the scene.

Suddenly the scene that they had loved in early rehearsal, a scene brilliantly written by Alvin Sargent, became in their eyes a terrible scene that needed a total rewrite. They would try to do the scene and then stop in the middle saying something like, "This is terrible, and it doesn't work." The whole shoot came to a complete halt. It was getting dark, we were losing the light, and nothing was happening. All my efforts to help got us nowhere. Even Bill Sackheim, our producer, who was so persuasive he could convert the Taliban to Judaism, couldn't break the logjam. One hour passed, two hours. I felt increasingly inadequate and panicked as the day faded away. Soon Jack Marquette, the cinematographer, held up his light meter and shook his head. The light was gone. Now we are a full half-day behind and I am in big trouble. People have gotten fired over less. I don't sleep well. Carrie and Michael call me at 2 a.m. worrying about the scene but getting nowhere.

The next morning we try again. Surprisingly, the scene goes like clockwork. It is very full emotionally and quite good.

Why would it work one day but not the day before? What had changed? I didn't get any better as a director. I certainly got a lot older. What I did learn, and have seen many times since, is that many highly charged emotional scenes frighten conscientious actors who want to be truthful. If they feel they are faking it, they balk and shy away from it like a horse at a high hedge jump. In this case Carrie Snodgrass and Michael Brandon needed to walk away from the scene and sleep on it overnight before they had unconsciously internalized the emotions and reached a comfort zone. They could also have found many other ways to stall shooting the scene. Some of the most popular choices are: hiding in the trailer and not coming out. Complaining that the wardrobe doesn't fit or isn't right. Or the makeup is wrong, the hair is wrong. Natalie Wood stopped a film shoot of *This Property Is Condemned* for hours while drivers were dispatched to get Jungle Gardenia perfume that she "had to have" to get the right mood. Patience is required in huge quantities.

A similar thing occurred on *Saturday Night Fever* in a scene between Travolta and Karen Lynn Gorney when John discovers that she has a boyfriend in Manhattan. As they drive back to Brooklyn they argue. We spent the afternoon driving in a car, shooting their argument. Though they both gamely struggled through the scene, nobody was happy with it. At 6:30 the next morning I went to the lab to look at the film. The performances were terrible. But I knew it was not the actors' fault. I also knew we had to re-do it. Because I didn't have time to go out in the car again I re-staged the scene on a sidewalk later that morning and we shot it again... in one hour. Nothing was changed, except the staging was much simpler. Yet there was a night and day difference. One was truthful, one was fake.

The point is that sometimes giving the scene a rest and moving on to shoot something else is the wisest thing to do. If you whip it till it bleeds, the exhaustion and desperation show through. Also, very interestingly, the second time around, it only takes a fraction of the time it took originally.

They Are Not There

Dennis Haysbert: "We all know that some actors tend to relax too much when the camera is not on them. And they don't give the on-camera actor as much as they need."

When an actor knows they are going to be on-camera, they focus their attention to do the best they can. But when the camera turns around to shoot the other character they are off-camera, and they will forget everything they have been saying for the last two hours.

The actor is so relieved to have gotten through their close-up that they will totally relax and lose their concentration. Next thing that happens, they totally screw up the other actor unintentionally.

Even worse is the actor who goes AWOL and won't do his off-camera dialogue for the other actor who now has to act with the script supervisor. What's wrong with that? Acting with script supervisors is like trying to dance with a crash dummy. It completely throws the actor off and makes them look bad in the scene. Script supervisors are not actors; it's not their job.

The AWOL actor is rude and unprofessional. The "I'm too tired" excuse is pretty lame. Do they think that nobody else is tired, just them? Of course not, they are just selfish recti. The damage done is twofold. One actor has to try to act in a vacuum. Secondly, the scene loses a lot because one side of the conversation is not as good as the other side.

In an interview for *Hollywood Life* in 2005, Jack Nicholson told Craig Modderno about his commitment to doing the off-camera dialogue with his fellow actors.

Jack Nicholson: "I love acting. I really do. I look at acting as a team effort where everyone's doing his or her best to try to make the team win. I don't want to sit in my trailer. I'm there to work and have fun. It's good to disarm people by coming on the set with a non-star, let's-have-fun attitude."

Kurtwood Smith: "The star of the movie, Tom Berenger, came in on his day off to do the other side of a phone conversation for me. Those are the kinds of people you look up to, not people who are holed up in their trailer."

A more aggressive form of this selfish behavior is the actor who actually does the off-camera lines, and tries to mess up the on-camera actor by changing line-readings, acting silly, giving no emotion. This is not the same behavior that actors like Robert De Niro or Jack Nicholson do. They are genuinely trying to keep the scene fresh and do more than just parrot back lines.

Penelope Ann Miller: "A lot of times I ask other actors I am in a scene with, 'Would you mind going really big, even though you're not going to do it in your take? Just so it really scares me. Really scream at me or swear at me or really do something that's going to throw me off, so that I get a real reaction that's not naturally and not rehearsed or stale.' I learned that from De Niro, because he does that a lot."

I'm Not Saying This

I was very fortunate to direct Lane Slate's clever comedy, *Isn't it Shocking?*, with Alan Alda, Louise Lasser, Ruth Gordon, Edmond O'Brien, Lloyd Nolan, and Will Geer. With actors like these, a director's work is easy. One day Ruth Gordon, seventy-five years old and very short, comes up to me and stabs at the script with her finger. "I don't like this line." She stares at me and waits for my answer. I knew that Ruth Gordon was not only one of the treasures of the American theatre as an actress; she was also a talented playwright. She and her husband, Garson Kanin, wrote *Solid Gold Cadillac*, a long-running Broadway hit. Much of the play's success was due to the very witty dialogue Gordon and Kanin had written. If I played this right I could get Ruth Gordon to write a clever line for me. "Well, Ruth," I said, "what would you rather say instead?" She stopped and fixed me with a crooked little grin, then put her finger in my face and waggled it about. "Oh no", she said. "I get paid for that."

Since I wasn't about to rewrite Lane Slate's perfectly good dialogue, she was a pro and said the lines as written. It was important for her to express herself but she drew the line at writing for free. The fact that I listened to her seemed to matter more than getting her own way.

James Woods: "I remember I had an actor say to me, 'I don't like this line in the scene.' I said, 'Well, let me tell you something. I've been acting all my life, and here's something I know because I've been hearing it for thirty years. The one line every actor doesn't want to say in every scene is invariably the key to the scene. So here's the answer I give when I'm directing: a) I'm not cutting it, and b) find a way to make it work and make it mean something.' Now, that's sometimes a little bit of a horseshit answer. But it's amazing what happens when they're busy trying to make this line work. By the way, they may be right that it doesn't actually work. But in the process of trying to make it work, all sorts of miraculous other great things happen, and often times they make it work."

When an actor springs "I don't like this line" on you it's a great time to call for backup. If you are really lucky you will either have the writer close at hand on the set or be the writer yourself. This is a fantastic way to cut through the crap. If the cast respects the writer's talent, so much the better. There is strength in numbers when the writer is present. On TV episodes the writer is in his office frantically writing the next show. But he'll always take your 911 calls. The two of you can huddle with the actor and solve the problem.

Judge Reinhold: "I had an actor friend who was working for David Kelly. He went into his office and said, 'My character wouldn't do this.' David Kelly said, 'Yes, she would. I know it for a fact because I wrote it.' That's the challenge. You have to make it work. I feel like I owe the writer and director. If I have apprehensions, I really owe them a chance to try to make it work. I do."

Kurtwood Smith: "Some actors start thinking, 'My character wouldn't say this or that.' This makes no sense. They didn't invent their character. They don't write their characters' lines. Instead of rewriting it as something that feels good for me, I should look at the scene and try to figure out what is it that I'm not seeing. How can I make this something that my character would say as opposed to just throwing it out the window to begin with?"

Many directors stupidly fear the writer will interfere if they're allowed on the set. The Directors Guild and the Writers Guild have been at each other's throats over this for years. I'm not getting in the middle of this jihad. Writers have been present on my sets for over thirty years whenever they wanted and very few problems have ever arisen. They are almost always collaborative colleagues who want to make the best movie.

But there is one rule to establish right at the beginning with the writer: **Only the director can be permitted to talk to the actors about their acting.** Acting is hard enough without getting mixed signals from different people. On one of my films the actors started playing scenes in very strange ways. When I asked them what they were playing, they said the writer had told them this is how they should do it.

The writer, who was just trying to help, told me what he said to the actors. I knew what he wanted to achieve. I also knew that the specific words he used were intellectual and un-actable. As the actors had struggled to understand what he wanted, they totally misinterpreted what he intended. I took the writer aside and told him that I would be happy to try anything he wanted with the actors, but it was important that it come from me. Not because I wanted to be the big mucky-muck, but because I can find a way to word what he wants with active, playable directions. Remember *Project Greenlight*, where two directors give seemingly contradictory directions to the same actors at the same time. The look on those actors' faces says it all. "What do I do? Whose direction am I supposed to follow?"

Unfortunately, any director that directs a sitcom has to face interference from writer-producers every hour of every day. Unlike in a movie where the director is at the top of the food chain, the writer/producers are the show-runners who, in their eagerness to succeed, micro-manage every detail of their show. The director is a sophisticated traffic cop with little hope of working with the cast one on one. The writers constantly talk to the actors and give them directions. When the shows are big hits and run for years one feels the show-runners are doing something right. That doesn't make it easy for the director who has to check his ego at the door.

Robert Butler: "My ego was such that I didn't appreciate the collective direction that goes on in those shows. I was rehearsing *The Dick Van Dyke Show* in particular, I remember, I would just begin to glimpse that the rhythm was goofy, and if we took more time here… and I would just be getting to that point, and four writers and the producer would all come up. Those guys knew about a thousand times more jokes than I'll ever know in my life. But those people, watching that rehearsal, would immediately step in and start engineering the fix, which was partially the material, but partially the direction of it. That's the way those shows worked. I didn't really like it. You have to have a real patient temperament, because it's direction by committee. They rewrite them, restage them, rethink them, re-conceptualize them all of the time. It goes on during the whole week."

I worked with Steve Tesich, the writer of *Breaking Away*, on an epic cycling film, *American Flyers*. Steve himself was a great cyclist who could out-ride all of us weakling actors and director. He was on the set every day all day. When actors had concerns he was right there to help. Often after he had explained a scene to an actor their concerns would melt away. Never mind that I had just finished telling them the same thing before Steve arrived. The fact that he was the creator, the writer of this film, was a very powerful way to calm their concerns. And when changes had to be made, he could do it right there.

When an actor says, "My character would never do this," he really means, "I don't want to do this!" The writer has carefully thought out the story and the actions of the characters. If the writer says that's the way the character is, then that's the way the character is. The actor's job is to find a way to interpret the character, not re-write it. People do all kinds of contradictory things in their lives. The sweet suburban mom drowns her children. The saintly priest…. Whoops, don't go there.

Jeremy Kagan: "Sally Field, speaking at the Sundance Lab to an acting troupe, talked of the actor having a responsibility to do the work, not to negate, not to object, to do the work. If the director asks you to do something that you respond to negatively, your job is to find a way to get past that response. That's what the job is."

Drama depends on the contradictory nature of characters. When the contradictions are smoothed out, the character is made blander. Why are most movies so predictable? Why are most TV series so dull? Because the characters have been homogenized into stereotypes: the hero, the villain, and the heroine. Even a ten-year-old can predict the end of the story.

I'm Not Doing This

Worst-case scenario. The actor *flat refuses* to do what you need to do. All your best people skills have been for naught. Now you have to make a judgment call. Get the AD to help you think of other things to shoot. Let the producer know there's a problem. Don't keep it a secret. But whatever you do, never let the actor see you sweat. Shoot something, *anything*, and do it as though the loss of the scene today is nothing. Don't give the actor the power. You are still in charge, at least until the actor's agent and manager try to get you fired.

Steven Soderbergh: "It's hard because sometimes the dynamic of the relationship makes it difficult for them to understand why you're making a certain request. Your job is to have the whole movie in your head. That's not their job. Their job is very, very specific and by design pretty myopic. And after you've exhausted all of the sort of rational explanations, I guess at the end of the day it really comes down to whether they trust you or not. That's a pretty mysterious issue, this issue of trust. It's the most important thing that you can have with an actor or your crew or the studio or whatever."

In an absolute worst-case situation you may ask yourself: Can I shoot this scene without photographing this troublemaker and get his coverage later? As I was having my set-to with Richard Pryor, even though I was wrong, I was thinking how we could shoot the rest of the movie without him if he actually went home. It's been done plenty of times before when an actor can't or won't be present. We only have to remember a few of the truly tragic accidents that happened during shooting. Brandon Lee on *The Crow*, Natalie Wood on *Brainstorm*. Even Ed Wood's *Plan 9 From Outer Space* continued shooting after the death of Bela Lugosi; Wood's dentist stood in for Lugosi. The incidents were tragic but even under those circumstances the films got made.

When the actor holds the script in your face and says, "This dialogue is crap," or "My character would never do that," or "This action isn't believable," all your antennae have to be up and functioning. You may have discussed and rehearsed the scene carefully before shooting and heard nary a peep from the actor. (Some of them are perverse: "I just happened to discover this last night going over the script.") Don't even bother asking, "Why didn't you call me last night so we could talk about this off the set?"

The first day of directing on any show is like being set upon by rabid vampires determined to suck you dry. The whole cast and crew descend as you walk on the set. Be ready for a panoply of weird behavior: nausea, cold sores, allergic reactions to makeup or bad hair days... and that's just from the crew. The actors have wardrobe catastrophes, hissy-fits, temper tantrums, acting out, and pissing contests. Though 99% of this can be attributed to first-day nerves, all of it becomes your problem.

Oliver Stone: "'I won't take my clothes off.' 'Yeah, well you bloody well read the script and you saw the contract.' With the script, you know, there's no surprises here today. On *Alexander*, Angelina Jolie and I had a misunderstanding on the first day. Not about nudity. We were head-butting right away. She's a strong lady. She said, 'I can't say that.' It was a line about 'Am I so old?' to her son. 'Am I so old?' I said, 'What do you mean you can't say it? It was in the script.' And she said, 'Yeah, but we rehearsed it and we agreed to cut it.' I said, 'I don't remember that.' Maybe she's right. But I said, 'Okay, we'll do it your way.' And right away there was no fight. She did it her way twice or three times and I let her hang in there. And she may have felt that there was something in the air that was just not quite coming together. Certainly she saw my face between takes, which was not disapproving, but just cold and quiet and neutral and dealing with the other actors... And then out of the blue she just said, 'Let's do it your way.' And she did it. And from then on we had a great relationship. Because I think that she understood, like any actor would understand, if the director doesn't trust you, you've lost an ally for the whole movie. And it's going to be a struggle. If an actor is going to do that, then I have to put up with it, but the actor is also going to suffer."

Even level-headed actors are nervous stepping into a new character with a new director. They are grappling with any number of new things: The character, their dialogue, their wardrobe and their makeup, other actors. This is why rehearsal time and bonding time are so critical. Even the most professional actors, however, may behave peculiarly on the first day of a film.

When an actor comes at you with any complaint, question, or request, don't let him put you on the defensive. Put him on the defensive, never with sarcasm, never belittling their concern. Make them do some Napoleonic staff work and answer their own questions. Psychiatrists have been pulling this dodge for decades. Answer a question with a question.

No matter what the actor asks, answer back "What do *you* think (*you should do... your character wants...* and so on)?" If they reply, "I don't know," ask, "Well, if you *did* know, what would you think?" Believe it or not, this works. It forces them to articulate their problem.

Look at what the script says the character does now and in the past. What he has done and what he does now are **actions**, not feelings. Actions lead to feelings. It's crucial that a director must know the history of a character's actions inside and out to be able to defend them. That is what gives you the ammunition to have these difficult conversations.

Talented actors are very smart. It's not easy to manipulate them with double-talk. Our thinking has to be based on the **actions** of the characters in order to defend what the writer has written. Not their **feelings**, because the feelings come out of the actions.

They're Not Very Good

Whose fault is this? Did the producer or the studio or the network force the actor on you? Did you screw up on your own? You're not the first or the last. One thing is for sure; they didn't just show up on the set. No matter, the actor is there, you are there, and the picture is shooting, the meter is running.

Forget sticking your thumb in your mouth and calling for Mommy. What are you going to do? Now. Right now.

What are the choices? Not a lot. 1) You can fire the actor right then and hold up the shooting of the scene till you find somebody better. 2) You can write them out of the scene. 3) You can keep shooting till you've exhausted whatever they are capable of and wrung as much out of them as you can. 4) You can shoot plenty of coverage on the other actors in the scene so you can cut around the bad one.

JB: "What do you do when you are against the clock and some guy is terrible?"

Mel Gibson: "I don't know. You just keep going. You make sure that you've got plenty of coverage. Sometimes you can make really good things happen from someone who didn't seem like they would work at all. The scissors can do amazing things for performances, as you know. I'm sure you had to do it with me on *Bird on a Wire*."

In my Directing Fundamentals Class at Chapman University, a beginning director brought in a scene from Spike Lee's movie *Do the Right Thing*. A young man delivers a pizza on a hot summer night to his old girlfriend who ordered it in order to get him up to her apartment. He figures he can grab a quick bit of sex. But she just wants some company; it's too hot and sticky for sex.

The actors were beginners and the director has cast the woman's real-life boyfriend to play her boyfriend in the scene. Because there is very intimate behavior between the two, he thought they would be more comfortable together than strangers would be. The trouble was that the man had barely acted before.

When the scene started she got him into the apartment and he just stood there holding his pizza, when he should have been trying to hold something else. He needed to play a very simple objective of crudely seducing her. But he wasn't playing anything.

I had the director tell him to try to put his arms around her, to kiss her, to fondle her. Her goal was to keep him away from any physical contact because it's too hot to mess around. She was doing her job but because he was so inexperienced and so terrified, he couldn't respond at all. He was worse than wooden. Spike Lee wrote a beautiful scene but it was totally destroyed because one actor could not live in the moment for even a nano-second. The director's fatal mistake was casting a non-actor without sufficient time (years probably) to work with him. The lesson is that we cannot create pearls from dirt. We may know all the fancy directing techniques, but they only work on a human being who is responsive, who is relaxed, and who has their emotions on the surface. In this case the only constructive thing to have done was to re-cast the boyfriend. Never forget: 80% of directing is casting good actors in the first place.

What If They're Really Crazed?

Richard Donner: "There's an actor — I won't name him, he's a wonderful actor. He was going through a divorce and I didn't know it. We got into it on a set. We rehearsed a scene the night before and left the camera and the lights set up and came back in the morning. I changed a camera angle that morning because I saw something different. He came in, looked at the new set-up and he went at me in front of the crew, screaming, 'How can you do this? How can you change this after we rehearsed it last night?' He started coming at me. And I figured, 'If he's going to hit me, I'm going to hit him back.' The crew grabbed him and separated us and he stormed off and went to his dressing room. So I left them to finish up and I went down there and knocked on his door. He said, 'Stay out of here.' I said, 'No, I'm coming in.' He said, 'Stay out of here.' I said, 'Look, I've got to work with you for another six weeks or something. I'm not going to leave this be. I'm coming in.' He said, 'If you come in, I'm going to pop you.' I said, 'Then I'm coming in.' and I came in and he said, 'Damnit, I told you not to come in.' I said, 'I'm here. We've got to work together or we're going to destroy the picture and each other.' I said, 'What's the problem, man? Are you unhappy with what I did?' He said, 'No, it's got nothing to do with you. I'm being divorced.' I said, 'Oh, I'm sorry.' He said 'I was on the phone all night and I was drinking and I got pissed off and I'm angry at the world.' I said, 'Hey, I'm not a divorce counselor. That's your life and I'm sorry. Why don't we work something out between us, so when you come in the morning, if you're feeling terrible, tell me. Give me a hand signal or something and I'll shoot long shots. And if you're feeling really bad, I'll find something else to shoot. If it's medium-bad, I'll do a medium shot and if you're in good shape, I'll do the close-ups.' And he started to laugh. And he said, 'Yeah, sure, that will work.' So, that's the way we did it. I'd go to his dressing room and have a cup of coffee and see how he was. 'Oh yeah, I'm okay,' or 'Oh man, I'm a mess today.' I'd say, 'Okay, I've got it.'"

Playing the Lottery

How many takes are enough? One, two, twenty, fifty. How many do you have time for? Is what you have good enough? What if one actor gets it right in one take and the other needs seven? Are you wasting time and film doing more takes and it's not going to get any better? If you only have one take, what if the lab screws up? What if you get it in plenty of time but it's not very good? So many questions, so few answers.

Oliver Stone: "Trying to get both actors to be good on the same take is tricky. But I find that's not an issue. Intensity is better on one or two or three takes. And I think actors... again, I trust them. They get ready. They know. They know that this matters, and they don't want to screw around either. Like you said, Russell Crowe. They just want to get it. They want to nail it. That's what makes them feel good. I've never seen anybody more nervous than Michael Caine or Anthony Hopkins before. Or Christopher Plummer."

Leonard Goldberg, the prolific producer of *Charlie's Angels, Double Indemnity, Sleeping with the Enemy,* and *WarGames,* called one day for a bit of advice. He had some dailies from a film he was producing and didn't know what to do with them. Each scene had many takes, too many takes. One particular shot was of two people walking up the stairs. No dialogue. Just walking up the stairs. There were nine takes of this one action. Nine. Identical. Clones. Dolly, the sheep. And they were boring too.

Goldberg asked, "Do you know what's wrong? I need to tell the director something, but what?" If all the takes were alike, the director either didn't know what he or she wanted, or the actors were incompetent or willfully ignoring directions. Since the actors were clearly talented it seemed that the first choice was the problem. The director was unsure and took a "play the lottery" approach to directing: Just keep shooting takes till you get a winner or run out of time. Some directors were famous for shooting this way. George Stevens, the director of *Giant* and *The Greatest Story Ever Told*, and William Wyler, who directed *Ben Hur*, were Academy Award winners who shot till they dropped. Was this director adopting their style? Possibly. But certainly not a good idea on a limited budget and certainly not a good way to inspire an actor's confidence in the director. **Why keep doing takes if you don't know what you want to be different?** It's okay to make wrong choices in an effort to find the right one, but to keep on doing the same thing over and over is pig-headed.

The solution to this problem was relatively simple: the actors needed to *run* up the stairs. Why? Because the story demanded it. The story says there is something upstairs they are both eager to see. Therefore, they hurry up the stairs. Solutions usually come from looking at the story closely for what it tells you. That's what has to happen in every shot, every take. Every single one is there for a specific purpose, otherwise it won't work! If a director hasn't thought the story through carefully he'll keep playing the lottery.

When a shot or a scene's not working, stop and debug it. If the director is out of ideas: huddle with the actors. **Go back to the two turnkey questions: 1) What is the story of the scene? 2) How does each character feel about it?** The answers to these questions give birth to ideas that can bring the scene alive. One thing is sure: doing the scene over and over wastes film, wastes energy, wastes money, wastes morale.

Mel Gibson: "I remember there was a scene, and I won't even tell you what movie, but we did forty takes, and it wasn't very good. I needed the actor to get to a certain place with it, and it just wasn't happening. It wasn't because he wasn't good. It was my fault because I wasn't communicating it in the right way. He didn't quite understand where he needed to go. It took me forty takes before I said the thing that made him click. I'd keep talking to him and wonder what I needed to say. It's easy to give somebody a line reading, but you don't want to do that. You want them to get there themselves. I swear it was like forty takes. We did the wide shots and things like that. I saw he wasn't getting it through all of that, and then the mid-shots. 'Okay, let's move into the close-ups. We'll have to get it here.' He was starting to get really edgy and worried, We kept going outside, and finally I said something in a conversation, and I referred to a play that we'd both seen, and that he'd read. I said, 'Remember that scene in that play with that character?' I related it to what he was doing in the scene. He immediately went, 'Oh,' and he immediately went in and did it, beautifully."

What happens when you know what you want and have to keep pushing the scene towards success? I was asked to help out on a film years ago where the director had been replaced. The first day I had to re-shoot a scene that had been shot earlier. The two young stars of the movie were nearly paralyzed with fear. The director had been replaced, were they next? Their scene needed to be light, charming, and playful. It should have been about two kids shyly flirting and getting to know one another. What we had now was two actors channeling department store dummies. The cameras rolled. The first take was as animated as Mount Rushmore. Actors, like athletes, need to warm up, to relax. So we did a couple more takes and a couple more, and a couple more. There was no relaxing going on. These actors were in the deep freeze. I got really nervous. This scene was the first thing the studio would see the next day and it better be good. My stomach started to churn.

Having had the benefit of seeing how the scene went off the tracks the first time, it was clear that it was being played too seriously. The characters needed to have fun. We already know it's no good to say, "Come on, kids, have fun with it." **A specific action or task** was needed that was organic to the scene.

Since the scene was in the boy's bedroom we scattered some of his dirty underwear around the room, on the lampshade and at the foot of the bed. We messed up the bed, and trashed the room. When the two actors came in the room he would realize what a pigsty it was and be embarrassed. He was excited to have this girl with him and wanted her to like him. Now he could react to this new situation and try to hide his dirty underwear, straighten the messy bed and kick the trash out of sight. All the while trying to act cool. The girl now can be amused by his antics and at the same time be uncomfortable alone in a strange boy's bedroom. Her job was to calm herself by pretending to ignore him and checking out the posters on the wall, the books in the bookcase.

Now the scene started to loosen up. But they were still stiff. So now I have to become Bozo the clown, never a problem for me. I tell stupid jokes, stick carrots in my nose, tickle them, anything to get a reaction. At one point to release the tension I took both of them by the hand outside the stage and challenged them to a race around the stage. The winner would get $10; the loser would have to sing a song for the crew that the winner would pick. We would run into the stage and roll the cameras. Of course I lost, I'm not stupid. They made me sing "The Happy Wanderer," one of the dumbest songs ever written.

The takes quickly got better and better. By take 14 the scene was alive and charming. Would the studio buy it?

The next day the studio executives came to the stage after they saw dailies of the first day. Watching this grim group come on the stage was like watching a jury come back from deliberations. God forbid they should smile, people might want more money. They stopped the shooting and said they had an announcement. There was a strict rule against alcohol on the lot but they were so happy with the film they were passing out champagne to celebrate. We drank a quick toast and went back to work charged up.

Of course the rest of the day was a disaster because we were too wasted to work. And the next day the movie was cancelled and we were all fired.

Just kidding.

Scene Stealers & Bad Boys

Scene stealing is an infamous tradition among actors. An actor makes sure that the focus of the scene goes to him even though he might be in the background. Obviously the move is a ploy for attention.

In director Robert Altman's film *McCabe and Mrs. Miller*, Warren Beatty kept leaning against newcomer William DeVane in a bar scene, causing the audience to shift their eyes toward Beatty's drunken character. After a while, Altman had enough and told DeVane not to hold Beatty up. Next take, Beatty leaned against DeVane, who backed away, letting Beatty fall on the bar. According to Altman, Beatty ceased trusting him and has never said a kind word about the film to anyone.

How to deal with scene-stealers is always a problem. If they are in secondary roles it's fairly easy to be blunt with them and tell them to stop what they are doing that distracts from the main focus of the scene. If their behavior is something that adds color to the scene and supports the scene then it should always be welcome. But when it steals focus and seems to be done for its own sake, then it has to be eliminated.

Jenna Elfman: "I've never had anyone try to steal a scene from me. Frankly, I've never thought about it before. If I'm going to be acting with someone, I want them to be the best they can be and I'll be doing the best I can and we'll both look good."

Usually whatever the stealer does is just distracting. English actors treat it as a game and love to steal scenes. Perhaps it comes from performing in theatre where after many performances even the most dedicated actor can get bored and start to think of mischievous ways to amuse himself during the play. If there's a good side to scene stealing, it keeps the other actors on their toes. In *Dracula*, Donald Pleasance was playing the doctor of an insane asylum. W.D. Richter wrote the role with tongue firmly set in cheek. Pleasance saw his chance and came to me seemingly in total innocence, and asked if he could use a small bag of hard candies as a prop.

When Pleasance came on the set he had his little bag of candies with him and ate them during the scene. But not at random. He would wait to the end of his line and then pop one noisily into his mouth. He knew the editor wouldn't cut away from him until he had put the candy in his mouth… thus giving him more screen time.

Sometimes he would bedevil the other actors by offering them candy while they were speaking. In one "tearful goodbye" scene, Pleasance kept thrusting the bag into Laurence Olivier's face. Olivier, who had a Ph.D. in scene stealing himself, kept pushing the bag off camera.

James Woods inherited the scene-stealing mantle from them. He is so good at it that other actors take out theft insurance.

James Woods: "If they do that to me, it's so tiresome and boring that I, with all due modesty, have the skills to take their kneecaps off after about four words. They try to steal a scene, I go, 'Oh, we're going to go that route. Great.' We can go the easy way or the hard way. And I love when they elect to go the hard way because I'm naturally gifted for warfare. I'd rather cooperate, but if you want to compete, look out. Because you're bringing a knife to a gunfight."

Mel Gibson: "Jimmy Woods? He's brutal. If you want to mess with that guy he'll walk all over you. He can. He's a brilliant actor. He can upstage the hell out of you if he wanted to."

In *The Hard Way*, James Woods, playing a cop, has been cornered by the killer, Stephen Lang, high above Times Square on an elaborate 3D billboard for a movie starring Michael J. Fox's character.

We have lined up a shot over Woods' shoulder onto Stephen Lang. Suddenly the assistant cameraman, Vinnie, a grizzled New York guy, turns to me with a distressed look on his face. "Boss," he says, "Mr. Woods wants me to put the focus on him." I look over at the two actors and see that Jimmy has managed to turn his head totally around on his body just like Linda Blair in *The Exorcist*. Now he is telling Vinnie to put the focus on him. The wonderful thing about Jimmy Woods is that he is not mean-spirited; he is like a little kid who loves to be a brat occasionally. If you call

him on it he never gets defensive, but smiles as if to say "you caught me."

This behavior can be funny but can also easily ruin a scene. On the one hand it's good to encourage the cast to be inventive; on the other hand when the inventiveness reaches a point that it distracts, then it has to be curtailed. It can be stopped easily by laughing out loud and busting the actor in front of everyone. Treat it as a joke. Once the actor's caught red-handed, he'll back off.

If it is the star who is stealing the scene, things are a bit trickier. Many stars are not used to being told "No." They get defensive, they lash out, and they get hostile. But in any case the first line of defense is to talk about how their behavior is hurting the scene. By itself it may be a good idea, but in context it doesn't work. An example could be a woman telling a really sad story and the scene-stealer deciding to blow his nose really loudly.

Years ago, a television series called *The Name of the Game* ran on NBC for several seasons. Tony Franciosa was one of the stars. At the time cigarette advertising was just coming under fire. Actors could still smoke on camera, but the cigarettes would have to come from a fictitious-looking pack. The prop man would take the actor's favorite cigarettes and put them in a phony pack ("Kofin Nayl" was a favorite). Franciosa would somehow forget to use the dummy pack and would pull out a real pack of Marlboros to the total dismay of the prop man. The executives at Universal first blamed the hapless prop man, then went to Franciosa and politely asked him *again* to use the dummy packs. Franciosa, however, continued to misbehave and there was little anyone could do.

Ranald McDougall, the executive producer and a soft-spoken professorial man, announced he would have a go at this problem. The other execs snorted at his naiveté. When he approached Franciosa and told him why he was there, Tony got angry and said he was sick of this cigarette baloney and had no intention of changing. McDougall smiled, "I agree, you can forget about it, it's not a problem any more." Franciosa was taken aback. "You can show the pack or not, it's OK," McDougall said as he started to leave. Then he turned at the door like Lt. Columbo and said, "Oh, just one thing. Whenever you show a real pack we'll have to cut away from you."

After that day the real packs were never again seen on-camera.

Meltdown in Malibu

Shrinkers have told us for years that speaking in front of people is one of the most traumatic events in many people's lives. To get over this terrifying experience is something that can take years. We see actors on TV effortlessly doing their work; newscasters blithely working through the Evening News; even evangelists and sportscasters making the whole thing look easy. But we don't believe in ourselves enough to be able to carry it off ourselves. We don't like the way we look, or our voice, we think what we have to say is stupid or we won't be able to remember it.

Actors and others who want to be in the public eye often have to resort to therapy, even hypnotism, to conquer this fear. Even after years of experience, actors who have never been afraid can be seized with stage fright. When I was very young my mother started me acting in local theatre in Birmingham, Alabama. After the usual stint of Christmas pageants and school plays, when I was ten years old I got my first paying job, as a girl. But hey, it paid $10 a performance. A year's allowance for me. I put on the wig, pulled on the dress, and thus transvestited stepped to the apron of the stage of *Dirty Work at the Crossroads* to launch into singing a heartfelt rendition of "Father, Dear Father, Come Home to Me Now." What do you want from me? I was ten years old.

Now jump ahead twenty years and I had become terrified appearing before people. No easy sashaying onto the stage, no ad-libbing freely, just pure stark terror. What happened?

Simple. I had grown up and realized that this acting stuff was serious. People had magically gained the ability to look holes through me, destroying any confidence I had. I gave up acting and hid behind the camera as a director. My failed acting career is not the point (though I'm still available). The point is that even people who are good at acting can go through psychic changes that reduce them to stuttering imbeciles on stage.

Recently I ran smack up against the opportunity to work with one of these terrified souls. Doing an episode of *Just Legal* with Don Johnson, a talented and accomplished actor, we cast an actor — "Bob" — for a scene with Don. He read well and had a good reputation. On the day of shooting, the rehearsal went well. The cinematographer, the gaffer and grip then took over to light the set. When they were ready, the actors, now in wardrobe and makeup, came on to the set for a final rehearsal. And suddenly our "Bob" couldn't even say his name. Though he had few lines to say, he couldn't remember any of them. Since he had to look at a piece of paper at the beginning of the scene we could write some of his lines on the paper. Hopefully by the time he had said those he would be settled enough to get through the rest of the scene. No such luck. "Bob" was so terrified that he had also lost the ability to read! We were in a real pickle.

Schedules are always important in film, but none more so than in TV. A show has to be shot every seven or eight days, not only to make the airdates but also because that's all the money the producers can afford. We could not take time to replace the actor. We could not postpone the scene and come back tomorrow because we were not in the same city the next day. Finally, we could not take all the time we needed with him because we had other important scenes to shoot that day. Everyone on the set saw what was happening and the room got *very* quiet.

I took him aside and calmed him as best I could. I never let him see me sweat. Instead I told him not to worry, that we had plenty of time. Not! Meanwhile Don Johnson and I were exchanging sighs and eye-rolls.

We started shooting and "Bob" would get a couple of lines into the scene and totally forget everything. We cut the camera and started again... and again... and again. After several terrible takes we had nothing that was usable, he couldn't even read his lines from the paper he was holding. At this point I moved to Plan B, "Wedding Vows technique": *one* line at a time.

This means that our hapless actor would say one line, then Don Johnson would say his. If "Bob" didn't get it right, I would ask him to say it again, and again and again. It's not enough to just get the line reading right, the actor has to look good too. No "deer in the headlights" look in their eyes. Once I got a good line reading we would move on to the next line and go through this over and over again. By the time the scene was finished even Don Johnson, who had been brilliantly supportive, was exhausted from the tension. The actor felt horrible about his performance and slunk from the set.

The next day the editor, Steve Lang, quickly cut the scene together out of the miles of film we shot. Looking for good line readings was the proverbial needle in the haystack problem. Steve did such a good editing job that if you were to see the show you would not ever know there had been any kind of a problem. "Bob" will get another job on the strength of this show.

What can we learn from this incident?

1. Terrorized actors don't respond easily to more terror. It will do no good to show panic, speak sharply, or yell. The actor will only get more scared.

2. Quiet reassurance and calm is the only workable way to go.

3. Once the camera is rolling, don't cut it except to change film or tape. When the camera rolls, a calm settles over the set. Keep that calm going and you can work peacefully and quietly. The minute the camera is cut, the crew runs around to get ready for another take and the panic can start afresh. The actor just gets more nervous and mad at himself.

4. Work through the scene one line at a time. When the actor blows a line, quietly ask him to do it again… and again, until he gets it right. Then move to the next line. Remember they have to look good too. If flop sweat is all over their face, you give the game away.

5. Get two cameras on the scene if possible and shoot two different angles and sizes simultaneously. When a line is right, it is right in two cameras and will edit much more easily.

This technique not only works with terrorized actors, it works with older actors who are having genuine trouble remembering lines. They are not terrified, they have short-term memory problems. They may have been acting all their lives and their memory is deserting them when they need it the most. And they hate it and themselves. But again, no matter how much agony it may be to shoot the scene, a talented older actor will come off like a champ. Other people then wonder why you were complaining about how tough it was to shoot the scene.

Drinks, Drugs & SOBs

A sensible person would think that people who got to do one of the most fun and best-paying jobs on the planet — acting — would not want to destroy themselves in the process.

Well, think again. It happens all the time. How? By drinking on the job, doing drugs, partying all night, coming to work hung over and by being miserable SOBs. Just to make it really fun you can have these joyful personalities in any combination you want. Not only actors, but directors and many others are prone to this self-destructive behavior. We all know the names of famous actors and directors who are always going back — again — to rehab and jail. How many lesser names are there who do the same thing? A lot. Quite a lot.

What do you do when they come onto the set? It's tough, really tough. Working with a drunk or druggie or party hound is worse than working with "Bob" the forgetful. At least "Bob" *wants* to do his best; the others don't respect what they are doing. How else can you describe a person who isn't there, who has chosen to send a complete idiot alter ego to work in their stead? How can you describe somebody who can't wait to make everyone else's life as miserable as theirs?

You can try to do the "Wedding Vow" technique with a souse or junkie, but you are committing yourself to having to do this every time the actor is in a scene. Shooting more takes only means they get worse and worse as they get more and more hammered. Oh, you think you can keep them from hammering themselves? Think again. They are so much cleverer than you at sneaking their favorite poison you'll never win. You can assign big-baby sitters to mind them and it only slows them down a bit. Booze can be hidden in toilets, injected into oranges, mixed in soft drink bottles. Drugs are even easier to hide. One sweet young thing even managed to corner the market for cocaine in South Florida and funnel it straight up her nose. There was nothing left for the rest of the crew!

Having dealt with stoners and lushes several times over the years I know there is no easy solution to this problem. You can keep trying to work with the impaired actor, muddle through the shoot, and doom your film to a very compromised performance at the same time.

I frankly believe there is only one sensible solution: tough love. The minute you see there is a problem, bring out all the guns. Call your producer. Call the actor's agent. Get them to the set right away and have an intervention with the actor.

The bottom line of the intervention is "Get straight or get replaced — now." Then send them home for the day to sober up. If they show up soused again, then get rid of them. Harsh? You bet. That's way better than the piece of filmed crap that results.

Pay or play? Let them sue.

I started work on a TV pilot years ago and realized by 8:00 the first morning that we had a drunk for the lead. A drunk that had been approved and vetted by at least six hundred layers of Show Business Bureaucracy. I called my producer, who showed up immediately, was horrified, and went to work right away convincing the studio and the network that we had to shut down and replace the bum.

Check out their response. "Well, don't panic, let's look at the dailies and see how he is." The next day their response was "Well, yes, it's sort of bad… but let's get somebody to watch him and keep him off the sauce." The next week it had changed to "Well, maybe we can cut around the bad bits." The bad bits? It was all bad bits!

The story of the pilot followed a blue-collar family's tough life. So we had lots of other "members of the family" who could carry some of the load. We didn't have to keep the camera on this bum the whole time. This inspired one of the studio Brain Surgeons to rationalize: "Well, we don't have to depend on him. The network will see how good the show is and we can replace him if the pilot sells." And so it went for twenty days of shooting. Every day on the set was like an uphill climb into an avalanche.

What were they thinking, not replacing him? Would you like to know? I'm going to tell you.

They thought they would save money by not replacing him. Then they wouldn't have to re-shoot and "the editor could fix it." Can you say "bullsh…"? They figured they could make the problem go away with flashy cutting.

The final film was really good… except when "the bum" came on screen, which was in every scene. The hapless editor had gotten rid of most of his slurring of lines, but there was nothing she could do about his half-asleep, weaving about, out-of-itness that was as subtle as ketchup on a white sweater. Still everyone sat there and said, "Gee, he looks pretty good now, you can hardly see the weaving." The weaving? You could smell the vodka fumes coming out of the TV set!

Then came the day of showing the final film to the president of the network.

Only then did reality set in. He took one look at it and said "Are you f...g kidding me? This is a joke, right? I just spent two million dollars of our money to watch a drunk for two hours?" The show was shelved and never seen again.

Finally, what happens if nobody will respond to your demand to replace the actor? Then quit the film. That's right. Quit the film. It's an impossible environment and it will only reflect badly on you. When people see your movie, they don't care that the actor was drunk, drugged, or out of it. All they know is that it's crap. And who do they blame? Not the actor. They blame you. And there is nothing you can say to change that unfair perception. You are screwed.

Live a Little

With all actors, method or no, if there is no life experience under their belt, there is an empty well to draw from. We can use "as-ifs," but if we haven't lived a little we have no well of experience to use. When we go to the high school play and watch *Life with Father* or *West Side Story*, we are amused by kids pretending to be adults. We get an idea of the way they picture adults. When many young adults start acting they only have television and movies to draw from. Their performances are faint copies of photocopies of faxes of carbon copies... etc., etc.

This makes for shallow acting. This is why in the theatre, older actors are often cast in young roles. In films that looks phony. It takes a lot of suspension of disbelief to accept Robert Redford and Barbra Streisand as college students in *The Way We Were*. Sydney Pollack finessed it by casting the other students surrounding them with "older" actors. In *Porky's* there are more high schoolers with receding hairlines than in any teen film ever made.

In *The Man in the Iron Mask*, Leonardo DiCaprio plays a young Louis XIV, the Sun King of France in 1750. In spite of his considerable talents and appeal to young women, it was a huge challenge for him to play Louis XIV. Why? Wasn't Louis XIV very, very young at this point? How much life experience can you have at sixteen anyway? In the case of Louis XIV, a lot — he was crowned at age five. Since the day he was born he was trained to be king, how to appear around his subjects, how to feel comfortable in his world of absolute privilege. When we watch Prince William and Prince Harry in England we know they are just teenagers but see how they carry themselves as future monarchs. It would be a tough assignment to portray one of them truthfully.

At Yale, cast in Moliere's *The Miser* as a seventeenth-century loan shark, I floundered through rehearsals. The dialogue and emotions seemed simple enough. But I had no genuine approach to the character. Paul Widener, the director, one day made everyone wear the high-heel shoes in rehearsal that we would wear in the play. Seventeenth-century buckled shoes with inch-and-a-half heels. Try walking in those. I clomped up and down the hall night after night during rehearsals, walking stupidly. In frustration I resorted to actor copout #4: make my stupid walk part of the character. Good thing it was a comedy, because the walk was hilariously stupid. I also was given very thick glasses to wear. So thick that I could only see a blur in front of me. I would have to launch myself on stage on my cue and hope to hell I was talking to the right actor. In performances I got huge laughs and applause. I thought I had succeeded admirably.

Constance Welch, the beloved Yale Drama School professor of acting, was not amused. She announced that my entire character was built "on a pair of shoes." Certainly, she said, the character I "created" had *none* of the characteristics of a real moneylender of the time. Nowadays, with more life experience, I could conjure up a pretty disgusting and seedy character that could still be funny and creepy. Hopefully it would be closer to Fagin in *Oliver Twist* than Pauly Shore in a dress. I came at the character from the outside and gave it no depth or truth at all.

Outside or Inside

The technique of coming at a character from the outside can work really well and is perfectly valid. Everything that surrounds a good actor will influence their performance. Even the most internal of actors put a great deal of thought into their wardrobe and their props. They know that a good costume will have a tremendous effect on their behavior. An actor can easily learn to use both external and internal techniques at the same time. "Whatever works" is the key phrase. There is no right or wrong here. The "truth" is not what is important, "the appearance of truth" is. Nobody cares if the actor really feels the emotion or not. *Does it work for the scene?* That is the question. If the actor feels the emotion so deeply that he is almost overcome, but the audience doesn't get it, the whole thing is a bust anyway.

This is where film acting gets very tricky. The camera is such a powerful reader of people that an actor may seem to be doing very little, yet what emerges on screen is absolutely perfect. Strangely enough, an actor may reduce the crew to tears and get applause on the set but when his performance is seen in dailies, it is over the top and unusable. John Travolta says that some directors complain he isn't giving enough in a scene. It's too bland, they say. Travolta knows himself so well that he can say, wait till you see the dailies. When the director sees the dailies, John is proven right. Don't think you can rely on video assist to tell you how much is enough and how much is not. Video assist is only the roughest of guides to what the camera really captures. Subtle emotion doesn't penetrate a 17-inch monitor.

Jan de Bont: "In the old movies, like with Cary Grant, there were some actors who even with just a little smile, changed the whole mood of a scene. Gene Hackman is very good at that. He knows what is expected in a close-up. He doesn't give anything more. You never see him do anything big in the close-up. Harrison Ford does so little in his face, and it's always perfect. He knows that… you have to do so little. There are not many who truly understand the science of the close-up. He's definitely one of them."

Paul Newman has worked his entire career to minimize his acting, believing less is more. It works for him because there is something always happening inside him so powerful it needs no embellishing. The magnificent simplicity of his work in *Road to Perdition* is extremely powerful, as it is in *Nobody's Perfect* or *Our Town*.

Summary

1. When a scene doesn't work from the actor's point of view, run through the checklist. Are they too tense? Don't know their lines? Don't understand the scene? Understand it but just indicate it? Don't know the real emotion? Afraid of the emotion? Don't want to play it as written? Don't want to play it at all? No good? Really crazed?

2. If they didn't learn their lines, stage the scene with them carrying their sides, then assign someone to run lines during lighting. Afterwards tell them this is not acceptable.

3. Cut a break for older actors who have real trouble remembering lines. Their performance will still be terrific.

4. If they don't understand the scene, use the crowbar technique, "What do you want? How do you get it?" Pick active verbs. Directing is Socratic.

5. Correcting indicating means two things: getting the actor to understand what the emotions really feel like and helping them to find that in themselves. Try improvisation, not using the written dialogue.

6. Use the "as-if" technique to help the actor better understand the emotions of the scene. "As-ifs" from your life will not be nearly as effective as ones the actor comes up with from their own experience.

7. Fear of failure causes more bad acting than almost anything. An actor uncomfortable with the situation may cover by giving very little to the scene, hiding in the trailer, complaining about the director.

8. Actors who don't care about their performance and try to walk through it have to be yanked up short. Again, aside from everyone else you are going to appeal to his or her sense of professionalism and pride. It's never about money.

9. Acting is not a one-sided thing. It is the actor's obligation to help other actors in the scene, on-camera and off-camera, as well by giving as much of themselves as they can. Doing the off-camera dialogue is as important as doing the on-camera dialogue.

10. If an actor doesn't want to say the dialogue as written (something else that could have been caught in rehearsal), they should talk to the writer, who can explain why it was written that way. The two of them can work it out. If the writer is not present the key question to ask the actor is: "What would you say instead?" Then shoot it both ways.

11. The actor who won't do the scene at all is one of the greatest problems the director will ever face. There are no formulas or quick fixes for this dilemma; each situation is completely different. Very often the problem is quite minor and easily fixed. The actor has built it up in his mind to be more important than it really is. Sitting down in private with the actor and talking through the problem ought to reveal the sticking points. Make the actor present solutions to the problem.

12. When no simple solution presents itself, then more drastic measures have to be considered: involving the producer and the actor's agent, cutting

around the actor, deleting the scene, replacing the actor, bringing attorneys to bear on the problem.

13. Bad actors in small parts can be shot around (over the shoulder, in silhouette, in a thunderstorm) so that their bad performance can be minimized. Re-voicing is only a partial fix akin to giving aspirin for a brain tumor. Replacing them on the spot or re-shooting is a better solution but not always practical.

14. The number of takes needed for a shot is completely up to the director. Clint Eastwood only wants one take, Warren Beatty wants fifty. A good rule of thumb is: Always have good reasons for doing another take. And let the actors know the reason. Or make up a reason. The more takes that are done, the more the life is drained out of a performance.

15. Scene stealers can be handled by busting them on their behavior. They know what they are doing and can be teased out of doing it.

16. Whether an actor works internally as in the Stanislavsky Method, externally as with many English actors, or a combination of the two, as with Michael Chekhov's techniques, does not matter. What matters: Does the performance work for the film and does it blend stylistically with the rest of the cast?

VideoVillage Idiots

In 2001, while preparing a film with Jeanne Tripplehorn, *My Brother's Keeper*, I announced to a shocked crew that there would be no video assist on the set. There would be no "video village"; no headsets passed out to every VIP and all the hangers-on that haunt movie sets. The producer, Guy McElwaine, said with his charming smile that it was okay with him because it would be my ass in a sling if we had a problem. The AD said in disbelief that he had never worked on a movie that didn't use video assist. Was it even possible? I reminded him that over eighty years of great movies had been made without video assist. Didn't he think that, just possibly, we might stumble through our movie without it as well?

Before the video assist monitor came along thirty years ago, everyone on a set had to depend on the camera operator to tell them if they had the shot or not. When Jerry Lewis began directing movies that he also starred in, he wanted a way to look at what he was doing right away and not wait till the next day for dailies. A huge video camera was lashed to the even bigger Mitchell 35mm camera, then the gold standard for motion picture cameras. The video camera fed images to a reel-to-reel videotape deck as big as a washing machine. The tape alone cost $200 a roll. Plus four video technicians were added to the payroll. No wonder it was infrequently used on movie sets.

In the late 1960s Panavision and Arriflex began to shrink their cameras and it became easier and less expensive to shoot on locations away from big sound stages. But the cumbersome video assist device was seldom considered for inclusion on these shoots. Directors resisted the innovation more than the bean-counters. Directors had always watched and listened carefully to what was being shot. Don't need no stinking video. A poll of working directors in 1970 showed almost nobody wanted to use video assist. In addition to the expense, it could take control away from the director. Stars and producers could waste all kinds of time watching takes and haggling over details. Schedules would go out the window. Costs would go up. The inmates would be running the asylum. It might be okay for Jerry Lewis and other big deal actor/directors, but the rest of us could soldier on without it.

In 1976 Sony introduced the Betacam and JVC introduced VHS technology. Instead of expensive two-inch tape, they used much cheaper half-inch tape. Panavision and Arriflex started building tiny video cameras into their equipment as an additional option. Of course the image was ultra-cheesy: grainy black-and-white and hard to see. Cinematographers wanted no part of the junky images that appeared on TV monitors.

It was a good tool, however, for action directors, second unit directors, and stunt coordinators, who could find out immediately if they had gotten the shot. This not only saved time, it made for a safer set. Till then, dangerous stunts were frequently repeated because the camera operator wasn't sure if he had gotten the shot. Now there was no need to endanger stuntmen by repeating stunts that worked well the first time.

Today: a different world. Color video cameras are routinely built into every camera. LCD monitors are hooked on the side of the camera for the focus pullers. It's a rare set where video assist is not in use.

So what moron would insist on banning such a terrific tool? The difference is that the director who sits (or hides) behind a TV monitor removes himself physically and emotionally from his cast. Actors need an audience. Even if it is just one person. Actors don't perform well in a vacuum.

Michael Ritchie, the talented director of *Downhill Racer, The Candidate,* and *The Bad News Bears,* spoke often of the need to connect, to be close to the actors where they can see you and feel your presence. Ritchie went back to the old technique of the director sitting on the dolly underneath the lens.

Anyone who has ever acted understands the actor's psychological need for an audience close at hand.

Ruth Gordon: "An actor has to have compliments. If I go long enough without getting a compliment, I compliment myself, and that's just as good because at least then I know it's sincere."[1]

Theatre actors believe they can sense what the audience is feeling. If an audience is unresponsive in the theatre, the cast will grumble about the "bad audience." Matinee audiences the world over are notorious for being unresponsive and noisy at the same time. Each audience member seems to bring shopping bags into the theatre that they can rustle loudly whenever they are not coughing or answering their cell phones. Try acting with that going on. The very same cast may perform again that evening with a different audience that is responsive and appreciative. As a result the cast's performance energizes and sparkles noticeably. **When the film director is hidden behind a monitor, often inside a black tent, he becomes either a non-presence or an imperious one.** This Wizard of Oz approach is especially off-putting to actors who feel as if some annoying Supreme Being is ordering them around.

Jeremy Kagan: "As much as you can, be close to the actor while you're shooting. I watch some of the directors on *The West Wing*, who just sit behind the damn monitor. And they literally scream over the walls. I'll never do that. I always talk to the actor face to face. "

There is one other delightful benefit to this approach. The absence of "video village" means the absence of the irritating crowd of people that gather like moths around the monitors where they talk out loud during takes, make snotty jokes about the actors, second-guess, kibitz, and make all around nuisances of themselves. When video village is gone, the village idiots are gone. Deprived of their TV entertainment, they find more constructive ways to spend their time. I have witnessed disasters where a frustrated director mutters something negative about a performance under his breath. This is overheard by one of the village idiots and conveyed right to the maligned actor. The actor, unable to accept this was said in the heat of the moment, takes it very personally and refuses to trust or work with the director again.

Ohmigod, They Want to Come to Dailies

Should we let actors see dailies or not? Are you just paranoid or are actors really out to get you? If you are opposed to actors seeing dailies, you are likely

---

[1] Ruth Gordon, *My Side: The Autobiography of Ruth Gordon* (New York: Harper & Row, 1976), page 92

to be worried about loss of control. If you are okay with it, you probably have confidence in your own ability and those of your actors to handle what they are seeing.

I've been letting actors come to dailies since the day I started directing in 1971. I have never had a serious problem because of this. Many times I've used it to solve a disagreement about which take works best.

Actors are ambivalent about seeing dailies. If they are objective and methodical in their approach, they like to see what they did and how well it worked. If they have concerns they nearly always come to discuss them with the director. They don't come to fight, they come to share ideas and look for guidance.

Actors who operate on a more intuitive, improvisational level tend to stay away from dailies. They don't like watching themselves, as it makes them very self-conscious.

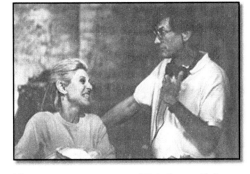

Anne Bancroft was an actress who combined both elements. She approached her roles from an emotional level and then was methodical about what she prepared. After she worked on *Point of No Return* for two or three days, I invited her to the dailies. Her reply was interesting. She said that she did not like to look at herself any more on screen. This beautiful woman, whom time had rendered even more beautiful, could not make peace with what she saw on screen. Her beauty was not that of a *Vogue* model, shallow and plastic; her beauty was one of great soul and depth. Reassuring and complimenting her could not defeat the sadness that enveloped her when she looked at herself on film.

Matthew Broderick in *WarGames* was equally skittish about dailies but for a different reason. He was frightened that he would see bad acting from himself. One day Ally Sheedy and I dared him to come to dailies. He lasted for about five minutes, then bolted from the room. I thought that would be it. But surprisingly, the next day he showed up on his own, stayed the whole time, and came every day thereafter. Mel Gibson, Richard Dreyfuss, Michael J. Fox, Candice Bergen, Jeanne Tripplehorn, Roy Scheider, Jenna Elfman, John Travolta, and John Cusack, to name a few, all take great interest in the dailies. They are strong personalities who want to see how their performance is working. I run an egalitarian set that tries to treat everyone as openly and equally as can be done in what is really a benevolent dictatorship. To tell actors they cannot see the dailies is to evince a lack of trust in them as artists. Nowadays even the dailies seem to be sold on the streets of Beijing and Hong Kong the next day. So if one billion Chinese can see them, why not the actors?

Summary

1. Video assist is a great tool for many things on a film set. However, it can isolate the directors from the actors. A director who relies on video assist must work very hard to stay in contact with his cast before and after takes.

2. Talking to actors from any kind of control booth over microphones or yelling is very off-putting. Personal and private contact with the actors is always the best way to give them directions.

3. Establish on the first day of shooting who can be around a video-assist monitor: director, script supervisor, AD, sound mixer, video playback technician. Anyone else should be brought in on a need-to-see basis, e.g., a makeup person who has to see if the makeup is working.

4. Let actors see any dailies they want. Nowadays most film companies don't project the dailies, they use DVDs. An actor can watch these privately.

Wait, You're Not Done

Finishing shooting is by no means the end of the director's work with the actor. There is still editing and ADR (automated dialogue replacement), and possible retakes. Just when you thought that was enough, the star may want to "improve" their performance. Treat any of these steps lightly and you'll get a nasty surprise. Depending on the star, you may have a partner you never bargained for. As if editing suites were not small enough already, wait till the six-hundred-pound gorilla plops himself down in front of the Avid.

Most actors move on to other work when their job on a film is done. If they are needed again, they are usually happy to oblige. First, they have a chance to improve their performance. Secondly, they are curious to see what they've done. Third, they get paid.

Everything we've said about working with actors still applies in postproduction, with a couple of new wrinkles. The most common reason for calling an actor back is to replace dialogue tracks that have excess noise from traffic, airplanes or air conditioners. For a skilled experienced actor, this is easy. Many can repeat the acting they did months before without stress. John Travolta and Mel Gibson can reel off huge paragraphs in one take with perfect lip sync. Kevin Costner is exceptionally good at not only replacing his original dialogue but also improving it immensely. In *American Flyers* he would constantly find ways to re-phrase dialogue, add new dialogue, and enrich the original far beyond just fixing a poor recording. LL Cool J, in *The Hard Way*, had never seen an ADR stage in his life. But as a talented musician he realized right away that he could improvise and improve his dialogue. He took a very good performance and made it sparkle. Here are artists who maintain their creativity and playfulness until the very end.

Some actors resent having to do it at all. Anthony Quinn, a spontaneous actor, would cause no end of grief for the ADR crew. Afraid he could not re-create his performance, he balked at the whole process. He would insist they open the windows so he could breathe fresh air. Reality check: ADR stages don't have windows. Other actors are scared by the process and can't seem to get it right. That really takes patience on everyone's part. If an actor loves to improvise dialogue filled with "ums" and "aahs" he'll have a tough time matching what he did originally.

But no matter the situation, it is very important for the director to be present at these sessions. Why? Isn't it just a mechanical voice replacement? Yes and no. It's much more than that. Surprise, surprise, acting is still needed. The actor has to re-create his character's state of mind and the mood of the original scene months after first acting it on camera. That's much tougher than it looks. Getting back in the mood of the original shooting day can really be a bitch. The ADR crew only cares about one thing: does the new dialogue lip sync with the original? Screw the acting, that's somebody else's problem. Without the acting being as good as the original, the result will be flat, mechanical, and soulless.

There is a reason why foreign movies dubbed into English often sound so terrible. The actors hired to replace the original voices are great at matching lip movements but not so great at acting. Woody Allen's hysterical film *What's Up Tiger Lily* is a funny satire of bad ADR. The characters' mouths keep flapping long after they stop speaking. And what they are saying makes no sense at all. Lots of foreign Biblical epics from the 1960s are almost as funny, even without Woody Allen. On the other hand the Germans and the French are geniuses at dubbing. For *Stakeout*, they made Dreyfuss and Estevez look like they spoke perfect German and French.

The director can be the quality controller. His presence can help alleviate the fears of actors uncomfortable with the process. All the bonding that went on during the shooting comes back to help out now.

In ADR sessions over the years I have held Joan Crawford's hand while she nervously learned a whole new technology. I have picked up Richard Dreyfuss physically in a bear hug to get a strong reaction in a fight scene;

yelled at Madeline Stowe and Goldie Hawn to startle them. I have calmed panicked young actors who think they can't do it at all and are ready to run away from the session. I have teased, cajoled, tricked, implored, begged, and had fun with actors getting them to do their best work. In other words, I am re-creating the playground environment that was on the set. Would anybody else other than the director do this on an ADR stage? Not bloody likely. Sessions without the director can be dry and dull, something to slog through like a cold swamp. After all the care and hard work that went into shooting, it only makes sense to be present to keep the movie on track. If the director goes to the final sound mix and doesn't like the actor's ADR tracks, it is his own fault.

Invading the Editing Suite

All actors are very concerned about their performance from the first time they read the script all the way through the finished film. Some are so concerned that they want to go into the cutting room and see that the best parts of their performances are being used. Of course this is completely a subjective judgment that can have varied results, not all of them good.

A good example is with John Cusack in the HBO film *The Jack Bull*. Cusack was not only the star but also the producer, and his father, Richard Cusack, had written a brilliant screenplay. He asked to come to the cutting room after seeing my director's cut. He and I sat at the Avid for eight hours straight without getting out of the chairs. He looked at almost every take of every scene he was in and we discussed the merits of his performance. Though the changes we made were relatively minor in relation to the whole film, they were extremely important to Cusack as a performer. Because he was the producer, he had the right to do this. But because he is an intelligent, tasteful man he had the good sense not to get crazy with the film as some actor/producers have been known to do. Barbra Streisand, for example, has been said to cut out all the close-ups of her co-stars and only use medium shots of them instead. The obvious result is to put much more emphasis on Streisand. Whether this is a good idea or not is a matter of opinion.

Paul Mazursky was finishing a film, *Faithful*, starring Cher when he got a call that Cher wanted to edit her own version of the movie. Mazursky, who brooks no baloney, said he would happily listen to her ideas but he didn't want her in the edit suite. Too late!

The producers had already rented a cutting facility, hired an editor, and given her a copy of the rough cut. Working with her editor, she produced a "Cher version" of the film. Mazursky naively thought the studio would see there was no comparing the two. His cut was in service of the movie; Cher's cut was probably in service of... Cher. Surprise, surprise, the studio announced they loved the "Cher version." Mazursky pleaded for them to preview both versions to see which one played the best. The studio agreed. Afterwards, the results were tallied. And... audiences liked Mazursky's version the best.

Paul smiled to himself. Problem solved, right? Wrong! The studio opted to release Cher's version anyway!

I bet you're thinking, how can that be? Don't they want the best *movie*? Doesn't the audience's clear preference for one version over the other count? This probably shows you haven't worked in Hollywood very long.

No mystery here: The studio wanted Cher to do publicity for the movie. If they didn't use her version, they feared she would refuse to publicize the movie. Simple as that. They arrogantly assumed that the movie itself didn't matter if they had tricked audiences into showing up.

Mazursky tried to take his name off the movie, but the studio refused. Why? Because Paul Mazursky is a big name internationally and the studio could sell that. Cher for the U.S., Mazursky for the rest of the universe. Mazursky was screwed.

Norman Jewison, Academy Award–winning director of *In the Heat of the Night*, *Fiddler on the Roof*, and *Moonstruck*, heard about this insanity. He called all the "A" list directors in Hollywood and asked them to write a letter to the CEO of the studio saying if Cher's version were released none of these directors would ever make films for that company. Since this would deprive them of every good director in town, the company blinked. Mazursky's version was the one seen in theatres.

Curiously, that film studio is no longer in business. Paul Mazursky continues to make wonderful films.

Kevin Reynolds directed Kevin Costner's first film, *Fandango*. A cult hit, it put Costner on the road to stardom. So Kevin Reynolds was a logical choice to direct Costner in *Robin Hood*. After the filming, Reynolds was very publicly barred from the editing room while the movie was re-edited. We could assume that Reynolds would never want to hear the name of Kevin Costner again.

So it came as an even bigger surprise when Reynolds was hired to direct *Waterworld*. Of course this was before Costner was hired as the star. The grapevine had it that Reynolds' contract stipulated Costner's name could not even be mentioned as a possible star for the movie. Well, isn't that ironic. Kevin Reynolds must've thought lightning couldn't strike twice.

The movie was a nightmare to make because of working on the open Pacific Ocean. At least it was peaceful in postproduction where the editing progressed. Until one day… ZZAAPP! Reynolds was again publicly barred from the cutting room.

Thankfully few movies come to that kind of an impasse. But unless you're Spielberg it could happen to you. Never forget that most movies are primarily about money, secondarily about money, and thirdly… about money. Art always comes in last. If movie investors think a movie will make more money if it smells like dog-doo, don't be surprised if you detect a foul odor flowing from your local Cineplex.

If a star insists on invading the cutting room and the studio allows it, you have two options: you can resist and risk getting removed from the movie or welcome the actor in and sit by their side at the computer. Don't get all arrogant and huffy, it will only cause more problems. Instead co-opt them, be their best friend. If you stick around you have a better chance of damage control. Sit with them as a collaborator while they root around through takes of their own performance. They very often have to discover for themselves why you and the editor made the choices you did.

Thank God for Attention Deficit Disorder. Very often both actors and studio executives play with a film for a while, then get bored and leave. If you're lucky, a few harmless changes get made and your nemesis disappears into the night on the hunt for more fun things: booze, broads, or crystal meth. Never let an adversarial situation solidify. You are likely to lose. Norman Jewison can't bail everybody out.

Summary

1. In postproduction, maintain the same good relationship with your actors you had in shooting. If you had a bad relationship, take time to mend fences.

2. ADR requires the director's full attention. Unless the acting is as good or better than the original the performance will be rendered flat, mechanical, and soulless.

3. Protect your editing rights. That means they have to be spelled out clearly when the film is begun, not afterwards. The Directors Guild of America contracts are very specific and fair in protecting the director. However, many non-DGA film producers will try every trick to avoid giving the director any rights.

4. If stuck in a situation where you have unwanted help in the cutting room, don't quit. Hang around and try to be helpful, not obstructive. Don't be a pain. You can minimize the damage if you are there every day. (This is called Devious Directing.) If the film turns out well, you have been a great paramedic. If the film turns out badly, you can always blame the kibitzers and remove your name. If you get pouty and go home, the producers will take that as a sign that they can do anything they want to the film. And they will. And you won't like it.

Some Final Thoughts

Working with actors is never dull. If it is, you've probably cast the wrong people. That's the fun of it. You never know what unscripted dramas will greet you when you arrive on the set every morning. But remember that a creative actor is not necessarily a compliant actor. You want them to think, you want them to come up with ideas. You want them to be part of the creative process. Because you are not God. You are not all-wise and omnipotent. Your frisky cast can either lift your script to heights never envisioned or crash it on the rocks below.

So right now you have to banish all that negativity about actors from your mind. Cursing them never got a good performance. Yelling at their agent won't make your film any better. Making them a creative partner, albeit a limited one, gives them some leeway to create, and gives you the control you need as captain of the leaky vessel known as a movie. A vessel that's always threatening to sink or run aground.

Frank Langella: "One last thing I would say to any director — young or old. Don't tolerate any actor who is rude, selfish, unprofessional, unprepared, or insulting to you or anyone else on the set. Slap him down early. If he has any integrity, he will stop the behavior and respect you for taking charge. So will your crew. If they sense your authority has been undermined, you've lost them for good. Be a loving, benevolent boss — set a standard of behavior and keep your real feelings to yourself. Everyone wants you to be God!"

If you have teenage children or can remember your own teenage years, you recognize the power struggle between parents and their "wanting-to-be-free-rebellious-children." It's fair to compare that to working with actors.

You're the coach, you're the Mom or Dad, you're the leader. You are not the dictator. You are not Oz, the Great and Terrible. Enjoy your time with your actors. It's some of the best times you'll ever have. And let's face it: if it were easy, anybody could do it.

Steven Soderbergh: "My goal is for an actor to go, 'I think I did some of my best work on that movie, and I don't even know how it happened.' To me, if I heard that from an actor, that would make me slaphappy. Because then I feel like they were in that unconscious place where you're just doing it."

Further Reading

Directing Actors. Creating Memorable Performances for Film & Television by Judith Weston (Michael Wiese Productions, 1999)
Judith Weston's book effectively encapsulates many of the concepts that great directors and acting teachers have used for decades.

Leader Effectiveness Training (LET) by Dr. Thomas Gordon (Perigree, 2001)
What does this have to do with film? The principles of working with people, communicating with them effectively, and resolving conflict is the same in business, marriages, child-raising, and even filmmaking. This book, or its parent, *Parent Effectiveness Training (PET)*, are invaluable tools for learning people skills.

The One-Minute Manager by Kenneth Blanchard, Ph.D. (Berkley, 1983)
This thin little book is a jewel that should be handy on every executive's desk. More stress and conflict can be resolved with the simple techniques outlined here than through reading vast tomes of psychology.

Picture Credits

John Frankenheimer (courtesy Doug Hyun)
Michael Ritchie (courtesy Lauren Ritchie)
Mary I. Badham (courtesy Henry Badham)

Chapter 1
Jenna Elfman (courtesy Jenna Elfman)
Stephen Collins (courtesy Stephen Collins)
Saturday Night Fever bridge/Michael Hausman (courtesy Paramount
    Pictures)
John Badham/John Travolta (courtesy Paramount Pictures)
Richard Donner (courtesy Richard Donner)
John Badham/Richard Pryor (courtesy Bonnie Leeds)
John Badham/Rob Cohen (courtesy Bonnie Leeds)

Chapter 2
Tom Mankiewicz (courtesy Tom Mankiewicz)
Mel Gibson (courtesy Joe Lederer)
Peter Hunt (courtesy Melody Rock)
Martin Sheen (courtesy Martin Sheen)
Kurtwood Smith (courtesy Kurtwood Smith)
Oliver Stone (courtesy Oliver Stone)
Jeremy Kagan (courtesy John Badham)
Ed Asner (courtesy Ed Asner)
Judge Reinhold (courtesy Judge Reinhold)
David Ward (courtesy David Ward)
Jan de Bont (courtesy Jan de Bont)

Chapter 3
John Badham/Rod Steiger/Jason Patric (courtesy Jane Cragg-Barber)

Chapter 4

Michael Chiklis (courtesy Michael Chiklis)
Roger Corman/Raul Julia (courtesy Roger Corman)
Phil Feldman/Jason Bernard (courtesy Bruce Talamon)
Malcolm McDowell (courtesy Bruce Talamon)
Gary Busey (courtesy Drop Zone/Paramount)
Elia Kazan (courtesy DGA)
Marlon Brando/Penelope Ann Miller/Bruno Kirby/Matthew Broderick
    (courtesy Penelope Ann Miller)
Britt McKillip (courtesy Vanessa Ruane)
Frank Langella (courtesy Bob Penn)
Martha Coolidge/Geena Davis (courtesy Martha Coolidge)

Chapter 5

Brad Silberling (courtesy Brad Silberling)
Rob Cohen/John Badham (courtesy Bonnie Leeds)
Saturday Night Fever poster (courtesy Martha Swope/Paramount Pictures)

Chapter 6

Sydney Pollack (courtesy Sydney Pollack)
Leland Orser (courtesy Leland Orser)
Jeanne Tripplehorn/Corin Nemec (courtesy Vanessa Ruane)

Chapter 7

Gregory Peck/Mary Badham (courtesy Leo Fuchs & Veronique Peck)
Randal Kleiser (courtesy Randal Kleiser)
John Travolta/Karen Lynn Gorney (courtesy Paramount Pictures)

Chapter 8

Hal Holbrook/Michael Tolan/John Badham (courtesy David Levinson)

Chapter 9

Johnny Depp/John Badham (courtesy Bruce Talamon/Paramount Pictures)
Johnny Depp in Nick of Time (courtesy Bruce Talamon/Paramount
   Pictures)
John Cassavetes/John Badham (courtesy Lawrence Bachmann)
Paul Pape (courtesy Paramount Pictures)

Chapter 10

Richard Dreyfuss in yard (courtesy Gregg Champion)
Mel Gibson/Goldie Hawn (courtesy Joe Lederer)

Chapter 11

John Travolta/Donna Pescow (courtesy Paramount Pictures)
Michael J. Fox/John Badham (courtesy DJ Caruso)
Lawrence Olivier (courtesy Bob Penn)
John Badham/Richard Dreyfuss (courtesy Lawrence Bachmann)

Chapter 12

Donald Pleasance (courtesy Bob Penn)
James Woods (courtesy James Woods)
John Badham in The Miser (courtesy Peter Hunt)

Chapter 13

Michael Ritchie (courtesy Lauren Ritchie)
Anne Bancroft (courtesy Bruce Talamon)
Matthew Broderick, Ally Sheedy (courtesy Ralph Nelson)

Chapter 14

John Cusack (courtesy HBO/Joe Lederer)

Index

About the Authors

JOHN BADHAM has earned the reputation of being an "actor's director" through a career impressive in its range and diversity. In 1977, he guided a then-unknown John Travolta to worldwide fame with *Saturday Night Fever* (a cultural milestone that launched the disco era and went on to become one of the top-grossing films of all time). His career hit another high point in 1983, when two films he directed that year, *Blue Thunder* and *WarGames*, received four Academy Award nominations. Since then he has collaborated with such luminaries as Laurence Olivier, Kevin Costner, Mel Gibson, Johnny Depp, and James Garner in films that have won both critical praise and box office success. Other films Badham has helmed include *Point of No Return* (1993), *Short Circuit* (1986), *Bird on a Wire* (1990), *Stakeout* (1987), *Another Stakeout* (1993), *American Flyers* (1985), *Whose Life Is It Anyway?* (1981), and the stylized *Dracula* (1979).

Badham is also a prominent television producer and director. He served as an executive producer for the Steven Bochco drama *Blind Justice* (2005) and directed several episodes. He has also directed episodes for *Heroes* (2006), *Crossing Jordan* (2006), *Standoff* (2006), *The Shield* (2003), *Just Legal* (2005) and *The Streets of San Francisco* (1972). He received two Emmy nominations for his work on the '70s series *The Senator* and *The Law*. His telefilm *Floating Away* (1998), starring Paul Hogan and Roseanna Arquette, won the Prism award for its portrayal of alcohol abuse. Other projects include HBO's *The Jack Bull* (1999), Showtime's *The Last Debate* (2000), Lifetime's *Obsessed* (2002), and CBS's *Footsteps* (2003). He is Professor of Media Arts at the Dodge School of Film and Media, Chapman University in Orange, CA.

John Badham may be reached through his website at www.johnbadham.com.

Photo by Carl Gottlieb

CRAIG MODDERNO is a journalist/filmmaker who formerly was an editor for *Penthouse* and *US* magazines. He wrote, produced, directed and did the interviews for the original documentary *The Graduate at 25* which was included on the DVD and video of the classic film *The Graduate*. He acted in the Samuel L. Jackson toplined movie *The Great White Hype*. Now residing in Hollywood, where he was a writer/producer for TV's *The Merv Griffin Show* and a reporter for the *Los Angeles Times* and the *Oakland Tribune*, Mr. Modderno currently freelances for the *New York Times*, Reuters, *Hollywood Life* and *DIRECTV — The Guide*. His three thousand–plus printed bylines have also appeared in *USA Today*, *USA Weekend*, *Details*, the *Washington Post*, *Hoop*, *Cosmopolitan*, *TV Guide*, *TV Guide Online*, *Hits*, *Playboy*, *DGA Magazine*, *American Film*, the *New York Post*, the *Contra Costa Times*, the *Los Angeles Daily News*, Mick Martin and Marsha Porter's *Video & DVD Guide* and *Rolling Stone* — the only writer other than filmmaker Cameron Crowe to have been published several times in that magazine as a teenager.

DIRECTING ACTORS
CREATING MEMORABLE PERFORMANCES
FOR FILM AND TELEVISION

JUDITH WESTON

BEST SELLER
OVER 45,000 COPIES SOLD!

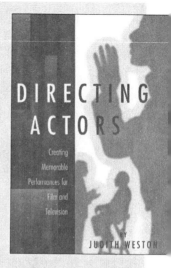

Directing film or television is a high-stakes occupation. It captures your full attention at every moment, calling on you to commit every resource and stretch yourself to the limit. It's the white-water rafting of entertainment jobs. But for many directors, the excitement they feel about a new project tightens into anxiety when it comes to working with actors.

This book provides a method for establishing creative, collaborative relationships with actors, getting the most out of rehearsals, troubleshooting poor performances, giving briefer directions, and much more. It addresses what actors want from a director, what directors do wrong, and constructively analyzes the director-actor relationship.

"Judith Weston is an extraordinarily gifted teacher."
> – David Chase, Emmy® Award-Winning Writer,
> Director, and Producer *The Sopranos,*
> *Northern Exposure, I'll Fly Away*

"I believe that working with Judith's ideas and principles has been the most useful time I've spent preparing for my work. I think that if Judith's book were mandatory reading for all directors, the quality of the director-actor process would be transformed, and better drama would result."
> – John Patterson, Director
> *Six Feet Under, CSI: Crime Scene Investigation,*
> *The Practice, Law and Order*

"I know a great teacher when I find one! Everything in this book is brilliant and original and true."
> – Polly Platt, Producer, *Bottle Rocket*
> Executive Producer, *Broadcast News, The War of the Roses*

JUDITH WESTON was a professional actor for 20 years and has taught Acting for Directors for over a decade.

$26.95 · 314 PAGES · ORDER NUMBER 4RLS · ISBN: 0941188248

MICHAEL WIESE PRODUCTIONS

Our books are all about helping you create memorable films that will move audiences for generations to come.

Since 1981, we've published over 100 books on all aspects of filmmaking which are used in more than 600 film schools around the world. Many of today's most productive filmmakers and writers got started with our books.

According to a recent Nielsen BookScan analysis, as a publisher we've had more best-selling books in our subject category than our closest competitor – and they are backed by a multi-billion dollar corporation! This is evidence that as an independent – filmmaker or publisher – you can create the projects you have always dreamed of and earn a livelihood.

To help you accomplish your goals, we've expanded our information to the web. Here you can receive a 25% discount on all our books, buy the newest releases before they hit the bookstores, and sign up for a newsletter which provides all kinds of new information, tips, seminars, and more. You'll also find a Virtual Film School loaded with articles and websites from our top authors, teacher's guides, video streamed content, free budget formats, and a ton of free valuable information.

We encourage you to visit www.mwp.com. Sign up and become part of a wider creative community.

Onward and upward,
Michael Wiese
Publisher, Filmmaker

If you'd like to receive a free MWP Newsletter,
click on www.mwp.com to register.

FILM & VIDEO BOOKS

SCREENWRITING | WRITING

And the Best Screenplay Goes to... | Dr. Linda Seger | $26.95

Archetypes for Writers | Jennifer Van Bergen | $22.95

Cinematic Storytelling | Jennifer Van Sijll | $24.95

Could It Be a Movie? | Christina Hamlett | $26.95

Creating Characters | Marisa D'Vari | $26.95

Crime Writer's Reference Guide, The | Martin Roth | $20.95

Deep Cinema | Mary Trainor-Brigham | $19.95

Elephant Bucks | Sheldon Bull | $24.95

Fast, Cheap & Written That Way | John Gaspard | $26.95

Hollywood Standard, The | Christopher Riley | $18.95

I Could've Written a Better Movie than That! | Derek Rydall | $26.95

Inner Drives | Pamela Jaye Smith | $26.95

Joe Leydon's Guide to Essential Movies You Must See | Joe Leydon | $24.95

Moral Premise, The | Stanley D. Williams, Ph.D. | $24.95

Myth and the Movies | Stuart Voytilla | $26.95

Power of the Dark Side, The | Pamela Jaye Smith | $22.95

Psychology for Screenwriters | William Indick, Ph.D. | $26.95

Rewrite | Paul Chitlik | $16.95

Romancing the A-List | Christopher Keane | $18.95

Save the Cat! | Blake Snyder | $19.95

Save the Cat! Goes to the Movies | Blake Snyder | $24.95

Screenwriting 101 | Neill D. Hicks | $16.95

Screenwriting for Teens | Christina Hamlett | $18.95

Script-Selling Game, The | Kathie Fong Yoneda | $16.95

Stealing Fire From the Gods, 2nd Edition | James Bonnet | $26.95

Way of Story, The | Catherine Ann Jones | $22.95

What Are You Laughing At? | Brad Schreiber | $19.95

Writer's Journey, – 3rd Edition, The | Christopher Vogler | $26.95

Writer's Partner, The | Martin Roth | $24.95

Writing the Action Adventure Film | Neill D. Hicks | $14.95

Writing the Comedy Film | Stuart Voytilla & Scott Petri | $14.95

Writing the Killer Treatment | Michael Halperin | $14.95

Writing the Second Act | Michael Halperin | $19.95

Writing the Thriller Film | Neill D. Hicks | $14.95

Writing the TV Drama Series – 2nd Edition | Pamela Douglas | $26.95

Your Screenplay Sucks! | William M. Akers | $19.95

FILMMAKING

Film School | Richard D. Pepperman | $24.95

Power of Film, The | Howard Suber | $27.95

PITCHING

Perfect Pitch – 2nd Edition, The | Ken Rotcop | $19.95

Selling Your Story in 60 Seconds | Michael Hauge | $12.95

SHORTS

Filmmaking for Teens | Troy Lanier & Clay Nichols | $18.95

Ultimate Filmmaker's Guide to Short Films, The | Kim Adelman | $16.95

BUDGET | PRODUCTION MGMT

Film & Video Budgets, 4th Updated Edition | Deke Simon & Michael Wiese | $26.95

Film Production Management 101 | Deborah S. Patz | $39.95

DIRECTING | VISUALIZATION

Animation Unleashed | Ellen Besen | $26.95

Citizen Kane Crash Course in Cinematography | David Worth | $19.95

Directing Actors | Judith Weston | $26.95

Directing Feature Films | Mark Travis | $26.95

Fast, Cheap & Under Control | John Gaspard | $26.95

Film Directing: Cinematic Motion, 2nd Edition | Steven D. Katz | $27.95

Film Directing: Shot by Shot | Steven D. Katz | $27.95

Film Director's Intuition, The | Judith Weston | $26.95

First Time Director | Gil Bettman | $27.95

From Word to Image | Marcie Begleiter | $26.95

I'll Be in My Trailer! | John Badham & Craig Modderno | $26.95

Master Shots | Christopher Kenworthy | $24.95

Setting Up Your Scenes | Richard D. Pepperman | $24.95

Setting Up Your Shots, 2nd Edition | Jeremy Vineyard | $22.95

Working Director, The | Charles Wilkinson | $22.95

DIGITAL | DOCUMENTARY | SPECIAL

Digital Filmmaking 101, 2nd Edition | Dale Newton & John Gaspard | $26.95

Digital Moviemaking 3.0 | Scott Billups | $24.95

Digital Video Secrets | Tony Levelle | $26.95

Greenscreen Made Easy | Jeremy Hanke & Michele Yamazaki | $19.95

Producing with Passion | Dorothy Fadiman & Tony Levelle | $22.95

Special Effects | Michael Slone | $31.95

EDITING

Cut by Cut | Gael Chandler | $35.95

Cut to the Chase | Bobbie O'Steen | $24.95

Eye is Quicker, The | Richard D. Pepperman | $27.95

Invisible Cut, The | Bobbie O'Steen | $28.95

SOUND | DVD | CAREER

Complete DVD Book, The | Chris Gore & Paul J. Salamoff | $26.95

Costume Design 101 | Richard La Motte | $19.95

Hitting Your Mark – 2nd Edition | Steve Carlson | $22.95

Sound Design | David Sonnenschein | $19.95

Sound Effects Bible, The | Ric Viers | $26.95

Storyboarding 101 | James Fraioli | $19.95

There's No Business Like Soul Business | Derek Rydall | $22.95

FINANCE | MARKETING | FUNDING

Art of Film Funding, The | Carole Lee Dean | $26.95

Complete Independent Movie Marketing Handbook, The | Mark Steven Bosko | $39.95

Independent Film and Videomakers Guide – 2nd Edition, The | Michael Wiese | $29.95

Independent Film Distribution | Phil Hall | $26.95

Shaking the Money Tree, 2nd Edition | Morrie Warshawski | $26.95

OUR FILMS

Hardware Wars: DVD | Written and Directed by Ernie Fosselius | $14.95

On the Edge of a Dream | Michael Wiese | $16.95

Sacred Sites of the Dalai Lamas– DVD, The | Documentary by Michael Wiese | $24.95

Printed in the United States
135156LV00001B/1/P